Developing Managers
Through
Project-Based Learning

Developing Managers Through Project-Based Learning

Bryan Smith and Bob Dodds

Gower

Published by
Gower Publishing Limited
Gower House
Croft Road
Aldershot
Hampshire GU11 3HR
England

Gower
Old Post Road
Brookfield
Vermont 05036
USA

Bryan Smith and Bob Dodds have asserted their right under the Copyright, Design and Patents Act 1988 to be identified as the authors of this work.

British Library Cataloguing in Publication Data
Smith, Bryan
   Developing managers through project-based learning
   1. Project method in teaching   2. Business education
   3. Executives – Training of
   I. Title II. Dodds, Bob
   658.4′07′1245

   ISBN 0 566 07723 X

Library of Congress Cataloging-in-Publication Data
Smith, Bryan.
   Developing managers through project-based learning / Bryan Smith and Bob Dodds.
      p. cm.
   Includes index.
   ISBN 0–566–07723–X (cloth)
   1. Management—Study and teaching. 2. Management—Study and teaching—Case studies. I. Dodds, Bob. II. Title.
HD30.4.S65 1997   96–46414
658.4′07124—dc21   CIP

Typeset in Century Old Style by Poole Typesetting Ltd and printed in Great Britain by Biddles Ltd, Guildford and King's Lynn

Contents

List of figures   vii
Preface   ix
Acknowledgements   xv

Part I   Inputs   1

1   Why Projects?   3
     Appendix: Honey and Mumford
     Learning Styles   18
2   The Management Development Context   21
3   Planning a Programme   41
4   The Value of Projects on Public
     Programmes   57
     Appendix 1:   The Younger
     Manager Programme   84
     Appendix 2:   Developing Tomorrow's
     Top Managers   86

Part II Outcomes   89

5   Six Case Histories   91
     Appendix: The Pacific Rim Project   104
6   Strategic Management at Allied Domecq   113
7   Developing Younger Managers with ICI   133
     Appendix 1:   Using technology to
     analyse outcomes   149
     Appendix 2:   Extracts from questionnaire
         to project owner   156
8   In-Company Programmes   159
9   Public Sector Projects   189

10   The International Dimension   215

Epilogue   The Project Orientated Organization   239
Index   257

List of figures

1.1	Criteria for choice of project	9
1.2	Conditions for successful completion of a project	10
1.3	Honey and Mumford learning cycle	12
2.1	Model of types of management development	22
3.1	Project-based learning infrastructure	42
3.2	Infrastructure following scoping	48
4.1	The Younger Manager Programme	59
6.1	A programme route map	118
6.2	The relationship of the project to current job rates	121
6.3	Linking the business agenda to the organization's potential for delivering outcomes to projects	124
7.1	Stages in the project lifecycle	135
7.2	Keyword search	149
7.3	Screen identifying owner of project	150
7.4	Developing self – project owner	151
7.5	Developing him/her – project sponsor	152
7.6	Achieving business objectives – project owner	152
7.7	Achieving business objectives – project sponsor	153
7.8	Hastening business change – project owner	153
7.9	Hastening business change – project sponsor	154

7.10	Developing other people – project owner	154
8.1	Sponsoring and mentoring model	176
9.1	North West Senior Management Programme	191
10.1	Culture dimension scores for selected countries	216
10.2	The cultural 'iceberg'	219

Preface

This book is aimed at helping those specializing in the development of people to value and realize the benefits of project-based learning. It will appeal to human resource and personnel professionals, management training and development consultants, and deliverers of learning in business schools, colleges and management centres.

Throughout the book we use the generic term 'people development'. Projects are placed within the context of other development activities so that the people development specialist can appreciate how to integrate the approach and achieve important business benefits.

The 'how to' approach is given strong emphasis through advice on establishing an infrastructure, scoping, getting started and the role of sponsors in contributing to learning and development.

The value of both individual and group projects in modular off-the-job programmes is highlighted, specifically in transferring and applying learning between modules. Contrasting experiences show how projects can be used at all levels of management, including at a strategic business level for senior executives.

The scope for projects in both private and public sectors as well as in international settings is described through successful case histories.

In looking to the future, the case is made for projects as a natural and powerful vehicle for performing and learning within the context of continuing change.

The book is organized as follows. In Chapter 1, we establish the case for using projects as a means of developing managers. We discuss the main problems encountered by people development specialists in integrating their efforts within a business context and delivering business results through people. We also describe tried and tested criteria and conditions for ensuring success when using projects as a developmental activity.

In addition, we explore learning processes, and the learning and organizational context in which projects take place, including change. We emphasize the role of the specialist in using learning styles and methods, as well as in helping project owners to capture and generalize learning and to exploit learning potential.

We encourage people development specialists to take stock of their own capabilities before embarking on project-based learning. This is particularly important in order to identify any capability gaps. The components of effective project-based learning are set out and placed in the context of a project as a vehicle, enabling a manager to undertake a journey resulting in both learning and business benefits.

In establishing the context for developing managers through projects, the logical starting point is an analysis of development needs. In Chapter 2, we link this type of development activity with a wide variety and range of learning methods including coaching, mentoring, self-development, action learning, teamworking and leadership. Other topical issues and approaches are also placed in the project-based learning context, specifically empowerment and business process re-engineering. Moreover, since projects are an integral part of many academic courses, we concentrate on a successful model for achieving effective integration.

All the above will be of value to the people development specialist in exploring tactics for linking project-based learning with other development activities.

Chapter 3 covers planning a programme and the infrastructure which needs to be put in place. We explore the multiplicity of possible roles which can be adopted by project sponsors, who themselves may well be learning. The greater the variety of roles exercised by the sponsor, the more likely the provision of extremely powerful learning for the project owner as well. The people development specialist may need to help sponsors initially to separate these different roles, e.g. coach and mentor from critic and assessor. Where sponsor and line manager relationships differ, particularly in establishing collaborative relationships and handling any possible conflicts, we examine the nature of those differences. The interests and contributions of other stakeholders are also put under the microscope.

We suggest some helpful tips for initial scoping of the project and for getting started. The whole infrastructure needs to be activated and seen as a clear benefit, not just a feature. There is scope for the people development specialist to frame the extent of involvement in project-based learning. Indeed, it presents an opportunity to be more influential in integrating project activity with business goals. We also list the pitfalls which both project owners and sponsors should endeavour to avoid.

In Chapter 4, we consider the value of projects on public programmes by drawing on the extensive experience of Sundridge Park distilled from two specific programmes: the Younger Manager Programme and Developing Tomorrow's Top Managers. Both programmes comprise two modules which are linked by projects. The programmes are designed so as to enable participants to apply as much of the learning as possible from the first module in carrying out their projects. We provide useful checklists for scoping and testing projects beforehand, and for facilitating questions and discussions following presentations of project results which project sponsors are invited to attend.

In relation to projects, the difference between the two programmes is that on Developing Tomorrow's Top Managers, the seniority of participants often enables them to involve members of their staff in the project, as a development experience – an option which is not normally open to participants on the Younger Manager Programme.

In this chapter, we also describe a number of project experiences, the results and learning from which is based on a recent survey of project owners and sponsors following completion of their projects. This generalized learning should be of immense value to the people development specialist.

In Chapter 5, six complete case histories provide the reader with a valuable record of benefits achievable and difficulties to be overcome in the project approach.

Chapter 6 positions projects at a strategic business level. It describes a strategic management programme carried out for high calibre executives of Allied Domecq, with Sundridge Park as the external provider. The programme is set within a business which is complex, experiencing rapid change and extending its global reach.

The programme helps executives to become more aware of strategic issues and business challenges, to explore their own capability and potential, and to achieve a return on investment in personal development by carrying out projects to help enable the success of the strategic agenda.

Rigorous project selection criteria include:

- identification of a strategic opportunity or threat
- stretch beyond current role organizational and functional boundaries

- capacity to deliver a valued return on investment, typically requiring a change in executive mindsets.

The project review process is equally rigorous, being in two stages and involving two levels of senior management. The first stage establishes the *quality* of the analysis and relevance of recommendations, as well as gauging adequacy of the presentations made to Group Chief Executives, Chairman and Vice Chairman (the higher level) as the second stage. Indeed, at this level, a convincing presentation is essential to influence and communicate to these key stakeholders. Moreover, such board level sponsorship of the evaluation process is valuable for future networking and personal visibility.

Described in Chapter 7 is the ICI Foundations of Business Programme on which, since the late 1980s, project work has been an integral part. At the time of writing, over 600 projects have been undertaken. The aim of the programme is to develop a broader understanding of business management issues in younger managers, predominantly graduate scientists or engineers. They have often spent their first years in ICI gaining experience in a production or technical role. Initially, project work was based on cross-functional business management issues, but more recently it has concentrated on the theme of change in the external and internal business environment. A good example of this shift in emphasis is the de-merger of ICI to create the biosciences company Zeneca.

A description of the approach, supported by examples, illustrates how technology has contributed to the management of the project process in the form of a PC database of current and past projects. Participants can access this database when refining the scope of their project and its use also aids the process of networking with owners of earlier projects.

We have provided tabulated data summarizing the outcomes and benefits of project work, from both project owner and sponsor perspectives.

Two case studies, including text from the original reports, exemplify the learning process. Both illustrate the importance of recognizing and addressing interpersonal and inter-team issues, as well as business performance requirements.

Chapter 8 describes the contrasting experiences of using projects for learning and development in three different organizations, with three different approaches. In each organization, the projects were carried out by teams as distinct from individuals.

The first is Volvo Car which was Volvo Concessionaires when the early courses were run. The programme was designed for junior/middle managers and was a closely tailored version of Sundridge Park's Younger Manager Programme.

The second was Gestetner, a multinational company, where the programme was designed for fast trackers from a mix of functional disciplines. Again, it was a two-module programme, specifically tailored to the company's needs.

The third, Lloyds Bank Insurance Services Division, was a three-level programme for the marketing group. There were three modules, with higher level participants sponsoring and mentoring projects for the next level down. Significantly, on the second module, 'gaining permission' to proceed was included where initial research and problem analysis, with alternative courses of action, were presented. Presentations at the third module covered the outcomes of implementation.

This chapter captures the varied experiences and roles of sponsors, together with the potential in the role where there is room for further development.

Chapter 9 explores the public sector and, like Chapter 8, it brings together three different types of experience, each one developed by a different management development provider.

The first describes a significant change initiative within the Inland Revenue, for which project-based learning was a key and integral element of the change process, with an external provider – International Training Services.

The second is based on a management of change programme for London Underground. It is a project management initiative in the human resources function with links to project-based learning. Internal management and an external consultancy combined to provide the impetus and direction for this programme.

The third is a project-based development programme carried out with the States of Guernsey Civil Service Board. Kennedy Robinson Business Development Limited was the external provider.

In Chapter 10, we examine three international perspectives for developing managers through projects. These bring together theoretical considerations and practical case materials.

First, we consider the impact of national culture in determining the approach to be taken when using projects for management development and develop guidelines for doing so. This review builds on the earlier work done by Geert Hofstede and others. We also explore the importance of bringing to the surface and discussing previously unstated differences in values and assumptions which impede effective cross-cultural working. Projects are used as a pre-cursor to a developmental stage in order to provide the opportunity for cross-cultural, experiential learning. This includes illustrative case material from a BTR company.

Secondly, we investigate how projects can provide a means of bench-marking performance in the increasingly global setting in which companies must operate. This is illustrated using practical case material from Scottish Nuclear Limited, which includes the benefits of broadening the awareness of managers to considerations of international competitive strategy.

The final part of the chapter illustrates the use of projects in the Renong Berhad group of companies in Malaysia. The Renong Management Trainee Scheme includes the Young Manager Programme on which a group project learning element has been a resounding success. We explore the reasons for this success, provide illustrative case material and describe the benefits obtained.

The book concludes with an epilogue describing managing and learning during times of continuing change. We begin by reviewing how most business operations are becoming increasingly more project oriented. We develop the idea of the project as the natural vehicle for performing and learning across a portfolio of activities, at both individual and organizational levels, and we examine the links between management through projects and management development.

We explore the opportunities for new ways of operating provided by advances in technology, including the capture and use of learning outcomes from projects. The concepts of organizational learning and links to project-based learning are examined, building on the work of Peter Senge and others. We provide practical recommendations for achieving an organizational culture which supports learning and development through projects.

In closing, we reflect on the recurring theme of change and explain why we believe that development through projects provides such a powerful means for managers to learn, grow and achieve success, both now and in the future.

We hope that this book will help people development specialists to recognize the benefits of developing managers through workplace projects, adding to their repertoire of development approaches in the context of continuing change.

Bryan Smith
Bob Dodds

Acknowledgements

In writing *Developing Managers Through Project-based Learning*, we have drawn on both our own experiences and those of others. Additional contributions from those who have used projects to develop their managers have greatly enriched our final product. We owe them a great debt.

We would like particularly to thank:

- Graham Morphey, an independent consultant who contributed significantly to Chapter 6.
- Graham Robinson, an independent consultant, for his 'editor free contribution on a Project-Based Development Programme in the Guernsey Civil Service' to Chapter 9.
- Graeme Fisher of the Inland Revenue for his help with Chapter 9 in allowing one of the authors to sit in on a set of Project Presentations, and for following up and updating core material.
- Paul Farmer of London Underground for the opportunity to discuss, in Chapter 9, his key project management initiative.
- Graham McGregor for his assistance with Chapter 7.
- Roger Headey and Tony Milne of Gestetner for the opportunity to discuss their project-based, fast track development programme, and for contributing to case material for Chapter 8.
- John Mills of Sundridge Park, together with Keith Gibb and Mike Todd of Lloyds Bank Insurance Services, for providing an account of a project-based programme carried out for the Marketing Group, also for Chapter 8.
- Alex Dickinson of BTR for supplying core material for Chapter 10.
- Haznah Mohammed of Renong Berhad (Kuala Lumpur), for help with case material for Chapter 10.
- Malcolm Hamilton of Heriot Watt University Business School, together with Peter James of the Ashridge Research Group, for their

contribution in Chapter 10 describing the Scottish Nuclear project experience.

- Miroslaw Gryszka of ABB, Poland, David Folkerd of London Electricity, Julie Shears of European Air Catering Services, each for their contributions to Chapter 4.
- Peter Beddowes of Ashridge Management College, for approving reference to the experiences described in Chapters 8 and 10.
- Chris Greensted, of the University of Strathclyde Graduate Business School, for his contribution about projects on academic courses in Chapter 2.
- Others, from a variety of organizations, who shared their views and experiences including Jim Morris, Neil Watson, Alan Wain, Geoff Higgs, Patrick Neate, James Ross, Alan Harley, Trevor Morris, Janet Wright, Frances Bee, Chris Hurley and Ian Greive.
- Nick Dwelly, who was formerly Quality Director at Sundridge Park and now operates as an independent consultant, for making a substantial contribution by constructively reading the manuscript and recommending changes. At the end of the long exercise that writing this book entailed, his energy and support were essential to its successful completion.
- Finally, Richard Dodds, Fiona Golle and Sandra Dwelly for sharing the onerous burden of typing the manuscript.

Bryan Smith
Bob Dodds

Part I

Inputs

1   Why Projects?

As organizations continue to downsize and rightsize, how are they to influence learning so that the necessary changes can be implemented effectively? How are organizations to optimize the transfer of learning to the work place and eradicate waste in training investments while contributing to priority business needs?

We believe that one answer to these and similar questions facing today's business managers lies in project-based learning and development. In this first chapter we identify the problems which those in specialist people development roles are encountering. We link the context of such experience to *project-based learning* by adopting a questioning approach. By this means, we seek to establish the business case for developing managers through projects.

This rationale – underpinned by our own strong beliefs about the timeliness and importance of project-based learning – will be supported by descriptions of the criteria and conditions necessary for successful projects.

Finally, we examine the learning processes and the learning context for the successful development of managers through projects.

THE RATIONALE: WHY LEARNING AND DEVELOPMENT THROUGH PROJECTS?

DEVELOPMENT

It is commonly accepted that the amount of management training in the UK is less than modest. The two and a half million managers in the UK receive the equivalent of one day's training each year. Even in a relatively

3

stable environment this would be inadequate. With today's pressure to learn a large number of new things, the turbulence of change in the manager's environment causes 'inadequate' to become 'disastrous'.

A response to this inadequate level of training is reflected, in part, by national initiatives to promote continuous development. These are strongly supportive of approaches which integrate learning with work. Growth in project-based learning and development will spearhead this initiative.

It is probably a truism that the pace and complexity of change has never been greater, even though this has been claimed to be the case for many centuries. As Heraclitus said in 600 BC, 'Nothing is permanent except change'. Indeed, there is a growing awareness among managers of the impact of change in their organizations. Changes in structure, systems, use of information technology, the marketplace and competition are real. In such a business environment, few would be so deluded as to think that being sent on a management course was a guarantee of long-term security. Increasingly, managers are coming to realize that such a training investment will only pay off if they apply what they have learnt when they return to their day-to-day work situations.

THE ISSUES FOR INDIVIDUALS IN PEOPLE DEVELOPMENT ROLES

As a consequence of delayering, rightsizing or downsizing (whichever piece of jargon you use), there are some significant questions which those in the people development business need to consider.

For a start, there are now fewer of such people with arguably more to do, and the 'more' consists of doing different things and doing things differently. A main question concerns how they integrate their efforts better into the context of the business and, in so doing, contribute to the delivery of business results through people development.

On the surface, this may not seem too difficult a question to answer, but placed within a context of rapid, complex change, where 'competing successfully' is an imperative, then it becomes much more challenging.

The people development specialist has different people or clients to serve. On the issue of competition, there is likely to be increasing pressure from the board (the main client group) for learning to be centred on the work place, to be faster, more effective and to have a clear and measurable impact on business strategy. He or she will therefore be tested on the delivery of business results through examining the cost effectiveness of on-the-job development opportunities.

These demands are mirrored in the clear shift of ownership for learning and development to individual managers. At present, most managers equate learning and development with external training courses. Although there is a place for such external provision, this is true only where 'value for money' can be provided through high quality tailoring to the needs of the business and its managers.

It is our proposition that these problems can be solved by integrating project-based learning within the company's armoury of learning and development methods. But, of course, the specialist is unlikely to be starting with a clean sheet. Managerial learning and development will be taking place in various forms, with the specialist exercising a number of different capabilities.

For specialists in emergent learning organizations, there will have been a shift in role emphasis from specifier of external provision, course organizer/booker, to facilitator of learning processes and provider of learning solutions. The role will be that of a consultant and expert in learning styles and methods.

CONTEXTUAL QUESTIONS

Irrespective of specific learning delivery approaches, the specialist will need to consider several broad contextual questions:

- Does the organization have a mission statement for management development which is integrated with business strategy? If it does not, then training and development could be seen as an end, rather than a means to an end.
- Is management development being used as a competitive weapon?
- Are the objectives of management development programmes driven by priority business issues?
- Am I clear about the organization's culture and any cultural change which is in process?
- Am I clear about the organization's stage of development and its pace of change? Can I see emerging characteristics of the organization's next stage of development?
- Are the knowledge and skills being offered to managers in development new and/or different from what they already possess?

Taking stock of current or existing capabilities will be a useful starting point. For the specialist with no experience of project-based learning, the

5

following questions are likely to arise:

- What is project-based learning and why should I make use of it?
- What does it deliver? When does it deliver?
- How is it different/better/preferable to what I am doing now?
- How do I get started?
- What links do I have with other development activities?
- How do I secure 'buy-in' from the relevant people, e.g. Project Sponsors?
- How will I know that it is working? What must I try to measure?
- What are the likely and less likely learning benefits (e.g. likely – managing change, problem solving)?
- What impact could it have on the career development of managers?
- What are the pitfalls? How can I avoid them?
- What new skills and knowhow do I need? For example:
  - business knowhow/functions
  - methods for measuring results
  - new technology for storage/transfer of learning
  - being more proactive, assertive – changing style
- What's in it for me?

If people development specialists can harness this opportunity for managers to start to value such self-managed learning, the richness of largely unrecognized on-the-job opportunities for learning can begin to be appreciated.

It may seem too obvious to state but a project, as a development method, concentrates on what managers really do. In theory, there should be no waste in respect of learning, providing projects are implemented effectively and efficiently. But of course, managerial reality is not tidy and ordered and it would be naive in the extreme to expect managers undertaking a project to behave in ways greatly at variance with the day-to-day reality. The studies of Stewart[1] and Mintzberg[2] on managerial work, and Kotter[3] on agendas and networks, has been influential in identifying what managers actually do. It is with such frameworks that project-based learning needs to be integrated.

This, however, is no simple task, particularly where a manager tries to treat a project as a totally separate activity from other priorities. Kotter's 'efficiency of seemingly inefficient behaviour' could appear to be at odds with old established models of managerial processes, i.e. plan, organize, co-ordinate, control, with the latter seeming vital for a manager undertaking a project.

There are no easy answers. As managers know only too well, 'life's like that'. However, the awareness of managerial reality can help managers to place the project in context. In turn, the project can test and strengthen links between such concepts and models, and the day-to-day realities of work. In our experience, no projects undertaken by managers are easy and straightforward, but then things which are valued and worthwhile rarely are.

If we accept the premise that most managerial learning takes place in on-the-job settings, then projects provide an important means of shifting the balance of management development activities back to on-the-job learning by dealing with the reality of managerial work. While formal management development processes – including performance review, succession and career planning – have their place, they can often seem to managers to be divorced from their everyday business world.

In a survey on how best to prepare managers for effective international operation, commissioned by Surrey European Management School in 1990 (Coulson-Thomas),[4] responses reveal a clear preference for integration of learning with work, the most relevant approaches being proposed as tailored company-specific programmes with a project component.

THE COMPONENTS OF PROJECT-BASED LEARNING AND DEVELOPMENT

PROJECT ELEMENTS

The project elements include:

- a project, which may be for an individual or a group
- a project sponsor, who may or may not have a line relationship to the project owner(s)
- criteria for project selection to be applied by sponsor and project owner(s)
- an off-the-job programme of learning which, typically, may be in modules with subsequent presentation of project outputs, including application of learning

7

- other key players (as part of an infrastructure), who may include consultant, trainer and/or support group
- IT support in capturing and sharing learning outcomes.

It is the sequencing and complexities in bringing these elements together which contribute to the richness of project-based learning and development.

THE PROJECT AS A VEHICLE

Project-based learning and development, whether with an individual or group focus, will claim a leading position in providing a twin-track approach which combines learning/developing with doing/achieving, ensuring powerful interactions between each track.

In this sense, *a project may be seen as a 'vehicle' enabling a manager to undertake a journey resulting in both learning and practical benefit to the business.* This analogy helps to illustrate the attraction and general applicability of projects. They are tangible, identifiable and can be described in terms of their starting point, their objectives and the end point of the journey. The benefits can thus be readily visualized in the eyes of both sponsors and managers. Furthermore, projects:

- provide a means for exploring unknown or unfamiliar terrain
- require the manager to think ahead about the territory to be explored and the approach to be taken
- provide the means to gather information and to record experiences, so as to develop an improved understanding of the terrain and reduce the level of uncertainty associated with making a further 'journey'
- require the manager to persuade others (e.g. sponsor, line manager, peers) of the benefits to be obtained from undertaking the journey
- provide, during the journey, the opportunity to put into practice existing skills and knowhow; also, lead to the recognition that additional skills and knowhow are required.

Moreover, projects provide the sponsor with a mechanism for agreeing and defining the appropriate 'terrain' for the manager to explore, allowing the scope of the project journey to be identified in terms of:

- the deliverables required of the manager and project, e.g. those areas which should be explored during the journey and the resulting outcomes sought

- the limitations to be imposed, together with areas not to be explored, allowing the sponsor to identify an appropriate learning environment for the manager.

Between the boundaries imposed by the deliverables and limitations, there remains the area of choice. Depending on how the boundaries have been agreed between sponsor and manager, there may be greater or lesser degrees of freedom available, varying according to the relative experience of the manager and the degree of 'stretch' that the sponsor deems appropriate for inclusion in the project.

NATURE OF PROJECTS

In our experience of projects, both individual and group, a *good project*:

- creates change and is a vehicle for managing change
- is bounded in scope and within a timescale
- requires the exercise of a range of key skills
- offers distinctive payoffs to sponsors and project owners, including learning benefits

1. Concerned with a significant problem within the manager's area of operation but, in solving, would involve gaining a broader understanding than the confines of the department or section.
2. Should include diagnosis of the problem, making recommendations and, where appropriate, initiating necessary action.
3. Should not be a problem which is so intractable that it is not capable of solution, nor should it be too complicated for one individual to effectively tackle.
4. Offers a challenge, provides stretch, and is not a set of tedious clerical routines.
5. Should not merely be concerned with gathering and collating information that yields little potential for learning.
6. Within the timescale it is possible for some real impact to be made on the problem and, preferably, a plan for implementation.
7. Should require involvement, co-operation and commitment of other colleagues.
8. Should not be directed at the solution of problems which are exclusively technical.
9. Likely to contain a 'people' element.
10. Should not be a puzzle to which there is a known solution.
11. May be linked to some planned or ongoing change.
12. Though primarily a learning vehicle, should yield some worthwhile benefits to the project sponsor and the organization.

Figure 1.1 Criteria for choice of project

> - Before starting, there should be adequate discussion with the line manager of the person undertaking the project (and the project sponsor if different) to ensure there is a common understanding, objective and interest.
> - Regular communication with the manager and project sponsor should be established.
> - The agreed time requirement (guideline 5 to 10 days) is 'protected' to avoid extreme frustrations or demoralization and, at worst, failure.
> - The participant should have a strong interest in the type of problem to be solved which is chosen as the subject of the project.
> - The person taking on the project should be given the freedom to approach the problem in whatever manner appears fitting.
> - The project should be defined as clearly as possible.

Figure 1.2 Conditions for successful completion of a project

- mirrors 'management in action', with all its inherent complexities and ambiguities
- possesses unique elements or may be totally unique (there are unlikely to be any templates of previous projects).

However, for a project to succeed, the initial choice needs to be made with great care. For this we advise, and have developed, a set of 'Criteria for Choice'[5] (see Figure 1.1 on page 9).

The criteria should be used by the manager, as well as the sponsor and line manager in considering ideas and suggestions for projects. In addition, we advise using a set of conditions for successful project completion (see Figure 1.2).

The following topics exemplify some recent projects undertaken on programmes at Sundridge Park:

- Develop marketing strategy for new products.
- Develop a strategy for open learning.
- Recommend and implement a downsizing programme.
- Carry out a market research survey to develop a new image and improve standards.
- Produce a strategy to help improve sales performance.
- Develop a plan for revamping inadequate service departments.
- Establish a PR strategy for the business and implement the initial stage.
- Develop and implement new or revised systems, several of which included the following elements:
  - management information

- cost control
- information technology
- stock control
- performance appraisal
- TQM.

A manager who perceives a project as a potential learning experience may need to identify with a certain business situation so that the project is seen as important and possibly mould-breaking, i.e. its outcomes will make a difference or, as we frequently declare to managers at the project formulation and clarification stage, 'nothing will be the same after the project!' Moreover, where a manager can perceive a project as providing a bridge into the reality of the work place, commitment and motivation will be high.

Projects, while containing some routine elements, will be developmental in nature. The emphasis is on *new* challenges, which raise new questions needing new answers. Also the structuring of projects, typically spanning several months, prompts greater tolerance and encourages questioning, rather than going for quick-fix solutions. Furthermore, while such questioning may lead to insights, it may also push at some of the boundaries or constraints, such as a non-developmental culture, i.e. 'this is the way we've done things here and it has worked well in the past'.

Not all projects can be strategic in nature; many may be at a tactical, operational level. However, where possible, the sponsor should show the manager the 'bigger picture' – the strategic fit of the project. This can certainly help in empowering the manager in situations where, initially, the project may not hold great appeal.

LEARNING AND LEARNING PROCESSES

Learning is a complex act. It involves understanding concepts, making distinctions, drawing inferences, perceiving, guessing, categorizing, handling ambiguities and uncertainties and generalizing from specific experiences, i.e. making sense of them. Learning relates to change, adaptability and the ability to question, to rethink. It is never passive – a learner either wants to learn or is willing to learn.

Projects provide a context in which such learning can take place, but effective learning *transfer* must be made possible. Off-the-job manage-

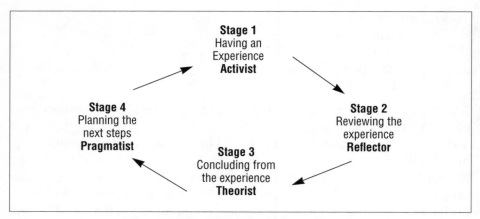

Figure 1.3 Honey and Mumford learning cycle

ment development programmes, which do not provide managers with the wherewithal to transfer learning fast and effectively to the work situation, will be an indulgence which organizations will not be able to afford. Ferocity of competition will necessitate a 'transfer it now' for off-the-job learning, as opposed to banking it for some possible later application. Therefore, infrastructures which enable organizations and providers effectively to collaborate in learning transfer will be at a premium. Coaching, mentoring, self-organized learning, action learning and project-based learning will be right at the heart of this movement to gain competitive advantage.

Among organizations, there is a growing awareness of the need for learning to be continuous and necessary for survival in the complex and rapidly changing business environment. If learning is to be continuous, there will need to be an increased emphasis on using on-the-job situations. Learner-centred rather than teacher-centred approaches will dominate increasingly. Projects, as vehicles for learning, can help to establish this. But such a paradigm shift will require an internal organizational re-education process, with project sponsors spearheading the change.

The notion of learning and learning processes, let alone reviewing what has been learnt from a specific task or activity, will be new for many managers. Indeed, a better understanding of learning processes, including a learning cycle based on original work by Kolb[6] and learning styles and preferences as developed by Honey and Mumford[7] (see Figure 1.3), can help a manager to learn more efficiently.

The learning cycle is a complete process, but the capacity of individuals to learn from each stage of the cycle varies. (These learning styles are reproduced in the Appendix at the end of this chapter for readers who are unfamiliar with them.)

Acquiring an increased awareness of learning style preferences before engaging in a project, can help to enable such preferences to be applied. Indeed, it will permit the chance to experiment with non-preferences. While most projects will tend to relate more to activist and pragmatist preferences, development and application of relevant theories, concepts and models can be emphasized during a first off-the-job module in a modular, project-linked programme. In addition, periodic reflection throughout the project can be stressed, with reflection further in evidence at the project presentation stage, when learning outputs are highlighted.[8]

Even with such understanding and awareness of learning style preferences, however, there may be cultures, values and reward systems in organizations which are unlikely to acknowledge or support such activity. 'Management concerns getting things done, moving from task to task.' Learning, if acknowledged, will tend to be perceived as just happening, as a natural part of doing work. Moreover, it may be relegated to 'what you do on courses'.

When managers perceive that what they are learning will help them to do better those tasks for which they are valued and rewarded, then a supportive learning culture will be in place in their organizations. But, too frequently in organizations, learning opportunities are not perceived. Recognizing and making use of opportunities for learning are critical to managers' effectiveness.

Such recognition can be aided by a project which is deliberately structured to yield learning outputs. Thinking about potential learning outputs at the incubation of a project can greatly aid managers in increasing their awareness of learning opportunities. In this way a project, as well as being a vehicle for learning, can be a catalyst for changing perceptions about everyday work activities. When managers think 'learning' as well as 'doing', and no longer see these as unrelated activities, then effective managerial and organizational learning will have arrived.

Experiences through which learning starts to become more valued by managers in an off-the-job environment can be emphasized and supported as the manager embarks upon the project. The aim is integrated learning and the project can provide a means of integrating learning with managerial work.

13

While a manager may be able to demonstrate the knowledge and skills acquired, there is often little or no understanding of how this acquisition has taken place. But the structure of a project can prompt learning through taking action rather than merely in planning to take action. Also, in requiring a manager to present project outcomes in terms of doing, achieving and learning, an awareness of learning processes may be heightened, i.e. when was learning most apparent? Why did it occur? How or by what means did learning take place? It is not sufficient to say, 'Here's a project – you can learn from it'. Both manager and sponsor are likely to treat the project (part of a modular linked programme) as an opportunity to achieve something to make a difference.

If managers are to value learning opportunities more highly, people development specialists will need to provide them with processes to capture and value learning outcomes throughout the project. One resource which some managers may find useful is a learning log, specifically tailored to the stages of the project and the learning cycle. On some programmes, we have found that 'reflectors' and 'theorists' will systematically complete their learning logs while 'activists' may have difficulty finding them!

For a small proportion of managers, learning is part of a planned process but, as mentioned earlier, most learning is accidental and incidental – it just happens. Projects provide opportunities for people development specialists to help managers make the learning process more conscious and, thereby, more effective.

While unpredictable learning may occur in carrying out a project, a more thoughtful and careful approach to the actual 'design' of potential learning, during the preliminary planning phase of the project, should pay dividends. Project owners might well ask themselves questions such as, 'Who are the people I need to influence? How shall I go about influencing them? What control mechanisms do I need to put in place? How shall I ensure a closed feedback loop of control?'

Of course, learning is rarely a solitary process. Managers learn from (and sometimes with) others. Specifically, there are opportunities to learn from bosses, colleagues, mentors, peers, subordinates, customers, suppliers, facilitators and even management educators. In embarking on a project, managers should consider who are the people (in addition to the sponsor) they can learn from and how involvement in the project can assist learning.

14

In our experiences with managers carrying out projects, progress has rarely been merely incremental. There have been times of feeling stuck and then subsequently making a breakthrough, often following a short period of detachment from the project. This may mirror the process of creative problem solving, which includes a stage of incubation, i.e. letting the subconscious reorientate the problem. Such blockages relate more to uncertainty and taking skilful action than to overcoming a lack of knowledge. A good deal of managerial behaviour is specific to a situation. A project can be testing for a manager in adapting to a situation which may be new. The value, of course, will come from generalizing the learning from such a situation.

As managers become increasingly involved in project-based learning, they will develop skills to manage complex, often messy problems with no clear boundaries. With such challenges, comprising as they do complexity and uncertainty, some difficulties, even failures, will inevitably be experienced. It will be vital that the learning is both *captured* and *generalized*.[9] It will be through projects which embrace tough challenges and stretch that the interchange between learning and change will be most effective.

LEARNING POTENTIAL

The learning potential from projects is immense. If we consider a wide range of learning opportunities, it is possible to tap into several in the course of carrying out a project. Here are some examples:

- handling relationships with the project sponsor, the boss, peers, colleagues and subordinates
- pushing at the boundaries of the job, identifying and exploiting the choices
- solving problems with others
- networking externally to obtain information/ideas and in the process developing the network
- being in a close coaching relationship with sponsor, boss and a mentor
- working with others in a team context, albeit temporary
- reading, expanding knowledge and awareness.

One can also position the project as a vehicle for applying and transferring specific learning from an off-the-job module. Areas of new learning could include:

- problem solving
- managing change
- planning and control
- time management
- managing and developing network of relationships
- influencing and persuading
- teamworking.

Through engaging in a structured process of learning, where a project is linked to an off-the-job modular programme with trainer support, the raised consciousness of the learning benefits among managers should help them to see and take advantage of any projects which can naturally occur in the normal work situation. In this way, projects on which learning previously has been patchy and ineffective, can become a highly effective and efficient means of learning and development.

KEY POINT SUMMARY

- Project-based learning integrates work with learning and minimizes waste in learning transfer from off-the-job settings to the work place.
- Projects provide a means of shifting the balance of management development activities into the arena of on-the-job learning.
- A project can provide learning for the project owner and bottom line benefits for the project sponsor and organization.
- A 'good' project creates change, is a vehicle for managing change and mirrors the complexities and ambiguities in the management role.
- The application of a set of 'criteria for choice' in project selection can help to ensure that a project is likely to be completed successfully.
- Topics for projects are wide ranging and can impinge on any and every aspect of a business.
- Projects may be at a strategic, tactical or operational level. Whatever the level, it is important for the project sponsor to show the project owner the 'bigger picture', the strategic fit of the project.
- Project-based learning, along with action learning, self-organized learning, coaching and mentoring are necessary to the pursuit of competitive advantage.
- An awareness of learning style preferences and learning processes is vital to the project owner in optimizing project-based learning.

- When managers think 'learning' as well as 'doing', and no longer see them as unrelated activities, then effective managerial and organizational learning will have arrived.
- Projects provide opportunities for people development specialists to help managers make the learning process more conscious and, thereby, more effective.
- Increasing involvement in project-based learning will enable managers to develop skills to manage complex and messy problems with no clear boundaries. This is the stuff of the present and, even more so, of the future.
- Projects can provide tough challenges and the risk of failure. What is learnt must be both captured and generalized.
- Learning potential from projects is immense. It can include building relationships, solving problems, exploiting choices, receiving coaching and expanding knowledge and awareness of the business.
- Project-based learning is a vehicle for releasing and focusing creative energy. The increasing instability which organizations are experiencing, and are likely to experience even more in the future, makes this an important need.
- The encouragement and application of creativity in organizations can be fostered through projects. Recognition and pursuit of the adaptive and/or innovative approaches appropriate to the existing situation will influence their success.
- Information technology is a powerful new means for supporting individual and group projects and for accelerating work place learning.
- As the pace of change increases, the ability of organizations to capture, and pro-actively build on, project-based learning will contribute to their responsiveness and competitiveness.

APPENDIX: HONEY AND MUMFORD – LEARNING STYLES

Activists learn best from activities where:

- There are new experiences/problems/opportunities from which to learn.
- They can engross themselves in short 'here and now' activities, such as business games, competitive teamwork tasks, role playing exercises.
- There is excitement/drama/crisis and things change with the range of diverse activities to tackle.
- They have a lot of the limelight, e.g. they can 'chair' meetings, lead discussions, give presentations.
- They are allowed to generate ideas without constraints of policy, structure or feasibility.
- They are thrown in at the deep end with a task they think is difficult, e.g. when set a challenge with inadequate resources and adverse conditions.
- They are involved with other people, e.g. bouncing ideas off them and solving problems as part of a team.

Reflectors learn best from activities where:

- They are allowed or encouraged to watch/think/ponder over activities.
- They are able to stand back from events and listen/observe, e.g. observing a group at work, taking a back seat in a meeting, watching a film or video.
- They are allowed to think before acting, to assimilate before commenting, e.g. They have time to prepare, a chance to read in advance a brief giving background data.
- They can carry out some painstaking research, e.g. investigate, assemble information, probe to get to the bottom of things.
- They have the opportunity to review what has happened, what they have learnt.
- They are asked to produce carefully considered analyses and reports.
- They are helped to exchange views with other people without danger, e.g. by prior agreement, within a structured learning experience.

- They can reach a decision in their own time without pressure and tight deadlines.

Theorists learn best from activities where:

- What is being offered is part of a system, model, concept, theory.
- They have time to explore methodically the associations and inter-relationships between ideas, events and situations.
- They have the chance to question and probe the basic methodology, assumptions or logic behind something, e.g. by taking part in a question and answer session, by checking a paper for inconsistencies.
- They are intellectually stretched, e.g. by analysing a complex situation, being tested in a tutorial session, by teaching high calibre people who ask searching questions.
- They are in structured situations with a clear purpose.
- They can listen to, or read about, ideas and concepts that emphasize rationality or logic and are well-argued, elegant, watertight.
- They can analyse and then generalize the reasons for success or failure.
- They are offered interesting ideas and concepts even though these are not immediately relevant.
- They are required to understand and participate in complex situations.

Pragmatists learn best from activities where:

- There is an obvious link between the subject matter and a problem or opportunity on the job.
- They are shown techniques for doing things with obvious practical advantages, e.g. how to save time, how to make a good first impression, how to deal with awkward people.
- They have the chance to try out and practise techniques with coaching/feedback from a credible expert, i.e. someone who is successful and can perform the techniques themselves.
- They are exposed to a model they can emulate, e.g. a respected boss, a demonstration from someone with a proven track record, lots of examples/anecdotes, a film showing how it is done.
- They are given techniques currently applicable to their own job.
- They are given immediate opportunities to implement what they have learnt.

- There is a high face validity in the learning activity, e.g. a good simulation, 'real' problems.
- They can concentrate on practical issues, e.g. drawing up action plans with an obvious end product, suggesting short cuts, giving tips.

REFERENCES

1. Stewart, R. (1982), *Choices for the Manager*, Maidenhead: McGraw-Hill.
2. Mintzberg, H. (1973), *The Nature of Managerial Work*, New York: Harper & Row.
3. Kotter, J.(1982), 'What Effective General Managers Really Do', *Harvard Business Review*, November/December, pp. 157–7.
4. Coulson-Thomas, C. (1992), 'Integrating Learning and Working', *Industrial and Commercial Training*, **24**, (10), pp. 18–22.
5. Smith, B. (1987), 'Meeting a Need: The Younger Manager Programme at Sundridge Park', *Journal of European Industrial Training*, **11**, (7), pp. 5–12.
6. Kolb, D.A. (1984), *Experiential Learning*, Englewood Cliffs, New Jersey, Prentice Hall.
7. Honey, P. and Mumford, A. (1982), *The Manual of Learning Styles*, Maidenhead: Honey.
8. Smith B. and Dodds B. (1993), 'The Power of Projects in Management Development', *Industrial and Commercial Training*, **25**, (10), pp. 3–9.
9. Smith, B. and Morphey G. (1994), 'Tough Challenges – How Big a Learning Gap', *Journal of Management Development*, **13**, (9), pp. 5–13.

2 The Management Development Context

ANALYSIS OF DEVELOPMENT NEEDS

The analysis of development needs is the logical starting point for this section. Needs can be identified by a variety of methods, and from a range of sources. For many organizations, the needs analysis process is likely to be keyed into a formal performance review or appraisal process.

While the people development specialist will want to encourage line managers to take responsibility for meeting the development needs of their people, it is likely that the specialist will retain at least an advisory, if not a co-provider, role.

In advising on methods to meet needs, the specialist will have choices to make. Such choices are likely to be influenced by any commonality of needs, e.g. several managers may need to be better at solving people problems or making presentations. Methods may be self-defining, particularly when considered on a piecemeal basis. However, where there are several needs, their collective provision may be less easy to identify. Here project-based learning is an option. For instance, take managers who need to expand their network of relationships, understand more about a related business function and solve problems more proficiently. Such a cluster of needs could be met easily through the project method.

Moreover, it is quite possible that if the specialist were to look across the business at how work is done, how change is managed and how new initiatives are introduced, it is likely that some pockets of project activity could be identified. While for such everyday activities the focus is about getting things done, it should be possible to integrate meeting development needs with project-based activities. Indeed, this would be a prime example of using what is there, rather than creating new structures.

A CONTEXT FOR PROJECT-BASED LEARNING

For the specialist, it can be useful to be able to locate project-based learning and development within a broader framework of management development types. Several such frameworks exist, from which we have chosen the Type Model developed by Mumford[1] (see Figure 2.1).

Project-based learning and development through modular linked programmes contains elements of both Types 2 and 3. While, initially structured as Type 3, projects strongly reflect the Type 2 integrated processes, with ownership being clearly more with managers than developers.

Type 1: Informal managerial – Accidental processes

Characteristics	Occur within managerial activities
	Explicit intention is task performance
	No clear development objectives
	Unstructured in development terms
	Not planned in advance
	Owned by managers
Development consequences	Learning is real, direct, unconscious and insufficient

Type 2: Integrated managerial – Opportunistic processes

Characteristics	Occur within managerial activities
	Explicit intention both task performance and development
	Clear development objectives
	Structured for development by boss and subordinate
	Planned beforehand or reviewed subsequently as learning experiences
	Owned by managers
Development consequences	Learning is real, direct, conscious and more substantial

Type 3: Formal management development – Planned processes

Characteristics	Often away from normal managerial activities
	Explicit intention is development
	Clear development objectives
	Structured for development by developers
	Planned beforehand and reviewed subsequently as learning experiences
	Owned more by developers than managers
Development consequences	Learning may be real (through a job) or detached (through a course) and is more likely to be both conscious and relatively infrequent.

Figure 2.1 Model of types of management development

LEARNING METHODS

There is a plethora of links among various learning and development methods. Such links can be described differently depending on the viewpoint taken. Our viewpoint is project-based learning and development.

One clear trend in learning methods, both on and off the job, is towards 'reality'. In off-the-job programmes, role playing using live situations and business simulations, in which the learning thrust is through 'high reality',[2] are increasing in popularity. This is often at the expense of more traditional lectures and some case studies, particularly where links with managerial reality are difficult for managers to make. While there is some growth in distance learning, the gregarious nature of most managers is likely to temper this trend in favour of an emphasis on developing the practical skills of managers, typically through problem-solving activities.

We have chosen just five learning methods to establish links with project-based learning and development. They are coaching, mentoring, self-development, action learning and teamworking. In addition, we have highlighted leadership development, because it provides further opportunities for the integration of project-based learning. Other topical issues and approaches are also included, for instance, empowerment and business process re-engineering. Projects in academic courses are also explored.

COACHING

Coaching is helping someone to learn in order to improve job performance.[3] It takes place on the job and starts from the premise that people can learn from everything they do, for example performing a task, solving a problem and, of course, carrying out a project. Coaching is just one of the ways in which an effective manager manages. It is not issuing instructions, telling someone what to do or prescribing how to do it; rather it is to do with helping, guiding, encouraging and allowing space to perform and do things differently.

Coaching is arguably one of the most undervalued and underused methods of development. This may be due in part to a misunderstanding of what coaching, as a process, involves and how skills, many of which a manager possesses, can be applied in a coaching relationship. However, limitations in the application of coaching may also be caused by the cultural beliefs about learning within the organization. Another limitation can be not knowing the learning styles of individuals.

23

A particular barrier may be the power sharing necessary by the boss, a perception of giving away skills and assets which are critical to the job and status. Indeed, with the increase in job insecurity which many managers are experiencing, the 'giving' element required may be replaced by a more self-centred 'holding on'. A useful definition is: 'Coaching is a form of on-the-job training, using work to provide planned opportunities for learning under guidance.'

So the choice is the everyday work environment, using real situations and work as a learning activity. Planned opportunities can be numerous including delegation, a work problem, the improvement of a product/ process/service, changes in job responsibilities, introduction of change, deputizing, guided reading, pre and post discussion when a course is attended, and projects, both individual and group.

Learning is at the core of any coaching relationship and rich benefits are realizable, providing tasks are seen as opportunities for learning as well as for achievement. For a manager, being involved as a coach can be a useful way of understanding learning more fully. It is still possible that many managers think others learn in the same way that they do.

On taking a coaching role, the manager can help learners to:

- gain greater awareness of needs and opportunities (activist)
- think about performance and development (reflector)
- develop new ideas and concepts (theorist)
- try out new skills and approaches (pragmatist).

The onus then is on the coach to provide appropriate guidance. In the context of project-based learning and development, the sponsor is ideally positioned to take on an occasional coaching role, which could typically involve testing the manager's thinking, steering towards sources of information and expertise and, maybe, opening the occasional door in this respect, without spoonfeeding the manager or giving solutions to problems on a plate. Among other skills, the coach will need to be an effective listener, able to use questioning techniques and give feedback which is valued and acted upon.

In all this there needs to be a sense of realism about what is possible. Over 30 years ago, Chris Argyris wrote: 'I can only be responsible for my own growth. I can never develop other people.' So perhaps a more accurate and succinct definition of coaching is 'assisted self-development'. But Argyris also said: 'In true development the emphasis is upon learning to learn.'

MENTORING

Mentoring has strong links with coaching, particularly in the core skills of listening, questioning and giving feedback.

Mentoring may be formal or informal and it is possible that formal mentoring is already an established requirement within an organization, e.g. professional development in acquiring chartered engineer status.

The distinction with line authority needs to be clear, since the mentor will not be the line manager. Formal systems can legitimize patronage and thus the transfer of skills and experience in providing support, signalling an expectation of progression and recognition of potential. While a valuable contribution to manager development, there needs to be awareness of the risk that a formal system will arouse resentment from those excluded.

Where a system of mentoring does exist, there are likely to be senior managers carrying out mentoring roles who could readily incorporate the role of project sponsor.

The mentor will exercise a wide range of roles in relationship to the protégé or mentee, which includes:

- encouraging two-way exchange of information
- listening to concerns and offering help where appropriate
- acting as a sounding board for ideas
- helping to plan strategies to meet personal goals
- helping to clarify performance goals and development needs
- recommending specific skills where improvement is needed
- acting as a role model to demonstrate effective management
- helping to expand personal network of relationships
- providing signposts towards sources of help and expertise
- representing concerns or specific problems
- urging involvement in high visibility opportunities within and outside the organization
- helping to understand political issues and systems
- giving specific feedback with a focus on constructive criticism
- helping to solve problems by showing new directions
- challenging opinions and beliefs, forcing reflection on decisions
- inspiring interest and displaying enthusiasm.

For the recipient in a mentoring relationship, there can be benefits from:

- increased confidence in the role and personal abilities
- improved networking of relationships
- being stretched, developing faster
- valuable career advice
- having a role model
- having support and a sounding board for ideas.

Of course, the mentor can also benefit from:

- increased job satisfaction in developing others
- increased influence (power)
- improved own promotion prospects
- identifying people to poach!
- increased self-development.

SELF-DEVELOPMENT

Self-development[4] is a process by which individuals:

- identify their personal development goals
- consciously take responsibility for planning and taking action to reach these goals
- develop and use methods of monitoring progress and assessing outcomes
- re-assess goals in the light of new business.

This process can be linked with a manager undertaking a project – the learning side of the twin track 'learning' and 'doing' approach.

The self-development concept, though not new, has become more prominent over the last 20 years. It can be traced much further back, a century earlier, to Samuel Smiles and his self-help treatise.

So, could self-development be a way of life? Is it fiction or is it fantasy? A minority of managers believe that self-development is indeed a way of life. They take responsibility for their own learning and development: it is an integral part of the way they manage. They seek out and use support resources, within and outside the organization. They are that rare breed of self-managed learners. They seek and welcome challenges as learning opportunities. They do not wait for the organization to develop them. They assert, as a right, the priority of their own learning. In organizations where such managers are in the majority, management development is focused on improving productivity, performance and competitiveness.

Pedler and others[5] have made the distinction between 'of' self and 'by' self. Self-development can be very demanding as well as lonely. A group of like-minded colleagues can provide the manager with support, help and challenge. Balance in such groups is important. 'Castle time away from the battlefield', as Harrison describes it, is important for taking stock, reflecting on actions, re-energizing and renewing confidence. However, it should not become a self-indulgent retreat. Critical review by colleagues of actions and non-actions should be carried out to provide a spur for subsequent actions and for taking on further difficult tasks with the benefit of new learning and insights. This 'group as a support system' reflects Revans' 'comrades in adversity' or Mumford's less brittle description of 'fellows in opportunity'. For such groups, membership is voluntary with individuals taking responsibility for identifying and pursuing development needs, but also for helping others identify and meet their needs. The lifecycle of such a group would be governed by the point at which needs are met.

Self-development, where learning is self-managed, has a great potential impact on the aggregate of learning within the organization. It is also a vital ingredient for any organization. But, of course, such learning is greatly enhanced when it is not just 'by' self, but with others. Some organizations have established self-development groups or self-managed learning groups, specifically linking individual needs into the business context with a 'present to future' business scenario. Such groups will usually have an advisor or facilitator. Benefits to be gained include an increased capability in learning to learn and in continuous adaptation. ICL has developed experience in self-managed learning over the last few years (see *The Power of Learning* by Mayo & Lank[6]).

While the process within self-development groups has application, a difference with project groups is signing on to the structure, outputs and timescales required. In the project-based learning context, where group meetings between modules take place, the process of sharing and helping achievement and learning is likely to be more conducive to cultures in which values of achievement and support are manifest, as compared with values ascribed to power and role cultures.[7]

ACTION LEARNING

Of all the learning methods discussed here, action learning has the closest relationship with project-based learning and development. Action learning is concerned with learning by doing and, defined thus, can make it appear deceptively simple.

An action learning programme[8] consists of a group of four to six people, described as a 'set', who learn with and from each other by tackling problems which they are committed to resolving. It can take several forms, including tackling a problem for a sponsor in a different organization, in a different part of the employing organization or even relating to a key problem/issue within the individual's job. The way a set is established and the influences on it are as follows:

- Each 'set' member has a sponsor – a senior member of the organization offering the problem and sponsoring the participant.
- There is also a 'set' adviser who helps the 'set' get on with its basic task of problem solving. The adviser does not solve problems for them.
- In addition, there is a group of people within each organization who can influence the solution of the problem. This group is sometimes called the problem owner or the 'client'.
- There may also be a development group, composed of representatives from participating organizations who, with the 'set' adviser, provide support during the life of the programme.

Action learning places value on 'learning to take effective action', not merely 'recommending action'. Some attempts at management learning overemphasize the ability to analyse and plan, but stop short of action.

Action learning brings together two elements: learning which has been acquired in a 'programmed' structured way, e.g. from courses, denoted by 'P'; and the questioning insights gained through experience, through discovery, denoted by 'Q'.

In an action learning 'set', members learn with and from each other, as well as from their own experiences. There is a clear premise that managers are more likely to learn from respected colleagues than from experts. The 'set' adviser's role is primarily facilitating 'Q', helping managers to develop skills of critical inquiry. A fundamental principle is that each manager, no matter how difficult the problem, will accept responsibility for the action taken. Managers learn most when they take action as distinct from merely studying how to take action.

For managers to make progress on their problem or project, they need to develop an appropriate level of self-awareness, together with a suitable preparedness for self-disclosure. In Johari Window terms, they need to have a very large arena, open to themselves and others. They also need to avoid distancing themselves from the problem/project. For 'set' colleagues to provide effective help they need to perceive the whole, i.e. the individual 'with' the problem.

Of course, problems do not stand still while awaiting the manager's solution. They are organic, changing and the manager will need to acquire detailed knowledge of what is going on. Managers will also need to be clear as to the abilities they can bring to bear on the problem and abilities they lack where the problem provides scope for learning.

Using an action-learning approach on a modular linked programme can be a more powerful form of learning if a number of one-day sessions between modules is arranged (typically over a six-month period). An action-learning assumption[9] that 'people only learn when they do something and they learn more the more responsible they feel the task to be' is well borne out in this type of programme.

TEAMWORKING

Teamworking skills are rated increasingly highly in surveys aimed at predicting future development needs of managers. Already, managers find themselves operating in several teams simultaneously, some of which are temporary. There is a growing need to become skilled at optimizing this mode of working for themselves, their people and their organizations. The link with project-based learning and development then is clear. Projects, whether individual or group based, will require managers to interact with others, frequently in a teamworking mode.

An initiative to improve teamworking skills starts from the premise that there are clear benefits to be gained through effective relationships in working together. In a growing number of organizations, recognition that this requirement is becoming a higher priority is evidenced through statements by top management about a 'one team' culture. Ideally, effective teamworking should start at the top with a team-building activity, but this is not the norm.

However, the people development specialist can initiate teamworking skills activities wherever there is a felt need. This can be where some discomfort, or even pain, is being felt by a number of people, which can be the trigger for the specialist to diagnose needs and gather, collate and feed data back to people who have the authority and will to embark on a team-working skill improvement programme. The content of such a programme, as well as the means of delivery, will be dependent on the outcomes of the diagnostic phase. However, typical issues which may be represented in this context are:

- balancing 'task achievement with team process'
- valuing and using preferences in styles and roles within teams
- identifying and developing characteristics of effective teams
- identifying factors which inhibit teamwork
- handling conflicts within teams
- recognizing, valuing and utilizing differences in teams
- using constructive feedback and review to improve team performance
- exploring personal effectiveness through teamworking
- monitoring and influencing behaviour with teams
- problem solving and decision making in teams
- working in temporary and permanent teams
- team and inter-team development.

To be effective, any teamworking activity needs to embrace 'reality' and 'risk taking'. This is achieved by moving from 'low' to 'higher' throughout the duration of the activities or workshops. Concentrating on the real problems of individuals and groups can be an effective means of both helping to develop teamworking skills and solving difficult problems for which solutions are valued.

Where there are initiatives already in motion to improve teamworking, there is likely to be a climate that supports project-based learning. Indeed, many of the skills will be essential to the successful establishment of project groups.

LEADERSHIP DEVELOPMENT

Leadership development is frequently a priority which the people development specialist needs to tackle. Designing and developing programmes in leadership skills is now standard fare.

While teamworking skills have emerged as a priority out of the massive restructuring which took place during the recession of the early 1990s, leadership skills have undergone a considerable shift as the role of the leader has, of necessity, been redefined. This is due to the complex, dynamic, ambiguous and uncertain environment in which leadership skills now need to be exercised; a far cry from the predictability of environments where reacting, responding and controlling through hierarchy typified acceptable behaviour for the leader. So leaders now function through teamwork, empower rather than control and create an environment in which decisions can be made rather than making all the decisions themselves. Leaders also create shared visions and are seen as role models in living the value systems underpinning the vision. Moreover, they invest heavily in the development and motivation of their people.

As with teams, the leader's tenure with an intact group can be short and uncertain, with more frequent changes in team membership being the only certainty. Without doubt a leader needs to be an effective manager of change and proficient at building and managing a network of relationships.

Where skills are being developed to match this scenario, there are clear and strong links with project-based learning. In the group project, effective leadership is vital to success. A group project also provides, usually in a short timespan, an opportunity for the leader to excel and to be noticed for achievement. Indeed, the group project can typically provide the opportunity to transfer and build new skills, which can add value after project completion.

TOPICAL ISSUES AND APPROACHES

As well as positioning project-based learning within the context of a range of development methods, the people development specialist needs to be aware of topical issues and approaches which are being proffered by authors and consultants or through conferences and seminars. Managers may well be aware of such approaches and, providing they are assessed to have more substance to them than merely being 'flavour of the year', it may be prudent to consider taking them on board.

EMPOWERMENT

Empowerment is one initiative which many organizations are exploring. Is it more than motivation dressed up in different clothes? It certainly has the potential to be so. To empower is to open up, give power, and thereby release the potential of people.

31

The main thrust is through having greater autonomy over how things are done, which gives immense scope for bringing about changes and improvements. Through empowerment, people are given more freedom and choices, more opportunities to take initiatives and risks, and to make decisions.

Properly enacted empowerment will support and promote learning from a wide range of opportunities and situations. Empowerment is at the heart of organizational change. Its relevance to project-based learning is very important. For the role of the project sponsor it is concerned with 'letting go', allowing as wide a range of choices as possible, but being available for any advice and guidance when the manager encounters discomfort with uncertainties. But the sponsor should not shelter the manager from challenges since, if properly scoped, the project is likely to contain several challenges and difficulties. This type of learning, when experienced within a project, is likely to be both measurable and capable of subsequent application with the managerial job.

Empowerment will not take root in organizations unless people can see the bigger picture. Top management will need to communicate inspiring visions and a display of confidence in people. But empowering statements will be no substitute for real, visible empowerment. In this respect, project sponsors have an opportunity to be role models to promote an empowering culture.

Of course, teamwork is at the core of the empowerment process. Where the people development specialist is involved in facilitating and supporting effective teamworking, there will be scope for spearheading empowered project teams; teams which can set their goals for a project, plan, co-ordinate and control their work methods and share in the design of the team's performance measures, even to the extent of setting measures of learning.

Empowerment is no quick fix. It requires substantial cultural change. It will only be effective where it enhances the organization's values; values about which people can feel a large measure of ownership. People will need to feel valued, that they are contributing to key business objectives and to the bottom line.

BUSINESS PROCESS RE-ENGINEERING (BPR)

The development specialist has for some time now found internal customers for services to be more demanding than external ones, particularly in tailored, value-for-money training and development solutions to business problems. Demand for value for money also typifies external customers, who require products and services to be delivered against rigorous criteria, e.g. quality, cost and time. Such competitive pressures are forcing organizations to make major transformations in their processes – transformations which cannot be achieved by the old methods of restructuring. Business process re-engineering is a vehicle for making the link between the organization's external positioning and its internal capability, including processes, competencies and behaviours.

The development specialist needs to be at the centre of any such transformation. BPR changes from 'function' centred to 'process' centred, from linear sequencing to parallel processing, from differentiation to integration and removal of anything which does not add value. All have people development and cultural implications. Indeed, many of the failures in BPR have been due to neglect of the people dimension in change. This has been particularly so where assumptions have been made that people will welcome radical change and that top management will be able to communicate effectively the rationale, which is likely to be interpreted as a threat to job security and working conditions.

Some form of project activity, whether individual or group, will be present as part of any BPR change strategy. Indeed, many re-engineering programmes find the changing of culture and people too demanding a challenge, so only processes and systems are changed, with predictable outcomes. There is an opportunity here for the people development specialist to claim the high ground by adopting a more holistic approach to change. Multi-disciplinary project groups can be part of a strategy for such radical change and, while many of the main architects of BPR come from a systems background, the people development specialist can have a key behavioural/cultural input. In addition, to be successful, BPR needs to sponsor and encourage creativity and innovation rather than drive it out through misperception, of which there is a real risk.

There are links here with empowerment. A commitment to empowering individuals and groups can form an important part of a BPR change strategy.

PROJECTS IN ACADEMIC COURSES

Projects have for some time been an integral element of academic courses for management qualifications. The model developed and used in guiding learning through projects at Strathclyde Graduate Business School for the Diploma in Business is both valuable and rigorous.

Project guidelines are offered covering purpose, benefits and project choice. Guidance is also given on methodology. Projects are problem based within the student's organization, with the likelihood of financial payback.

THE MAIN GUIDELINES

Main guidelines for the project are set out here.

Purposes of the Project

The project is an integral part of the Diploma course and, if properly chosen, it will serve the following purposes:

- Develop your understanding of the concepts, techniques and skills acquired on the course and your ability to synthesize them through their application in the work place.
- Assist you to develop your competencies as a manager.
- Develop your skills of writing and presenting a management report in a well-structured and lucid manner.

Potential Benefits to You and Your Employer

When approaching your project, we suggest that you think beyond merely satisfying the course requirements and consider the following:

- If you conduct the project with enthusiasm and endeavour, the result should be a source of personal pride and make a significant contribution to your ability to perform as a manager.
- Since the project will provide you with an opportunity to practise problem solving in your work place, it will give you an opportunity to make a positive impact on your employer.
- If the project is carefully chosen, with the assistance of your line manager, it could be financially beneficial to your employing organization, helping to defray the cost of your course and encouraging your employer to sponsor you on the next stage of your career development – the Strathclyde Master of Business Administration (MBA)!

Choosing the Project Topic

It is your responsibility to identify a suitable project topic with the approval of your employer and your Course Tutor. The project should be of interest and value to you and your employer, and should require the exercise of personal initiative and investigation. The topic chosen should reflect the broad purpose of the Diploma course, being relevant to a middle level line management position in public or private institutions, and should not be too narrow in focus. You should endeavour to make as much use as possible of the topics covered during the course.

You should discuss possible project areas with your line manager with a view to finding a problem area that will take you beyond your current job function and thus require liaison with a spectrum of people and functions within the organization. Ideally, the project outcome should be a solution to a problem and a proposal for implementing it – better still, a report on its successful implementation!

Company Mentor

Since the project is to be based in your work place, it is not feasible for SGBS staff to take a major role in guiding its progress. This element of the course is designed for you to develop your managerial competencies at work and it is therefore best guided by your peers and senior managers. It is therefore essential that you identify someone in your organization who would be willing to act as a mentor or guide to you for the duration of the project. This person may or may not be your line manager but should be in a position to guide you through the internal workings of the organization and open appropriate doors for you. They will obviously need to have an interest in your particular project area.

SGBS PROJECT SUPERVISOR

As stated previously, SGBS is not expecting to take a major role in guiding the project but you will be allocated a Strathclyde supervisor who will be available for advice by any appropriate media, e.g. telephone, fax, e-mail, post, etc. Depending on your proximity to Glasgow, you may or may not meet the supervisor face to face unless there is a number of Diploma participants within one company loca-tion. However, your project proposal should be submitted to Strathclyde for approval in the first place when you will be allocated a supervisor. Thereafter, you should have intermittent contact with the supervisor to discuss project progress and indeed to submit draft elements of the management report. Ultimately, the supervisor will be the Assessor of the project and it is therefore in your interest to main-tain contact with the supervisor. If it is feasible in terms of time and cost, the supervisor may be available to attend the project presenta-tion to your company's senior management.

TIMESCALE

Give careful consideration to the effort and timescale likely to be required in completing the project, to ensure that it will be manage-able in the time available to you (equivalent to four credits). It is not meant to be a large project and it might take about 150 hours work. It should be spread over a maximum period of nine months part-time working in parallel with your normal work.

PROJECT METHODOLOGY

Generally your project should include the following stages:

a) Identify and clearly define the nature and scope of the problem.
b) Identify and evaluate previous relevant work in your project area, e.g. review of academic literature or previous reports within the organization.
c) Identify the data required and organize its collection.
d) Hypothesize a model (not necessarily quantitative), use the data to build and test it and finally analyse it for a recommended solu-tion (or further information, e.g. a forecasting model).
e) Draw conclusions from the analysis and make recommendations for solving the problem, showing the costs and benefits of the recommendations.
f) Plan the implementation of the solution and then implement it.
g) Make a presentation to senior management showing how the problem could be solved and the value to the organization of so doing. Support the presentation with a management report.

Fuller project methodology guidelines will be issued by Strathclyde as you approach the project component of your Diploma.

PROJECT ASSESSMENT

The project will be assessed in *two* parts:

a) A 30-minute presentation to management of your findings and recommendations. Evidence of the presentation should be sent to SGBS in the form of photocopies of OHP slides and, perhaps, a video of the presentation. Your mentor will be asked for an assessment of the presentation.

b) A short report of around 6,000 words. The quality of what you write is far more important than the quantity.

KEY POINT SUMMARY

- Among development needs which can be identified by the people development specialists, there may be clusters of needs for which projects will be the most cost-effective development approach.
- Pockets of project activity are likely to be visible in how work is done, how change is managed and how new initiatives are introduced.
- It can be useful to locate project-based learning and development within a framework of types of management development, e.g. *Models of Types of Management Development* by A. Mumford.
- Coaching is a role which the project sponsor can take on, typically by testing the project owner's thinking, providing occasional guidance and offering the benefit of his own experience.
- Where a mentoring system exists, senior managers carrying out such roles could readily incorporate the role of project sponsor.
- In a culture which supports self-development, managers taking responsibility for their own development can identify and use (with the people development specialist's help) the project approach in meeting particular learning goals.
- Project-based learning and development has the closest relationship with action learning. Where a modular linked programme is used, one-day sessions in action learning mode can yield powerful results.

- Projects, whether individual or group, will require managers to interact with others, frequently in a teamworking mode; so the development of teamworking skills can be readily integrated with project-based learning and development.
- For group projects, it will be necessary to develop a range of teamworking skills if project outputs are to be successful.
- Also for group projects, effective leadership skills can be vital to success and can also provide a leader with the opportunity to excel and have achievements recognized.
- The essential 'letting go' required for real empowerment, when practised by the project sponsor, can open up a wide range of choices for the project owner. It can promote a culture in which learning, including learning through difficulty, can be promoted.
- Where there are several sponsors with respective projects, a support group can be of value in sharing experiences and in identifying and developing skills.
- Establishing an appropriate infrastructure can be instrumental to the success of a project. Organizational readiness can be an important criterion, and one which the people development specialist may usefully gauge and influence.
- The people development specialist can show a lead in ensuring a strong emphasis on 'learning through projects' as both the orchestrator of infrastructure and an ally to sponsors in helping to integrate projects with business goals.
- Project owners and sponsors need to be aware of the pitfalls to avoid, thus learning from others' mistakes rather than the costly process of learning from one's own.
- On academic courses, it is important for students to identify potential benefits of the project for themselves and the organization, as well as satisfying course requirements.
- A carefully chosen project can produce financial benefits, thus defraying the cost of any off-the-job course with which it is integrated. This could lead to further organization sponsorship of the individual's career development.
- The quality of an individual's project output, i.e. presentation to sponsor/mentor/line manager and written report, can be a key contribution to learning and development.

- There is scope for the people development specialist to contribute towards BPR initiatives by highlighting and facilitating essential behavioural and cultural change.
- Creativity and innovation can be encouraged by the people development specialist in BPR initiatives as a balance to any prescriptively driven interventions.
- Since the introduction of BPR invariably involves some multi-disciplined project activity, there is scope for the people development specialist to take a leading role by ensuring that learning is effectively captured and valued.

REFERENCES

1. Mumford, A. (1989), 'Model of Types of Management Development', *Strategies for Action*, London: Institute of Personnel Development.
2. Smith, B. (1987/88), *High Reality Business Simulations for Managers, Training and Management Development Methods*, Vols 1 & 2, Bradford: MCB University Press.
3. Smith, B. (1985), Management Action Checklist No. 6, *Coaching, Management Monitor*, Chichester, W. Sussex, Cromwell House Publications.
4. Delf, G. and Smith, B. (1978), 'Strategies for Promoting Self-Development', *Industrial and Commercial Training*, **10**, (12), pp. 409–501.
5. Pedler, M., Burgoyne, J. and Boydell, T. (1986), A Manager's Guide to Self-Development, 2nd edn, Maidenhead: McGraw-Hill.
6. Mayo, A. and Lank, E. (1994), *The Power of Learning*, London: Institute of Personnel Development.
7. Harrison, R. (1987), *Organisation Culture and Quality of Service*, London: Association of Management Education and Development.
8. Revans, R. W. (1982), *The Origins and Growth of Action Learning*, Bromley, Chartwell-Bratt.
9. Casey, D. (1976), 'The Emerging Role of Set Adviser in Action Learning Programmes', *Journal of European Training*, **5**, (3), pp. 3–14.

REFERENCES

3 Planning a Programme

Once a project is conceived it is important for the people development specialist to have a good grasp of who are likely to be the key stakeholders as the project progresses. The quality of relationships between the stakeholders themselves and their relationship with the project owner will be critical to the success of the project. Of particular importance will be the possible roles, activities and availability of the project sponsor and the corresponding contributions and benefits obtained by the project owner. Equally important will be the relationship between sponsor and project owner and how this relationship is initiated, monitored and developed throughout the duration of the project.

STARTING SIMPLE

For the people development specialist embarking on project-based learning the initial infrastructure may be rather basic. It may only involve the individuals carrying out the projects and their line manager, with the specialist involved in a setting-up and advisory role, as illustrated in Figure 3.1. Of course, there could be occasions when the specialist alone is involved, for instance where there is a graduate management trainee scheme for which the specialist is both organizer and project sponsor. Wherever possible, the specialist needs to optimize the opportunities for securing line management involvement with projects. Whether the specialist, line manager or sponsor is provider or orchestrator of the learning experience, there can be value in some initial formality and authority in establishing an infrastructure for getting started on the project. But, in having ultimate ownership for learning, the individual carrying out the project will have some freedom of choice to build and develop the infrastructure.

41

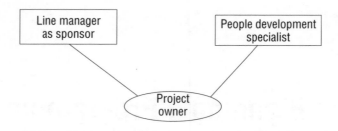

Figure 3.1 Project-based learning infrastructure

SPONSOR

Whether or not project sponsors are line managers, there will be a range of roles and activities which the sponsor may undertake. These roles are likely to include:[1]

- mentor
- coach
- adviser
- critic
- assessor
- learning facilitator
- sign-poster
- ambassador

Activities will vary according to the nature and scale of the project but, in our experience of working with sponsors, the following have been identified as important:

- Advising on the initial choice of project, by applying criteria for choice (see Figure 1.1).

    This initial identification/agreement of a project between manager and sponsor/line manager is in itself a critical success factor. We have found that when the 'criteria' are rigorously applied to project ideas/ possibilities, adequate screening ensures that projects chosen will have a good chance of successful implementation. This initial meeting is an opportunity to clarify individual and mutual expectations and to put in place an important element of the project infrastructure.
- Helping to scope the project, ensuring that what is to be attempted is feasible and realistic, and also sufficiently challenging and stretching (developed further in this chapter).

42

- Helping to sort and concentrate priorities, so that time is not wasted pursuing peripheral issues.
- Providing context; showing the bigger picture, where the project fits into the scheme of things.
- Sign-posting to main people and stakeholders.
- Advising on culture, political systems and power issues as appropriate.
- Coaching at specific stages and in situations involving difficulties or new opportunities
- Helping to solve problems, through coaching on problem-solving skills and techniques, but not actually solving problems for the project owner.
- Motivating, energizing the project owner when difficulties or lack of progress are experienced.
- Communicating imminent changes which may affect the project.
- Representing the project and its significance to peers and colleagues.
- Selling project outputs to key people as an ambassador.
- Ensuring appropriate rewards, e.g. acknowledgement for project achievement.
- Picking up and channelling any wider opportunities or ramifications from the project to appropriate sources.
- Helping to contextualize new learning so that learning transfer is effective.

Some of these activities may follow a logical sequence, but others may arise intermittently. The sponsor role presents an ideal opportunity to pass on experience, skills and knowledge in a coaching role within a structured format. Activities within the role will change in emphasis over the duration of the project. Initially, the emphasis will be to establish aims and purposes, testing against criteria of choice, providing guidance on project structure and timescale with some initial sign-posting and, where appropriate, opening one or two doors for access to information. Subsequently, activities may include helping to keep the project on track, advising on how to tackle roadblocks, keeping a focus on outputs (bottom-line and learning) and, where necessary, providing or sustaining motivation when progress falters and difficulties arise.

In programmes at Sundridge Park in recent years, 'thinking big' has been more in evidence in choosing projects. Sponsors are now more

43

searching in looking at the problems and opportunities in the business. This can mean that the 'bottom-line' output takes priority in the sponsor's decision-making process, thus placing a greater priority on project owners to take ownership for the learning process.

Towards the end of the project, a devil's advocate role may be adopted in rigorously testing recommendations and planned actions, as well as a support role in projecting outputs into the wider business arena involving other stakeholders.

Where the sponsor is also the line manager, a relationship with the project owner will already exist. However, being in a new 'project owner to project sponsor' relationship provides opportunities for the former to build the effectiveness of the relationship. The project provides a temporary and intermittent 'working together' opportunity, an opportunity for receiving coaching on which the manager should capitalize. Such one-to-one meetings will be prime time and it will be important to prepare carefully beforehand.

Since the project is intended as a learning experience, the manager should concentrate on how the sponsor can assist that learning. This does not mean going along with several problems, expecting solutions from the sponsor. It does mean seeking guidance and thoughts on possible approaches. The aim should be to gain from the sponsor's experience and insights. Such meetings should be purposeful and not merely routine progress monitoring against deadlines. Because they draw in top managers as sponsors, projects can often help to raise their level of commitment to management development.

It is still not uncommon for an organization to channel most of its management development efforts on junior and middle levels of management. There is frequently a tacit assumption that senior or top level managers and directors do not need it. If they did, how could they possibly be where they are today?

For sponsors, the multiplicity of possible roles may cause some initial conflict but, once the project relationship develops, there are no incompatibilities. Providing guidance on avenues to explore, while constantly criticizing gaps in thinking or planning, can be compatible within the same dialogue. The initial separation of roles, however, may help sponsors in structuring their approach to the overall role.

Project working can be a means of channelling individual, group and organizational learning.

Projects differ from much of the everyday work of an organization because of their temporary nature. Often they will be dealing with the new, the different or the unusual.

The project owner needs to recognize how the project fits into the bigger organizational picture. This can be where the sponsor may be able to help in making appropriate links.

To ensure commitment, sponsors must be able to see learning in practice by project owners. This can be more visible for group projects where behaviours such as handling complex change, teamworking and cross-functional/cultural co-operation can be seen in action. Indeed such project groups may model the behaviours required in tackling strategic business issues.

While the sponsor is the main stakeholder, it is important to be aware of the different interests of other stakeholders, how they may integrate and how they may change as the project develops.

SPONSOR AND LINE MANAGER

Functioning as a project sponsor is very different from operating as a line manager. Where the project owner is a staff member, the normal hierarchical/managing relationship may not be a relevant style to adopt, i.e. straightforward delegation. Where several dilemmas exist in a climate of general uncertainty and change, assumptions about clarity of goal and task may be unfounded.

Admitting and embracing ambiguity, and/or holding back from telling or instructing, may herald a different way of working for many project sponsors. This can also cause difficulty for the project owner who has been used to requesting and being given answers by the sponsor in their day-to-day relationship. It can mark a shift in relationship more towards partnership and away from hierarchy.

SPONSOR–LINE MANAGER RELATIONSHIP

Where the sponsor is not the line manager, there is a high chance of conflict in relation to the project. The sponsor is staking a claim to resources for which the line manager has overall accountability. There, therefore, needs to be a clear and mutual understanding between the sponsor and line manager as to how issues regarding priorities and deadlines are handled. The project owner is likely to experience conflicting pressures

45

between the day-to-day demands of the job and the longer term requirements of the project. While this mirrors the managerial reality of handling competing short and longer term pressures, it is likely to be an area where help may be required, as well as an attitude of give and take between sponsor and line manager. Depending on the scale of the project activity in the organization – e.g. several managers undertaking projects simultaneously – the people development specialist may have an intermediary facilitating role to play. A simple set of ground rules, agreed by line managers and sponsors, could be useful here. They might include the following:

- An initial scoping document, shared between sponsor and line manager.
- Critical events/activities in both the project and the management job identified, predicted (as far as is possible) and incorporated in the project plan.
- A comprehensive project plan, clearly identifying when resources are likely to be stretched. This information should be shared with both sponsor and line manager.
- The project owner should call on the sponsor/line manager if a serious conflict of priorities arises which cannot be resolved unaided.

Such a set of rules could help to avoid the situation where a line manager offers advice such as 'just find the time but not at the expense of . . .'. This response is quite common among line managers.

It can be testing for the manager successfully to integrate a project with the everyday activities of managing, while keeping both line manager and sponsor happy, particularly where the latter is taking on the role in a serious and professional manner.

Realistic expectations between sponsor and project owner is very important, especially where the former has no previous experience of such a role. While immense value can be acquired from feeling the stretch of a project, unrealistic targets can ultimately be demotivating for some project owners.

Although the project sponsor will have an interest in the 'task' or bottom line output, as well as the learning output, the line manager's interest will be clearly biased towards the learning output, in bringing added value to the project owner's development, e.g. new/improved skill or knowledge which can be applied subsequently. Striking a realistic balance between both sets of outputs is important.

PROJECT OWNERS – SKILLS

Although projects can provide for the practice and development of a wide range of skills, our experience to date suggests that a few important clusters of skills tend to achieve particular prominence. One such cluster centres around research methodology which, for some managers, means picking up skills learnt earlier but now relatively dormant.

For other managers, this might be a new skill area which necessitates locating internal expertise. A typical example would be a manager with no marketing experience seeking advice and expertise from market research staff in designing and conducting customer service surveys.

Another cluster concerns interpersonal skills including interviewing, influencing and persuading, which may develop into the need for a higher level of internal consultancy skills; skills which are becoming more important and prominent with the change being experienced by many organizations towards more open cultures. The whole area of mapping and building networks of relationships, including identifying and meeting stakeholder needs and expectations, is encompassed by this skills cluster.

Of course, the chief stakeholder is the project sponsor and handling this relationship well is essential to success. While realizing and releasing the role potential of the sponsor is vital, there may be occasions where it is necessary to confront issues which, if avoided, could result in unsatisfactory project outcomes. The skills of giving and receiving constructive feedback are important here.

OTHER STAKEHOLDERS

Although the sponsor is the main stakeholder for the project, there will be others whose success criteria are likely to be different. This is unlikely to be static: new stakeholders with different priorities may emerge, so project owners need constantly to keep the situation under review. New stakeholders might well have a declared interest which could raise the profile of the project within the organization, giving scope for it to become a more substantial development experience.

Stakeholders will have a number of common characteristics which include:

47

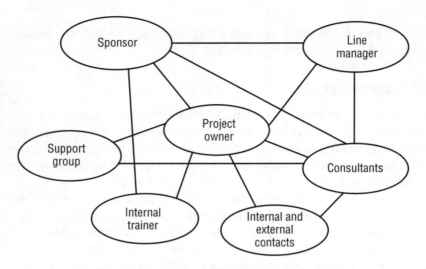

Figure 3.2 Infrastructure following scoping

- power or clout
- key information to contribute
- a degree of self-interest
- knowledge of the project and anticipated outputs
- approachability
- accessibility
- a preference for expectations to be met (no nasty surprises).

SCOPING

Scoping the project will determine the initial infrastructure which will become real once action starts. A typical infrastructure is represented in Figure 3.2. Scoping is unlikely to remain the same process throughout the project; it is more likely to undergo a number of iterations between sponsor and project owner. This can be important in clarifying just what is 'in' or 'outside' the boundary of the project, sorting the 'essential' from the 'nice' options. Even then, boundaries will be fluid to some extent, not least because things will change as the project proceeds. The organization does not stand still while the manager carries out the project.

It is at the scoping stage that the project owner's approach to 'thinking big' can subsequently have a valuable and valued pay-off. Since the project is likely to have an impact on a wide range of tasks, it is inevitably a disturbance. How big a disturbance the project owner is willing and able to tolerate or handle is a significant consideration.

This raises the issue of how well the project is integrated with other tasks and activities. It could be argued that the more separate it is, the more developmental it will be, e.g. insights into different parts of the business, breaking new ground. On the other hand, a degree of integration or fit with a specific ongoing objective can also yield development benefits, e.g. reaching out, but keeping your feet on the ground.

The project scope could highlight dilemmas in relation to the manager's day-to-day job. The sound practice of defining the objective, with a well-planned methodology and outputs tied to deadlines, might be at odds with actual management experience. Management objectives being undertaken on a day-to-day basis will vary from clarity to vagueness. The priority given to the project in its scoping may set it apart somewhat from other managerial activities. However, there can be dilemmas for the sponsor/line manager where distinctions need to be made between the project and the manager's line activities. A project will often cut across line responsibilities, so clear definition and differentiation is needed to minimize the risk of muddled activities and responsibilities.

All of this apart, some practical guidance will be needed to clarify the scope and get started. Assuming criteria for choice have been applied and a suitable project has been identified, the project owner will probably benefit from posing a few questions for clarification. These might include:

- What am I going to do?
- What difference will it make to how the company or I do things?
- How can I measure the difference in terms of what the company will value?
- Is it an isolated or an ongoing difference?
- What do I have to do to make this project successful (knowledge, skills, contacts, etc.).

Getting started and getting organized will be the next consideration. Again a checklist of questions may be helpful:

- Where will I start?
- How will I start?
- What resources will I need (time, access to information, commitment/ sponsorship)?

49

- How will I sequence my actions?
- Who can assist me with data gathering and expertise?
- Has anyone managed this type of project previously?
- How will I know I'm making progress?
- What problems will I experience and which ones are high/low risk?
- How will I secure people's commitment to do what I need?
- What early success do I need to achieve?

INTERNAL AND EXTERNAL CONTACTS

For some project owners this is likely to be breaking new ground. Project owners will be establishing and exploring new internal relationships, usually in parts of the business with which they are less familiar. Such contacts may be at different levels, and this 'occasion' of the project can lead subsequently to building valued relationships. In addition with the impact of delayering, learning opportunities can be utilized through this expansion and development of a network of relationships.

The extent of external contacts will depend on the project, but typically such contacts may provide opportunities for benchmarking. Again, depending on the project aims, external contacts may include educational, professional and consultancy bodies, as well as customers and suppliers, with possible subsequent networking advantages.

SUPPORT GROUPS

Where several individual projects are being carried out at the same time, for example as part of a larger development programme, there is an obvious benefit in establishing a support group. While content and context may vary widely, the *fact* of carrying out a project, with various successes and pitfalls along the way, can be a source of valuable learning, together with the added spin-off of occasional teamworking. This is where the people development specialist can play an active role, as well as possibly involve a number of senior managers who are committed to the people development part of their roles.

Moreover, when there are several sponsors with different projects, there is scope for setting up a support group to share experiences and identify and develop essential skills. Again, this is where the people development specialist might take the initiative.

50

INFRASTRUCTURE ISSUES

Establishing the appropriate infrastructure for a project is an activity which may be critical to the ultimate output of the project. The infrastructure should facilitate not inhibit; release not constrain. It should offer value to the thrusting, go it alone, assertive manager, while providing essential support to the manager who may lack some confidence.

Managing change is much in evidence in relation to project infrastructure. On modular-linked programmes (usually with a six-month gap between modules), the manager's job may change during the project, the sponsor may move out and there may be a new boss. So, managing changing relationships in the infrastructure can be an important activity for project owners.

Another key consideration is the readiness of the organization to support projects. Is the structure one in which a manager carrying out a project, often with a cross functional/departmental component, will be welcomed or will there be hostility? Will the culture, values and beliefs be supportive of, or antagonistic towards, such a venture? These are issues on which the people development specialist will need to advise and influence where necessary.

Putting an appropriate infrastructure in place is much more than drawing up a network of relationships covering the sponsor, boss, people development specialist, other stakeholders, colleagues, etc. It needs activating and becomes a benefit (not just a feature) in seeking to secure the desired project outputs.

LEARNING

As previously mentioned, there is a shift towards managers taking more responsibility for their own learning. The people development specialist is at the heart of business development: will be aware of current and potential project activity throughout the organization; will thus be able to identify where the development needs of an individual manager coincide with the needs of the business. The specialist should, therefore, be able to help managers both identify more strongly with the concept of being involved in projects and with making the right choices. The specialist should also, where appropriate, be able to establish the relationship between the manager and project sponsor.

Equally, the specialist could prompt managers to question themselves as to whether they are giving enough emphasis to learning through projects; whether they are being sufficiently productive in taking or making project opportunities; whether they are sufficiently at the forefront of change, for which projects are frequently the means of delivery.

At one level, the role of people development specialist can include orchestrating the infrastructure and monitoring progress towards project outputs. At other levels, it may demand a more active involvement in working with sponsors to secure meaningful change through full integration of projects with business goals. In this respect the specialist's clients will be managers, sponsors and the organization. The role may encompass successful integration of organizational and individual learning.

CLASSIFYING PROJECTS

As project-based learning becomes part of the organizational fabric it should be possible to produce a classification of projects which, with several dimensions or variables, will help when choosing and scoping them.

At the core of the project-based learning philosophy is 'innovation', breaking new ground, bringing new 'things' into being. The scope for innovation will clearly vary with the type of project. For instance, developing a new system, a process or a product will have more scope for innovation than a project which centres on bringing about necessary improvements. Some projects, when properly selected and scoped, can provide a spur to innovation and change. As Sir Paul Girolami of Glaxo says: 'Innovation should become an attitude of mind. It should permeate the whole business – research, products, production, administration, services and marketing. It is no good being effective in one department and not in another.'

Some typical project classifications are:

- Strategy – produce/develop/establish for:
  - marketing new products
  - improving sales performance
  - PR for the business
- Systems – develop/implement for:
  - management information
  - cost control
  - information technology
  - stock control

- performance appraisal
- TQM.

The type and size of an individual's job can influence substantially the choice and scoping of a project. The biggest variable is likely to be the degree of accountability for other people. The manager with little or no accountability for staff cannot command resources for the project. The project sponsor can do some door opening in terms of requesting co-operation and support from people in other departments or functions, but the main onus will be on the project owner to try to secure resources without the use of authority. In contrast, the manager with a team of people can readily command resources to collect and collate information/opinions from other departments and functions. The team manager also has scope to frame such contributions as development experiences for staff.

Managers experienced in managing projects, should be able to ensure a smooth running project together with stretching for more significant outputs. Regardless of whether the manager undertaking a project has people accountability, there will be valuable learning. However, the learning will differ depending on the nature of the project and the business sector concerned.

PITFALLS TO AVOID – PROJECT OWNER

Establishing the infrastructure, scoping the project and carrying out the project can be a fraught process. There are particular pitfalls which the project owner should seek to avoid, thus learning from the mistakes of others rather than repeating them. The main pitfalls are:

- Underestimating the importance of co-ordinating different resources, including people.
- Underestimating the time required for particular phases of the project.
- Unrealistic/over-ambitious planning.
- Not taking account of changes throughout the project.
- Not planning essential access to sponsor.
- Not keeping the purpose in view.
- Not fully appreciating the effects of various changes.
- Not securing a common understanding of expected outputs with the sponsor.

- Not being clear about who are the end users (clients) of the project where these differ from the sponsor.
- Not maintaining the appropriate balance between the project and other job priorities.
- Not recognizing the different outputs required from the project by the main project stakeholders.
- Not recognizing who needs to be informed on progress/implications at the start of the project and periodically during its implementation.
- Not balancing the outputs in relation to task, people, systems, structure – change in one area invariably impacts on one or more other areas.
- Not adopting a whole brain approach, e.g. too biased to left brain logic, analysis, form, structure.
- Not claiming/securing the requisite authority to match the account-abilities which the project requires.
- Not taking account of the informal power and political relationships.
- Not exercising leadership characteristics essential to project achievement.
- Not ensuring that high expectations are matched with managerial and sponsor support.
- Not taking account of unpredictable outcomes in the assessment of individual performance.
- Not recognizing a real constraint and/or perceiving a constraint which has not been imposed.
- Not recognizing or compensating for imposed lack of skills among the main people involved.

TYPICAL PITFALLS – SPONSORS

Sponsors are not immune to pitfalls, either. Again, here are a few:

- Allowing the end point for a project to be a set of recommendations, rather than pursuing action to make changes. If nothing is different as a consequence of the project, then success and potential for learning has been unduly limited.
- Not helping the project owner to cope with critical issues, e.g.:
  - foreseeing real difficulties which will be encountered
  - recognizing political pressures and understanding the power system.

- Insufficient attention being paid to the learning process during the project, e.g. an assumption that learning will happen.
- Not picking up (or helping the project owner to pick up) signals about change which, if ignored, could result in the project output being out of date or redundant.

KEY POINT SUMMARY

- There is a range of roles which a project sponsor can take on including mentor, coach, adviser, critic, assessor, learning facilitator, sign-poster, door-opener and ambassador.

  A key activity for the sponsor is to advise on the initial choice of project. This will be achieved by applying criteria of choice (see Chapter 1).
- Roles and outcomes of the project sponsor will vary over the time-scale of the project; role priorities will emerge and recede. There is an opportunity here for the people development specialist to help sponsors in getting to grips with, and effectively performing, the variety of roles.
- Involving senior managers as project sponsors can often help them to commit more to management development.
- Where the project sponsor is also the line manager, the 'sponsor–owner' role relationship may differ from the day-to-day 'boss–staff member' relationship. For some, it could mark a shift towards partnership and away from hierarchy.
- Where the project sponsor is not the line manager, there needs to be an understanding of how issues regarding priorities and deadlines are handled. An attitude of 'give and take' is fundamental.
- A set of agreed ground rules for sponsor and line manager is essential to avoid unnecessary conflict.
- Other 'stakeholders' in the project need to be identified, including their specific interests, requirements and what they may have to offer to the project owner.
- Scoping the project is a vital activity and will affect how developmental it can be. The boundary of the project needs to be as clearly defined as possible, while acknowledging the possible dilemma that it also needs to be fluid.

- Since a project is inevitably going to be breaking new ground, identifying internal and external contacts which will need to be made is an important early stage.
- Valuable learning can be derived from setting up support groups when several projects are being carried out within the same timeframe.
- There is scope for sponsors to look more searchingly at problems and opportunities in the business when identifying suitable projects.
- In today's business climate, sponsors are more likely to be looking for *business* benefits from projects, thus putting the onus on project owners to take ownership of *learning* benefits.
- With their wider perspective of the business environment, sponsors can help project owners see how projects fit into the larger organizational context.
- A classification of projects can be developed which helps organizations to choose and scope projects.

REFERENCE

1. Smith, B. and Dodds, B. (1993), 'The Power of Projects in Management Development', *Industrial and Commercial Training*, **25**, (10), pp. 3–9.

4 The Value of Projects on Public Programmes

Public programmes tend to fall into two categories:

- those concerned with a specific skill or knowledge set, lasting two or three days
- those with a far broader general management focus of two to four weeks.

In the second, an individual project can concentrate on learning and learning transfer.

A company's investment in an individual's development, where it includes a general management programme, needs to be as cost effective as possible, since such programmes are expensive. The inclusion of a project can help to make the investment cost effective.

Where part of the off-the-job learning can be carried out before work on the project starts, a large amount can be tested/used/transferred through the project. Learning about models and theories of managing change, then applying them in carrying out the project (which often involves some aspects of change management) is good practice in training effectiveness.

The best form of project-based learning is arguably where the project provides a link between two or more off-the-job modules. It then becomes integrative and not a separate 'bolt-on' extra.

As with selection and recruitment, if you make a bad decision regarding the initial choice of a project there is little you can do about it, other than the inevitable.

Offering a clear set of criteria for choice to the individual and sponsor can help to eliminate potentially inappropriate projects. Discussion of alternatives against the criteria can also help in making the ultimate choice.

When Sundridge Park first embarked on integrating projects into general management programmes there was a bias towards choosing projects which had a strong element of delivering learning outcomes. Over time, there has been a client driven shift towards a balance between learning outcomes and 'bottom line' business benefits.

In addition, there is now a trend in which programme participants are about to undertake, or have already started, a project in their normal work situation. There is, then, discussion of how the project may meet the criteria of choice offered for project selection and how the project can integrate with the timescale of the modular programme. Perhaps this trend is indicative of an increase in projects as a normal mode of working for managers. It is in such circumstances that the project may take on a higher profile than if it had not been linked to an off-the-job programme.

THE DEVELOPMENT OF PROJECT-BASED LEARNING AT SUNDRIDGE PARK

Project-based learning was initiated at Sundridge Park in 1986,[1] when the Younger Manager Programme was designed and added to the portfolio of Open Programmes. The innovative aspect of the programme design was a modular approach (two × one weeks) with a project linking the modules.

The programme was born out of the need to build the right foundation early in a manager's career, i.e. to establish good habits before bad ones could take hold. It concentrated on promoting early acceptance by managers of responsibility for their own development, it provided a broad base of learning, including the major business functions, key management principles and processes and the whole range of people skills.

The structure of the two modules, separated by a period of five to six months, was designed to optimize the potential for learning transfer. For example, problem solving, managing change and influencing skills formed part of the content of the first module. In addition, there was a project workshop day midway between the two modules. The outline programme is illustrated in Figure 4.1.

A salient decision of any organization is the selection of its managers. Similarly, in project-based learning, the selection of the project is of paramount importance. To this end, we identified the need to apply criteria for

58

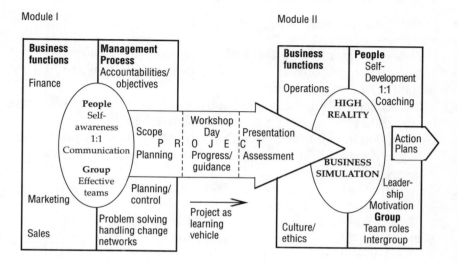

Figure 4.1 The Younger Manager Programme

the choice of project and to establish conditions for successful project completion (see Figures 1.1 and 1.2). For most projects selected for the programme, almost all the criteria were applied.

The results of a recent survey with managers and sponsors included an evaluation of the relative importance of specific criteria in project selection. This is referred to later in the chapter.

Occasionally, there has been a need to check the criteria and conditions between sponsor/participant and the programme director, but in the main this has not been necessary. On the *first* module, two sessions are devoted to the project. The first is to look at clarification of purpose and scope for the project, to test the methodology envisaged and the expected outcomes, i.e. what the project is likely to achieve for the participant's learning, career development and for the sponsor/company. This is carried out in groups of four to six, with a consultant as facilitator. Participants are encouraged to test each other's thinking on their projects. A checklist is used by the consultant in facilitating the session, as outlined below. 'Fellows in opportunity' or 'comrades in adversity' start to show during this session.

PROJECTS – SOME PROMPTS

- How clear is the purpose?
- How realistic/feasible is it?
- How are you going to go about it?
- What problems (if any) do you anticipate in devoting five to 10 days to the project?
- What sources of information and advice may you require? Will there be any difficulties in obtaining information/advice?
- How do you intend to integrate the project with your job priorities?
- Will you be preparing a time plan with check points to monitor progress?
- To what extent will you need to obtain information
  - from other people/functions?
  - from external sources?
- Will you need to persuade/influence people?
- Whose commitment will you need to proposed changes?
- How will you secure such commitments?
- What, for you, will be a successful project?
- Will your boss's/sponsor's view be the same?

One outcome from this session is the occasional necessity for the participant to go back to the sponsor to clarify/modify the scope of the project. Sometimes, the outcomes are over-ambitious or unrealistic within the timescale, or the project is too modest or small in providing for stretching learning benefits. The application of criteria and conditions, together with the scoping session, has resulted in projects which have been challenging, testing and provided learning and bottom-line pay-offs.

The second session, scheduled towards the end of the module, provides an opportunity to pick up and deal with any outstanding issues and to start looking towards the project workshop day and the second module during which project presentations, with sponsors in attendance, take place. There is also a video, with support material, which tracks a manager's progress on the project from the point of leaving Sundridge Park, at the end of the first module, up to the point where the final presentation is made. Relating a real project experience serves to help participants in making the transition back to the work place and starting work on the project.

THE PROJECT WORKSHOP DAY

A special day is set aside about midway between the two modules to provide participants with an opportunity to take stock and to meet any needs for advice, guidance, help or signposting. The scheduling is deliberate since, by this time, participants will have got to grips with their projects and may have encountered obstacles and, possibly, overcome them. Some may be moving towards completion, where main issues of concern are around the scope and focus of recommendations (and often involvement in) actions and conclusions.

At this stage, participants usually have sufficient project material to give a short presentation (10 minutes) on some aspect of the project. In so doing, they are able to benefit from a critical evaluation, including Closed Circuit Television (CCTV) feedback, of their presentation skills. In addition, in having experienced already the 'support group' concept in the project scoping session on the first module, they are able to operate in this mode in probing, testing and offering advice and suggestions to each other on their projects.

During this day, we offer advice on the structuring of the final presentation, visual aids and training. A presentation will last 20 minutes with the same amount of time for questions, discussion and sponsor assessment.

In the second module, the first afternoon is devoted to project presentations. Time is allowed beforehand for any last-minute preparations, checking of visual aids, rehearsals, etc. Group size for presentations is usually four to six participants (the original scoping groups from the first module where possible) plus sponsors and/or line managers and, occasionally, specifiers, i.e. human resource or training and development specialists. Each presentation is followed by a probing evaluative discussion of the project, initiated and facilitated by the consultant. The discussion centres on both the task/content output and the learning output. As a guide to the consultant in facilitating the 'process' part of the discussion, a checklist of questions can be useful (see below).

QUESTIONS FOR DISCUSSION

- What were the main satisfactions for you/what were the main frustrations? What did you do to try to handle them?
- What were the difficulties encountered? How did you overcome them?

61

- To what extent did working with/through other people figure in the project? How effective were the relationships?
- What is going to be done differently, or what different things will be done, as a result of your project?
- How do you feel about *'bottom line'* in relation to your project?
- What things did you learn during the project which will be of value to you in the short/long term?
- What was the most significant learning point which came out of the project?
- Did you have any 'learning through mistakes' experiences you would like to mention?
- What links, if any, were there between the learning from the project and the action plans you prepared/put into practice?
- Are there any general points (pearls of wisdom) you would like to leave with the group?
- With the benefit of hindsight, if you were about to start your project again would you do anything differently?

While often rigorous, assessments by project sponsors have given a level of validation to projects to the extent that, almost without exception, they have resulted in action leading to beneficial (often measurable) changes within the employing organizations.

In many cases, sponsors/line managers spend the complete half day listening to, and taking part in, the discussion of projects involving participants from other companies. Several have subsequently commented on the personal benefits gained from an appreciation of the problems and tactical considerations employed in managing situations of change across a wide range of industry, commerce and the public sector. Moreover, participants have valued the depth of experience and different perceptions offered in the project discussions by sponsors from other companies – enriching the learning experience.

Each presentation is video recorded so that the participant can review his or her performance later in the module. Following the end of the set of presentations, there is a critical review of the presentation skills where the participant is his or her own severest critic. What is apparent is the difference in quality of presentations by those who have attended the project workshop day and those who have not (the majority do attend).

For some participants, the presentation is the end of their project involvement but, for others, there is a continuing involvement in implementation. The end point of the project is not necessarily the presentation at Sundridge Park and presentations relate the stage of the project. Frequently, it is a set of recommendations or actions already taken.

What is important is not to 'run it up to the line' but to finish work on the project for the Sundridge presentation at least a week before the second module, thus allowing essential time for structuring and rehearsing the presentation.

Before the start of the project, managers gain an increased awareness of their learning style preferences, using the Honey and Mumford Learning Styles Questionnaire.[2] In learning styles terminology, most projects will tend to cater more for 'activist' and 'pragmatist' preferences than 'theorist' or 'reflector' styles. However, development and application of theories, concepts and models is emphasized. Periodic reflection throughout the project is stressed and high reflector styles are clearly in evidence at the project presentation stage, when learning outputs are highlighted.

Carrying out a project over a period of several months frequently mirrors the reality of managers' work patterns, that is, what they really do. While managers will often embark on their projects by adopting a classical Fayol approach of planning, organizing, co-ordinating and controlling (because it is a project!), the actuality, even at junior levels, often soon reflects Kotter's[3] 'efficiency of seemingly inefficient behaviour', as the project becomes part of the manager's agenda, interwoven with a network of day-to-day interrelated problems and issues. The idealistic intent of securing big chunks of time for working on the project is rarely experienced in practice.

The participant's level in the organization can influence the amount of control he or she has over the project, particularly its resourcing. It was in 1988 that a further new programme was designed: Developing Tomorrow's Top Managers. The rationale for this development was a perception of the spread of participants on the Younger Manager Programme, where approximately the top quartile were in the high-flier category. Such a population could be more effectively targeted and stretched by a new programme offering more depth and breadth in learning.

While the Younger Manager Programme was targeted at managers who had limited managerial experience, Developing Tomorrow's Top Managers sought to attract those who had a recognized level of managerial achievement and success and were, moreover, seen as likely candidates for board level appointments in the not too distant future.

The same model was adopted, except that the first module lasted two weeks. In addition, action learning was introduced into the programme and on each programme, extra project workshop days (one or two) were contracted with the participants. Some of these were hosted by a participant's organization. This came close to the practice of action learning sets and in many cases was valued by participants by the time they had reached project completion.

Predictably, many of the projects were bigger than those of the Younger Manager Programme and it was often the case that participants would include one or two of their staff on the project as a development experience.

For both programmes, the most significant differentiator of projects has been between projects which have the following characteristics:

- Part of the manager's actual job, but raised in priority by becoming integrated with the Sundridge programme.
- Linked to, but pushing out from the manager's job, i.e. going well outside what would be seen as the job boundary.
- Totally separate from the manager's job, i.e. being thrust into a different part of the business. For this category of project the sponsor is definitely not the line manager.

Over the last few years, over 200 projects have been successfully completed. They have spanned every aspect of business, with immense learning and bottom-line benefits. Some recent projects from each programme are listed below.

A SELECTION OF RECENT PROJECTS

THE YOUNGER MANAGER PROGRAMME

- Develop a prototype for a new management information system in one of three food processing factories.
- Develop a training and mentoring system whereby managers take on the roles of mentors to management trainees in an international airline.
- Carry out a strategic review for the marketing of training products in the Far East for a video/training material provider.
- Develop an integrated HR strategy for a large building society, with particular attention to securing the best fit of HR within the business strategy.

- Develop a control system at branch level for a retail organization to achieve greater financial efficiency and productivity benefits.
- Increase effectiveness of industrial and commercial marketing team through an improved focus on priorities and implementation of systems to ensure quality in a regional utility.

DEVELOPING TOMORROW'S TOP MANAGERS

- Examine the career development of functional specialists externally recruited into HQ roles of a large international brewery and hotel group.
- Identify promotional/sponsorship/marketing options which will distinguish an international bank in the markets in which it operates.
- Increase productivity (15 per cent) and profitability (20 per cent) in a large quarry redevelopment.
- Develop and implement an end user computing strategy for a large financial institution to enable the business to gain strategic advantage through the use of IT and information resources.
- Identify reasons for poor performance of a business within the group (recently taken over) and to restructure/re-engineer the business to make it profitable (large power group in Poland).
- Design and implement a computerized stock control system and restructure process control and material control to provide increased and effective support (large publishing group).
- Develop and introduce a Total Quality Management system into a large newspaper group undergoing substantial cultural change.
- Review of occupational health strategy initiatives with recommendations for desirable changes (large regional utility).
- Identify ways of substantially reducing the overhead cost base (delayering), while ensuring optimal effectiveness and profitability (large financial services institution).
- Recommend improvements in customer service based on a survey of attitude to power supply interruptions (large regional utility).
- Evaluate increasing a regional network in order to secure greater market share in a large car rental business.

A few years ago, one company, The Kingsway Group (supplier to the construction industry), in seeking to provide for top level succession entered into a development partnership with Sundridge Park. (The

65

following account is largely based on the article 'A Successful Development Partnership'.[4])

Six 'middle ranking' employees were identified as having senior management potential – some in junior line management positions, others in specialist functional roles. These six were removed from their positions in order to take part in an accelerated career development programme.

Their positions were permanently filled by internal promotion or new recruits. There was no commitment to the trainees to offer a particular job at the end of the training period, nor could there be a guaranteed return to the pre-training job. It was not the intention to groom individuals for particular designated jobs, but it was anticipated that some trainees would incline to 'general management' and others to top functional management (because of professional qualifications).

Such an open-ended contract, while not uncommon at graduate trainee level, required the six 'management trainees' to delegate, or forget about, job security as one of their motivation characteristics. In establishing a series of secondments of six months' duration as the core of the programme, it was important for senior managers in each division to be supportive of the programme and provide for both a testing/challenging secondment, while giving appropriate support in an occasional coach/ mentor role.

A steering committee, comprising three directors and the personnel/ administration manager were to supervise the training programme. The responsibilities of this committee were to liaise with departmental managers to ensure that a proper standard of training was obtained, to match trainee requirements with departmental requirements and to appraise trainees' progress. Each director was to act as an informal 'mentor' for two of the trainees. The training programme was of three years' duration.

Hands-on, rather than passive, secondment was seen to be vital. Sometimes this was achieved by temporary placement in suitable establishment vacancies and sometimes by designation of extra-establishment *ad hoc* tasks. The overriding intention was to provide in-depth experience of a number of management tasks, rather than a sampler of every individual function. Great use was made of projects in the different management functions.

Development opportunities and objectives likely to arise during the project were discussed prior to the secondment, and learning experiences reviewed at the end.

It was recognized that the on-the-job development thrust needed to be integrated with selective off-the-job development. It was at this stage that, based on a rigorous review of external provision, Sundridge Park Management Centre entered the scene.

With a concern for integrating off-the-job courses with on-the-job development a choice was made to 'test the water' by trying out the Younger Manager Programme at Sundridge Park Management Centre because it:

- matched the profile of the proposed trainees
- had a good coverage of the basic management topics
- integrated project work with course content
- encouraged trainees' involvement in planning their own career development.

The project element was also a main attraction of this programme in that it was perceived by the directors that completing projects within a six-month period would be a testing and challenging experience for the trainees. Indeed, directors gave a top priority to their attendance at project presentations on the second module. Their support was, on the one hand, greatly valued by the participants on the programme and, on the other hand, probably seemed to raise the adrenaline level, since presenting findings or recommendations to top management was both an opportunity for visibility and recognition, but also an occasion of high vulnerability.

The six management trainees attended the programme in pairs, and over a period of one year they had all completed the programme, including projects. The shared experience of the programme was highly valued.

Detailed below are descriptions of the six projects undertaken including comments from the particular management trainees.

CLIFFORD FUDGE, TECHNICAL MANAGER

Objective: develop a new market for concrete blocks produced by Celcon Blocks Ltd.

Traditionally, these building blocks have been used as a walling material, but a growing market now exists as an infill material in beam and block flooring for housing. The aim was to assess the size of the market, how to gain third-party approval and how to promote the product.

Recommendations

Recommendations from market and product research were as follows:

1. There is clearly a market which is growing.
2. Further R&D is necessary.
3. Customers' views on a new product should be sought.
4. Third party approval should be obtained.
5. Cost comparisons should be carried out.
6. Thermal insulation studies should be carried out.
7. Beam manufacturers should be approached.
8. A 'user' guide should be produced.

Current Position

The volume of material which could be sold for this application was seen as substantial. High profile promotion is continuing to take place in what is seen as an exciting new area. Third party approval is being actively sought, with the approval body's acceptance of our R&D facilities. Cost comparisons and thermal insulation studies have been carried out showing benefits over other types of material. Other aspects are awaiting the outcome of assessment, but the end result should be a new market at a time when the housing industry is rapidly declining.

JOHN TEBBIT, CORPORATE PLANNING MANAGER

Objective: investigation of the production, marketing and sales of non-standard shaped bricks (or special shapes) at Ryarsh Brick Ltd, one of the companies in the Kingsway Group and to identify ways of improving the profit contribution from special shapes.

The project was tackled using a multi-disciplined approach. Specialists tend to see the solutions as well as the problems as being within their domain, even if their solutions consist of merely treating the symptoms. A historical example of this was the medical profession's view of cholera in Victorian London. Despite doctors' treatments, cholera was not cured until civil engineers brought in wholesome water supplies.

'Other brick manufacturers were helpful in allowing me to look at their factories, enabling me to gain an industry-wide view. The collection, collation and assessment of the information presented no great difficulties once people had confidence in my motives.'

Recommendations
This report concluded that the special shapes business could be improved. Existing costing systems were not satisfactory, nor was the operation of the business. Some twelve recommendations were made to improve the position.

The report has not been acted upon in its entirety, but elements of it have been used. However, even if nothing had been used I feel that it would have been worthwhile. '*Real world problems tend to produce real world solutions, and that is what management is all about*'.

PAUL McGHEE – PROJECT MANAGER (SPAIN), HORMIGONES CELULARES SA

Objective: investigation of the procedural aspects and options for obtaining Kitemark registration for Ryarsh Brick Limited.

Recommendations
It was proposed that the company consider the possibility of obtaining an Agrément Certificate as this could be a first step towards obtaining the 'CE Mark', which would be beneficial if the bricks were to be sold in Europe.

The company decided to go for quality assured status first, and then apply for the Kitemark at a later date. The company is also considering obtaining an Agrément Certificate to cover the use of our bricks below Damp Proof Course (DPC).

The Building Materials Division of Kingsway Group has become more quality conscious generally since the project, with Celcon Blocks also adopting the principles of quality assurance.

STUART BRITTLE, WORKS MANAGER (NEW FACTORY), CELCON BLOCKS LTD

Objective:

1. Examine the need for a fifth aerated concrete block manufacturing plant.
2. Review implications of the decision to employ a different manufacturing style and the subsequent effect upon marketing because of the ability of produce variations on the current product range.
3. Assess the effect of the automation on the style of local management compared with other more labour intensive plants and the type of operatives employed.

Recommendations

The core of the project examined, and made recommendations in some detail on the procedures involved in production planning, recruitment and training requirements, needs for management information, and especially the implications for management roles and structure required to establish effective management within the plant.

JOHN DOYLE, GENERAL MANAGER, BRANTHAM ENGINEERING LTD

Objective: investigate the large amount of statistical information sent from each of the factories around the country to central offices at Grays and London – where it comes from, how it is presented and recorded and what it is used for.

Recommendations
From looking at the existing arrangements and talking to the people who both generate and use the information, a presentation was given which explained the specialist nature of the factories and why certain seemingly straightforward figures were not all they appeared to be; and also identified and compared various options for future developments.

Comparisons between the different ways of producing the same statistic at each site highlighted certain existing differences which were then looked at and in some cases amended.

'Personally I feel I gained a greater insight into the practical side of the business.'

GEORGE STRAW, SENIOR SALES EXECUTIVE, CELCON BLOCKS LTD

Objective: proposals for the marketing of the increased production of Celcon Blocks.

In line with the other three major aircrete producers Celcon are increasing production capacity to such a degree that during the course of the next two years a further 50 per cent of aircrete products will be available.

Competition will increase as production increases, and there will be a need for staff who can see the opportunities rather than be apprehensive about the changes.

Recommendations
It is against this background that recommendations for strengthening and improving the effectiveness of the salesforce have been made:

71

1. The salesforce in the 1990s will have to be more tightly managed in terms of objectives and accountabilities. Sales staff will need to be more adaptable, forward looking and skilled negotiators. A recommendation for intensive, across-the-board training was accepted and implemented.
2. With 50 per cent of the company's turnover in the hands of 20 accounts, it leaves the company extremely vulnerable. These are the accounts which will come under attack once capacity exceeds demand, and it will become increasingly difficult to maintain margins. Accordingly, the Board approves the appointment of two national sales executives.

A common factor among the projects was that they were all relatively 'big' and each one resulted in some change – in one or two cases, significant change. 'Things will never be the same again', was one comment. The project was, of course, only one element within the programme. The learning design feature of bringing together an understanding of key business functions and their interrelationships (the fundamental management principles, and the whole range of people skills), served management trainees well in supporting and facilitating the broadening of managerial experience they were gaining through secondments.

Of course it was not all plain sailing; mistakes were made in secondments/placements, but probably the most dramatic change was an attitudinal change towards training as a corporate investment. The management trainee initiative had a high profile within the company (dare we say it was elitist!). It also enjoyed the real power of top-level sponsorship, including directors using personal power to 'secure right placements'.

A not inconsiderable element of learning transfer came through the networking of relationships wherein secondments were of greater value in allowing management trainees to develop and build their network of relationships initiated on the Younger Manager Programme during secondments and placements. These networks continue to bear real fruit in achievements in their senior management roles. Perhaps one of the most significant pay-offs was in the costs/benefits area where the philosophy of growing your own with a little bit of help, has been well proved. It will of course never be a total answer nor should it be, but the early development of a group of 'young turks' who are now helping Kingsway through the 1990s is a significant development.

ASSESSING THE IMPACT OF PROJECT-BASED LEARNING

Recently we have carried out a survey several months after the presentation of project outcomes on the second module of a particular programme. The purpose of the survey was to discover the real impact of project-based learning, as assessed on reflection by the main stakeholders, i.e. project owner and sponsor/line manager. The methodology included topics for discussion and questionnaires. These are included below, with a summary of the most significant findings, some of which are subsequently elaborated through case histories.

TOPICS FOR DISCUSSION WITH PROJECT OWNER

1. How was the project chosen?
2. How useful did you find the 'criteria for choice'? Were certain criteria of particular importance? If so, which ones?
3. What benefits and difficulties did you expect?
4. What benefits were actually experienced and by whom?
   - in order of importance?
   - any unexpected ones?
   Can you give examples of:
   - learning benefits?
   - organizational/departmental benefits, quantified where possible?
5. Why did these benefits occur? What helped and hindered (give examples)?
6. What difficulties were experienced and by whom?
7. How were responsibilities for the project organized (sponsor, line manager, yourself)? How well did this work? Are there alternatives, better ways?

SPONSOR/LINE MANAGER QUESTIONS

1. What were your expectations of benefits from the project?
2. What were the benefits? To whom?
   Were there any unexpected ones?
3. Why did these benefits occur? What helped and hindered (give examples)?
4. What were the difficulties experienced (give examples)?
5. How were responsibilities for the project organized between the project owner, yourself, others?

73

6. How did the project impinge on the rest of the project owner's work while the project was in progress?
7. What was your own role in relation to the project?
8. In your opinion, how useful has the project been?

	Extremely useful	Very useful	Moderately useful	Of little use	Of no use
Developing him/her	———	———	———	———	———
Achieving business objectives?	———	———	———	———	———
Hastening needed change?	———	———	———	———	———

9. What scope do you anticipate for using projects for further development in the organization?

SUMMARY OF FINDINGS

TOPICS FOR DISCUSSION WITH PROJECT OWNERS

1. How the project choice was made

With a couple of exceptions, where the project was suggested by the proj ect owner, there was a 50:50 split between a joint project owner/sponsor –line manager exploration of choices *and* the project being proposed by the sponsor–line manager. However the choice was made, there was no real significance when compared to project outputs.

One useful observation from Jim Morris, Personnel Manager, York-shire Electricity, was that project choice can depend on how long the individual has been in the job; namely, if at the start, the project needs to be linked to, or be a core part of, the job; whereas if the individual is well into the job then the project can push out from it. Moreover, where the individual may be ready for a new job, then a project separate from the job could provide a wedge for such a move, i.e. into another unit or function.

2. Criteria for Choice

The criteria for choice checklist that follows was strongly valued:

1. It is concerned with a significant problem within the participant's area of operation, but which in solving would involve gaining a broader understanding than the confines of the department or section.
2. It should include diagnosis of the problem, making recommendations and, where appropriate, initiating necessary action.
3. It should not be a problem which is so intractable that it is incapable of solution, nor should it be too complicated for one individual to tackle effectively.
4. It offers a challenge, provides stretch, and is not a set of tedious clerical routines.
5. It should not merely be gathering and collating information which yields little potential for learning.
6. Within the timescale it is possible for some real impact to be made on the problem, and preferably a plan for implementation.
7. It should require involvement, co-operation and commitment of other colleagues.
8. The project should not be directed at the solution of problems which are exclusively technical.
9. It is likely to contain a 'people' element.
10. It should not be a puzzle to which there is a known solution.
11. It may be linked to some planned or ongoing change.
12. Though primarily a learning vehicle it should yield some worthwhile benefits to the project sponsor/organization.

All were perceived to be relevant and useful. Several project owners valued number 1, 7 and 8 as being particularly important.
Additional criteria mentioned were:

- Being business driven (Neil Watson, Brooke Bond Foods)
- To achieve a key appraisal objective (Alan Wain, Mirror Newspaper Group; Dave Folkerd, London Electricity)
- Raising the individual's profile (several)

75

- Reference to people element seen as important (Geoff Higgs, London Clearing House)

3. Expectation of benefits and difficulties

Benefits

- Raising the profile and re-establishing credibility of the IT department; getting managers to do things themselves, relieving pressures on IT staff; improving investment in technology and hardware; improving communication (Development/Implementation of End User Computer Strategy).
- Using one factory as a catalyst for change with the expectation of being able to communicate results more quickly/effectively (Introduction of Management Information System).
- To develop a programme (grow your own approach to supervisor development) which would be very beneficial to the company.
- To obtain a broader picture of group personnel and how it fits into the business plan together with a broader understanding of other parts of the business (Development of an Integrated H.Q. Strategy).

In addition, a whole range of 'personal skill' benefits were identified, e.g. interviewing, influencing skills, managing change, planning, coordination and control, networking and problem solving.

Difficulties

- Obtaining time and commitment from other managers for inputs to the project (several).
- Managing/carrying out the project as well as doing the day-to-day job (a majority).
- May not be able to challenge or change the status quo; too much resistance from key people (several).
- Scope too wide to make a meaningful impact on the issue (a few).
- Changing attitudes; suspicion from old culture (Introduction of Total Quality Management).
- Seeing/charting the way forward into unfamiliar ground (several, not own job projects).
- Lack of commitment to action from key people; directors (several).
- Feeling very exposed and vulnerable because of the high profile and the politics involved (a few).

- Selecting team members to assist with the project; the need to be wary of people who are easily available (a few).
- Gaining access to project sponsor (a few).
- Raising expectations of others to an unrealistic level and then failing to deliver (a few).

4. Actual benefits experienced (including learning and unexpected benefits) by those involved

Project Owner

- Greater clarity and understanding of other business functions and their interdependency with each other and with own function.
- Being a change catalyst.
- Visibility in presenting outcomes to directors/managers of other functions.
- Importance of maintaining the momentum of the project; not letting things slide.
- Using delegation as an opportunity for development of staff, e.g. in processing questionnaires, analysing and collating data.
- Raising the profile and activities of a department/function, particularly among senior managers.
- Presentation skills; projects provided several opportunities within own company as well as at Sundridge Park.
- Getting recommendations accepted through careful groundwork.
- Developing self in new job; gave a boost, accelerated development.
- Helped to improve relationship with sponsor/line manager through occasional working together.
- Able to practise specific 'Team Role' strengths, e.g. resource investigator bringing in key information.
- Importance of assessing frequently changing priorities.
- Receiving a bonus as recognition of success.
- Clear influence of project outcome on subsequent promotion.
- Greater understanding of what senior people want from own function.
- Being forced to challenge/test both barriers and constraints.
- Recognition and enhanced credibility.
- Prioritizing for strategy; greater understanding of SWOT analysis (Strength, Weaknesses, Opportunities, Threats).
- Techniques of report writing.

- How marketing and research functions carry out surveys, including development of questionnaires, analysis, collation and presentation of findings.
- The need to refer upwards as well as manage/collaborate laterally to get things done.
- The value in having a 'hands on' approach to change things.
- Never to accuse; to respond to, rather than react.
- Importance of keeping people involved; good/bad news – let them know as much as possible.
- Importance of having the right sponsor who, because of commitment and ability to give support when required, can open doors to specialists in other functions.
- Study of information flows raised questions about need for more broadly based information and how it should be collated/presented.
- Individuals being prepared to inconvenience themselves for the benefit of the team.

Organization

- Better customer service; fewer complaints (Mirror Group Newspapers).
- Structural changes in customer services leading to increased output, improved quality and greater skill flexibility (cross-functional teams, St Ives Printing Group).
- Importance of investment in PCs established; previously seen as incidental (London Clearing House).
- £10 million costs saved through delayering, with no damage to the business (Financial Services Organization).
- Development of expanded office network within M25 as a key competitive initiative (Avis Car Rental).
- The Strategic Review of Training Products (Far East) provided a standard for reviewing strategy in other regions (Longman Training).
- Decision by CEO to survey customers; 60,000 a year on a monthly basis, combining Operations and Customer Service requirements (London Electricity).

5. Why benefits occurred

- Out of necessity; systems had to be changed to provide greater value for money for customers.
- People feeling more involved and informed, which increased motiva-

tion and team spirit; helped by company culture and high level of loyalty, hindered by external day-to-day pressures.

- Having good people as part of a team and being successful in building an effective team.
- Having a supportive, helpful boss/sponsor (several).
- Pressure of competitor activity gave high priority.
- Project being outside normal role and at a higher level than normal work – very stretching.
- Commitment from people in other departments/functions.
- Valuing the project as a significant learning exercise.
- Good timing in choice of project; fitted with key, strategic initiatives (several).

6. Difficulties experienced

- Not realizing there were skilled people around who could help.
- Scope of project initially too broad; had to be narrowed in discussion with sponsor (few).
- Objectives not clear enough at start of project (few).
- Time constraint; managing own job while carrying out project (several).
- The phase change in type of activity, from interviewing a large number of people to analysing, collating data and drawing out main findings (a few).
- Handling internal politics; gathering/using sensitive data.
- Change in project sponsor; having to develop a new relationship (few).
- Change in focus of project due to internal organizational changes (few).
- Varying commitment to implementation among directors.
- Lack of knowledge (different business area) and feeling exposed; had to learn fast (few).
- Resistance to (perceived) change by people asked to contribute or provide views/information (several).

7. Organization of responsibilities for project

For most projects, the responsibility was given to the project owner. The sponsor's main involvement has largely been at the start of the project in choosing and agreeing the project, clarifying objectives and scope and,

79

towards the end of the project, in discussing and assessing recommendations and/or supporting involvement in implementation.

The role of sponsor has been that of 'being on tap', but with the initiative needing to be taken by the project owner, i.e. to set up monitoring/ review meetings.

There have been several occasions on which the sponsor has opened doors, particularly where the project owner needed access to people at top level. On a few occasions the sponsor has been able to offer skills or specific expertise but, for such contributions, the norm has been for the project owner to look for, and bring in from, other sources.

Some sponsors have provided a sounding board prior to the Sundridge presentation, i.e. giving feedback in rehearsal of the presentation and occasionally coaching for a key internal management presentation. Most certainly took responsibility for attending the final presentation of the project – clearly one indicator of sponsor commitment to the project owner.

SPONSOR/LINE MANAGER QUESTIONS

Since the questions largely mirrored the topics discussed with project owners, it is no surprise that there was a high coincidence of views expressed. We have therefore identified where there are different/ additional perceptions experienced by sponsors/line managers.

Benefits

While sponsors expected as benefits a similarly wide range of skills, several highlighted the greater exposure to people at a more senior level in the organization and increased knowledge of other business functions.

Several sponsors were also very clear about seeing the project as providing an opportunity to drive an important change forward, i.e. important to them in their own role. Sponsors experienced very few disappointments. Where they occurred, they were due usually to unforeseen change impacting on the project.

They also received some pleasant surprises from the impact of projects, especially in view of the relatively junior management level of project owners; a clear indication of project owners grasping the opportunity to excel.

An often quoted benefit by many sponsors was having more confidence in the project owner's abilities, put to the test and developed through the project.

Some sponsors, reflecting on why benefits had occurred, referred back to the initial choice and scoping, which had not always been an easy

80

process as it sometimes involved a few iterations. However, it was seen as an investment if benefits were to be secured.

Difficulties

Some sponsors mentioned the reality of the project owner having to prioritize data collection, rather than hanging on to the last minute and creating an activity overload towards the end of the project. Idealism versus realism was mentioned, as was the 80:20 rule.

Another difficulty noted by some sponsors was taking on personally all the activities involved in the project, rather than influencing others to participate and contribute.

Most sponsors had adopted a 'hands off' approach, e.g. 'get in touch if you need help'. For some this had resulted in not being available when a contribution would have been valuable. One sponsor suggested that a few dates in the diary would have been useful, with the project owner taking the initiative to use them if needed.

Some sponsors noted the difficulty of project owners not being sufficiently au fait with the politics, but with hindsight, were critical of themselves for not providing help in this difficult area.

Organization of responsibilities for project and role for sponsor

Responses here mirrored those from project owners. The only differences were of emphasis. Some sponsors mentioned help in managing the boundaries, ensuring top level support and access to key people.

Where projects moved from recommendations through implementation, a few sponsors had taken greater responsibility.

While allocation of responsibilities has not been a contentious issue, there has been more potential generally in the role and relationships of sponsor and project owner than has been explored.

Usefulness of the project

Sponsors' responses were split about evenly between 'extremely useful' and 'very useful' for each of the three areas:

- developing the project owner
- achieving business objectives
- hastening needed change

81

Interestingly, 'development' was not ranked any higher than the other two areas. Organizations are looking to secure a balance between business and learning outputs.

Scope for using projects for further development

Most sponsors claimed that projects were already in use as an internal development method. Several predicted an expansion in such use. One sponsor felt projects provided a means of developing people quicker and more effectively and, in anticipating further use for development, asserted that 'most work is project based'.

KEY POINT SUMMARY

- Linking a project to an off-the-job modular programme generally gives the project a higher profile in the company.
- The purpose and scope of a project should be clarified before initial planning. Applying a checklist to discussion is useful.
- A support group is valuable in clarifying and scoping the project, in monitoring progress on the project workshop day and in taking part in open discussion following project presentations.
- A 'questions for discussion' checklist is useful to the consultant in facilitating the project presentations session.
- Sponsors make valuable contributions and derive learning on managing change from their involvement in the project presentation sessions, i.e. in respect of projects from other companies.
- Participants learn from the depth of experience and different perceptions offered by sponsors from other companies in presentation discussions – enriching the learning experience.
- The project presentation can mean recognition for the participant, particularly with regards to the response and assessment by the sponsor.
- Different learning styles are evident at different stages of the project.
- The ideal of securing large portions of time for project work is rarely experienced in practice, since the project becomes interwoven with the manager's day to day agenda.
- Where a manager is ready for a new job, a project separate from the job can provide a springboard for the move.

- Project responsibility is vested in the project owner, with the support of the sponsor who should be available and ready to respond when needed.
- Many sponsors have realized a benefit from project owners being tested and developed through the project.
- There is unexplored potential in the role and relationships between sponsor and project owner.
- Projects can form part of an accelerated career development scheme for high-fliers, and are particularly valuable in broadening managerial experience at an early career stage.

REFERENCES

1. Smith, B. (1987), 'Meeting a Need: The Younger Manager Programme at Sundridge Park', *Journal of European Industrial Training*, **11**, (7), pp. 5–12.
2. Honey, P. and Mumford, A. (1982), *The Manual of Learning Styles*, Maidenhead: Honey.
3. Kotter, J. (1982), 'What Effective General Managers Really Do', *Harvard Business Review*, November/December, pp. 156–167.
4. Smith, A. and Smith, B. (1990), 'A Successful Development Partnership', *Industrial and Commercial Training*, **22**, (6), pp. 3–8.

APPENDIX 1: THE YOUNGER MANAGER PROGRAMME

OBJECTIVES AND OUTCOMES

By the end of the programme, participants will be able to:

- assess their early experiences against best management practice
- recognize the impact of the main business functions on their own department and the organization
- face future challenges and opportunities with greater confidence
- contribute more effectively to their career development
- use their new skills and knowledge to complete a clearly defined project within their organization.

CONTENTS

Personal skills of managing

- accountability and objective setting
- time management
- personal planning and organization
- planning and control systems
- problem solving and handling change
- networks of relationships

Major business areas

- finance
- marketing
- culture, values and ethics
- structure and systems
- manufacturing and operations
- information technology
- computers in business

Interpersonal knowledge and skills

- communicating
- interviewing and persuading
- presenting to groups

Leadership and self-development

- leadership, motivation and staff development
- development self-awareness
- concept of self-directed learning
- women and men working together
- teambuilding and development
- inter-group relationships

APPENDIX 2: DEVELOPING TOMORROW'S TOP MANAGERS

OBJECTIVES AND OUTCOMES

By the end of the programme participants will:

- have a broad view of business in general and their own business in particular
- recognize the relationship between key business areas and how they impact on their own function
- be able to contribute to the needs of other business functions
- have a framework of best practice
- have more confidence in building, directing and representing their team as well as in motivating and coaching staff
- be able to improve their interpersonal and networking skills
- have completed a major change project within their organization.

CONTENTS

Personal skills of managing

- accountability and objective setting
- personal planning and organization
- planning, co-ordination and control
- creative problem solving and handling change skills
- developing and managing networks

Individual development

- self-awareness and assessment
- learning styles, action learning
- self-development methods and skills
- stress management
- career management
- women and men working together

Staff development

- leadership styles and framework
- motivation and coaching skills
- teambuilding and development
- inter-group relationships

Interpersonal skills

- interviewing, influencing and persuading
- presentations and meetings

Business and the environment

- environment trends and pressures
- social, economic, political and legal influences on the business
- technological change
- corporate culture and structure
- vision, values and ethics

Marketing

- strategy, planning and orientation

Finance

- financial structure and accounts
- management reporting
- assessing financial strength

Operations

- operations strategy
- structuring for better service

Information Technology

- IT for competitive advantage

(Note: This chapter has concentrated on Projects in Public Programmes at Sundridge Park, with particular emphasis on project choice and benefits. The Public Programmes are examined in more detail in Chapter 5.)

Part II

Outcomes

5 Six Case Histories

The last chapter brought into view, through several project examples, the importance of project choice and how difficulties can be overcome and benefits realized for project owners, sponsors and organizations.

The following case histories describe some projects from conception through to implementation. Descriptions are based on responses to the topics/questions used in the survey.

BUSINESS RESTRUCTURING/RE-ENGINEERING – A LARGE POWER GROUP IN POLAND

The purpose of the project was to identify reasons for poor performance of a business within the group (recently taken over) and to restructure or re-engineer the business to make it profitable.

On both programmes – Developing Tomorrow's Top Managers and the Younger Manager – a project may have been identified before attendance on the programme. Miroslaw Gryszka (deputy managing director of ABB Zameck) was in discussion with his MD about poor performance of one of the companies within Air Pollution Control (APC) in Poland. They agreed it was essential to establish the reason(s) for poor performance and find actionable solutions. Miroslaw already had responsibility for restructuring/re-engineering business development so the project fitted well within this core activity. It was then that he selected the Developing Tomorrow's Top Managers Programme, which he saw as providing methodological support for the project as well as meeting his overall development needs.

Criteria

Criteria which he noted, albeit in retrospect, were that the project was:

- *very important* not only for the company but for the whole group
- seemingly *more difficult than any other*
- the *biggest challenge* for both the company and for Miroslaw personally.

Expected benefits

- very good shareholder perceptions of the company, providing the project was successful
- a big improvement in short-term company performance
- personal improvement/development through tackling such a challenge
- value in working with new people in a new environment with new targets.

Expected difficulties

- resistance to the project by the company and its people – 'someone from the outside is going to change their world'
- limited support from own functional managers because of a perception that they would want to concentrate on their own priorities.

Actual benefits

- For the company:
  - target was achieved and the future looks promising
  - better relationships with power generation customer
  - satisfied shareholders
  - confirmation of skilled management able to use opportunities.
- For Miroslaw:
  - experience in how to deal with an unknown environment, including people, organizations, markets and technology
  - self-confirmation 'I can do it now and in the future'.

An unexpected benefit was making a lot of new friends and building good customer relationships.

Specific learning benefits

- experience in creating a new business
- giving people targets is not limiting; they can have a wider vision

- from new people; how they do things
- managing a new team in practice.

Organization benefits

- synergy, i.e. the old organization supporting the new one and vice-versa
- a shortened learning period
- a leverage effect, where one product supported another and vice-versa
- creation of a new business area unit
- absorption of all assets and liabilities from the company taken over
- selection of a new MD from the company taken over
- training of key people to implement new procedures
- location of support for key functions in new businesses
- Miroslaw, as deputy group MD, becoming coach for the MD of the new business unit
- initial establishment of direct contact with all customers by Miroslaw.

Reasons for benefits occurring

- teamwork and with will to do better
- strong position of the company in the market
- strong support from top management of all parties involved
- a 'sound' product
- common understanding by all the parties involved.

Difficulties experienced

- the people from the taken over company had to adopt all procedures which were used in the parent company, their response was 'we're happy with our system so why change?'
- foreign partners (middle level managers) had difficulty understanding that someone new was responsible for the market some customers initially had difficulty understanding the benefits for them from having a new partner.

Organization of responsibilities for the project

- The project was carried out by Miroslaw with little reference to the Group MD.

93

Postscript
- The restructured company met its budget for 1994 and projected exceeded orders for 1995.

DAIRY RATIONALIZATION – DAIRY DIVISION CMCS

Derek Pattison was General Manager, Production. His project was to review the three processing dairies to determine possibilities for rationalization and then to develop and implement the rationalization plan.

Derek saw the project as a significant change management situation. It was also a great personal challenge, since he was fairly new in his job and came from a technical experience base. In discussions before selecting the project, the following criteria were specified.

Criteria
- a learning vehicle enabling skills from the programme to be put into practice
- opportunity for contact with all aspects of the business including some departments with which he had not previously worked
- presenting a different and practical opportunity in his new job with complete control of a key initiative.

He expected the *benefits* to be a broadening experience, expanding his network of contacts and involvement in commercial issues.

Expected difficulties
- uncertainty about where to go for what
- concern about whether he would be accepted by others in what he was trying to do
- consciousness of being closely observed
- the need to handle things well and not make any mistakes.

Actual benefits
Putting new learning into practice, for instance:

- scope to transfer learning quickly from first module
- networking with different departments and people in seeking help
- skills in how to start to build teams

- planning, monitoring, feedback and control
- experiencing the 'big picture'
- supplying leadership skills
- not being blinkered; thinking creatively
- handling change in respect of people taking on new roles and responsibilities.

An unexpected benefit was a contribution from a personnel specialist who produced important data on redundancy. This resulted in faster learning than there would have been otherwise.

Organization benefits

The project sent out messages about learning, being fit and lean and that there are no longer jobs for life. In concentrating resources on two rather than three sites, there were savings in capital expenditure as well as staff costs through redundancies.

The impact on the bottom line was not easy to measure because of other changes in the business. However, there were savings of £600k/year on personnel, as well as an upgrading of health and hygiene standards. The outcome was in line with the company's initiative 'An Agenda for Change' in moving towards a downsized, more flexible, workforce.

None of the expected difficulties occurred. The sponsor made an important contribution in providing guidance on how to approach certain influential people.

Organization of responsibilities

The project was carried out by Derek plus a team who assisted him. The sponsor was available for help and advice and there were regular progress reports and meetings.

Postscript

The project recommendations were implemented with the closure of one of the three sites. Subsequently (five months later), a review of cost savings was carried out.

The project was perceived as extremely useful in hastening needed change and in achieving both business objectives and self-development.

EUROPEAN AIR CATERING

Julie Shears is Sales and Service Manager with European Air Catering Services Ltd, which is contracted to cater for British Airways on shorthaul flights. Julie's project was to develop a training and mentoring system whereby managers took on the role of mentors to management trainees. The choice of the project was made by Julie herself, based on her observations that internal job moves by managers were leaving gaps which were difficult to fill through external advertising. Moreover, due to a lack of training and capability, there were few staff members ready to step into these supervisory management positions. Consequently, it was decided to explore the possibility of 'growing our own' managers. The scheme she designed included projects for the trainers, with the appointment of three operational managers as mentors to the trainees.

The *criteria for choice* provided useful basic guidelines. Considered to be particularly important were numbers 1, 2, 6, 7, 8, 10 and 12 (see list Figure 1.1, in pps 9–10).

Julie's *expectation of benefits* were that she would be able to develop a programme which would be beneficial to the company, while also developing her planning, training, recruiting and mentoring skills.

Anticipated difficulties were in getting other managers to find the time to be with the trainees and assist them with their projects. Julie also thought it could be a difficult time for her since she had been appointed only recently to her job.

Benefits were experienced by all managers and heads of departments, through a sense of teamworking which developed as a result of involvement in the programme. As Julie comments: 'The trainees continuously questioned and made us re-look at the way we operate.' The trainees benefited in being properly equipped with the necessary knowledge and training to take up future supervisory roles in the company. They had the time to familiarize themselves with the company, look at and analyse problems, without the additional pressures of running a section on a daily basis.

Unexpected benefits were realized through their projects. For instance, one trainee set up a stores procedure and computer program that could save the company considerable costs when fully implemented. He also trained the staff in how to use the program.

Particular learning benefits

- supervision of staff
- report writing techniques
- presentation of results to management
- use of computer packages.

Organization benefits

In addition to the savings on stores costs, training aids have been developed for checkers, ensuring consistent delivery to customers. In addition, customer complaints have been reduced as a result of reviewing routines in dealing with glass.

Benefits occurred because the trainees had time and support for their projects from management. The naivety of the trainees helped them to look at problems objectively and because they had management support they were not afraid to criticize.

An initial difficulty arose because mentors were not always able to give the time required to the trainees. At one stage, trainees became disorientated and unsure of where they were going, which led to some time-wasting. This difficulty has since been remedied through the establishment of clear goals, scheduled meetings and regular follow up.

Responsibilities for the project were laid down by Julie at a project meeting with managers, supported by her project sponsor (who was also her line manager).

The *sponsor's view* clearly matched Julie's responses to the topics. He emphasized the benefits to the management group in identifying training needs and the shortfall in training. He also stressed shared ownership and the need for clarity about what was to be achieved. Julie reflects: 'I guess we were all naive in believing that this was a straightforward project. We have, in hindsight, learnt a lot about training needs.' The sponsor saw the project as very useful in developing Julie and bringing about necessary change. In addition, while the project was additional to Julie's job, the sponsor did not see it as detracting significantly from her other objectives.

LONDON ELECTRICITY

Dave Folkerd of London Electricity's Network Services carried out a project with a customer focus. This aimed to achieve an understanding of the measures of performance and standards required by customers and to establish a bureau for customer needs and improve efficiencies of the department. The project was linked to his own performance review targets and was, in essence, an own job project.

The *criteria* were considered valuable, particularly through the interface with other functions. The project had both an engineering and customer focus.

Expected *benefits* and *difficulties* were mainly created by initially 'going it alone', trying to do everything. Subsequently, Dave discovered colleagues with expertise, i.e. designers and users of questionnaires in market research. So he approached them to help him conduct a survey into customer attitudes towards power supply interruptions and the service provided by LE in the event of an interruption.

Several *benefits* were realized. Early communication difficulties arose from not understanding other functions and their jargon/terminology. Once overcome, Dave was able to understand their contribution more clearly.

Moreover, there was benefit in expanding contracts with marketing, market research and customer services. As a consequence of the project both engineering and customer service realized they were not providing as good a service as they should. Customers valued being asked for their views.

The chief executive officer decided to survey customers on an ongoing basis (60,000 a year, on a monthly basis) combining operations and customer service requirements. Surveys are being carried out by agencies and independent assessment has been of benefit to staff in diagnosing particular problems, including communication. As a consequence, all emergency services jointers now have mobile phones. This improves the speed at which they can inform customer services of issues and concerns. The project has helped to bring operations close to customer services so that, together, they can resolve problems.

Another benefit came through having the support of a staff member in sending out questionnaires, collecting responses and tracking progress. The importance of setting clear and specific deadlines was well reinforced. The project has also hastened much needed change.

A *difficulty* was experienced in relation to timescales and not having control or influence over other people's priorities. The example quoted was that market research, because of other priorities, was not able to help Dave at a time to fit in with the project timetable. This led to a rush towards the end of the project to collect and present data.

The *sponsor* had very little involvement, but was pleased with the results. However, due to restructuring, the project did not achieve the aim of establishing a customer control centre within the operations function. The sponsor's main involvement was in giving occasional support, if needed, by monitoring through regular review meetings. The sponsor had thought Dave needed more awareness of the customer. As a final comment, Dave said, 'we are now committed to providing better customer service'.

FINANCIAL SERVICES

Projects can vary from being part of the current job to being totally separate from it. For one participant, Jim, in a financial services organization, the overhead value analysis project became his job for some months, in essence a secondment, but with no clear picture of what he would return to. The project also used the services of an external consultancy and arose out of pressure to improve services and reduce costs.

The objective was to identify ways of reducing substantially the overhead cost base while ensuring that the residual costs and activities were configured in an optimal way. The project was resourced from both the consultancy and internal resources. There was a part-time project manager from the consultancy, with Jim acting as a full-time project manager. The range of overhead activities reviewed was very wide, covering a total of 1300 staff with a cost base of £100 million.

The Developing Tomorrow's Top Managers programme fitted well with the project and the predicted timescale. In reviewing the project against the topic structure, the following reflections emerged.

Criteria were useful in providing constraints and also a challenge when one can't move the goal posts.

With regards expectations of *benefits* and *difficulties*, the whole project was expected to be difficult, with the pain coming from people losing their jobs. There was also a need to be careful about suggesting changes where one was prepared to be involved in change. Furthermore, there was the risk of deteriorating people relationships. It was difficult to convince people of the need when no apparent threat could be perceived, i.e. the previous year with record profitability. In addition, Jim felt very exposed and vulnerable: 'It could have been a big failure', he said. In addition, there was

99

uncertainty about 'implementation' because of the perception that not all the directors shared the necessary high level of commitment. For Jim, the project was a high risk/medium gain, but he saw it as an opportunity to achieve as well as for career development.

The project facilitated the reduction of costs and improvement in the quality of staff involved in the areas covered by the review, and to develop a more proactive business culture responding quickly to competition. On the total commitment issue, it was seen as important that 'if you say you're going to do it, you need to do it' or the credibility of directors will suffer. 'It can be too easy to find things for people to do', said Jim.

Real cost savings were difficult to estimate because of the need to prevent other costs creeping in. This can be prevented by senior directors pulling together and being tough.

The selection of team members for the project is important. There is a need to be wary of people who are easily available. Contributions to *actual benefits* were having good people to help with the project, successfully building a team and having a supportive boss/sponsor.

Difficulties encountered

- fading commitment among executives when it was time to implement recommendations, 'executives needed to accept that cutting costs means cutting people'
- an uncomfortable mix of part-time and full-time members on the project team, including consultants, which could have benefited from external facilitation.
- ambitions for the project probably being too big.

However, *outputs* were that the project ran to time, was considered by senior people as constituting success, and Jim received a bonus!

Learning points

- The importance of practice and rehearsals for a high level exposure in presentation skills, i.e. to the head of banking division. The sessions at Sundridge Park were seen as essential in this respect.
- A need to be aware of making the best use of consultants, e.g. on methodology. Consultants can become over-zealous, dismissive and arrogant.
- Being in a strong bargaining position for a short period can be a window of opportunity which needs to be exploited.

- Going for 100 per cent quality of output is unrealistic. Adopting an 80:20 rule is usually more feasible and acceptable.

STRATEGIC REVIEW OF MARKET POTENTIAL IN THE FAR EAST – A TRAINING PRODUCTS COMPANY IN THE UK

Carl Lumbard was International Development Manager of Longman Training. The choice of the project was agreed jointly between Carl and his line manager Mark Anderson. It was an own-job project, but attendance on the Younger Manager Programme brought it forward in priority.
   Carl's *expectations of benefits* were:

- improvement in organization skills, particularly time management
- improvement in interpersonal skills, specifically interviewing and questioning techniques
- learning how to collect and organize information
- acquiring a broader understanding of the company
- being able to make an informed decision about allocating resources into the Far East market.

Actual benefits

- learning about planning, the importance of reviewing and how to review and organize efficiently
- monitoring flexibility, since what is expected may not happen
- increased responsibility for taking decisions
- knowing how to develop alliances through communicating the importance of the project
- providing a focus for an action plan.

An unexpected benefit was that the project opened up new markets and challenged preconceptions of where the company could do business. An unexpected *difficulty* was in collating the information into a coherent useable form.

Reasons for benefits occurring

- the project provided Carl with challenge and stretch
- timing was appropriate; the right project at the right time
- the task suited Carl's competitive spirit and will to succeed

101

- the limited time for interviews pushed him to question effectively and probe when information was not forthcoming.

Difficulties experienced

- obtaining information and overcoming reluctance by some people
- assimilating and prioritizing information
- developing a standard reporting format
- making objective decisions.

Organization of responsibilities for the project

Mark Anderson provided some guidance in organizing information systematically and coherently for the report. This apart, Carl took responsibility for the project but with secretarial support for organizing travel and appointments.

Mark's *expected benefits* were that the project would improve Carl's interpersonal skills, particularly interviewing techniques, allow for greater exposure to senior people in the Longman group and help him to develop his presentation skills. The project was also seen to provide an opportunity to carry out an in-depth strategic review, a management activity with which he had not previously been involved. He did not anticipate any difficulties.

Actual benefits for Carl

- greater exposure within the company
- gradual development of interpersonal skills
- experience in completing a very detailed strategic review
- involvement with senior people

In addition, the project had greater impact than anticipated with recommendations implemented.

Reason for benefits occurring

- the project selected matched Carl's capabilities
- 'report writing' is an activity which is valued and supported by the company
- the timing was right; a strategic review was needed
- senior people supported it since it was aligned with strategic reviews being carried out in other regions.

Difficulties experienced

- time constraints, limiting the scope for detailed research
- slowness in decision making because of other priorities
- too wide a scope for the review
- objectives set at senior level not sufficiently clear and specific.

Organization of responsibilities for the project

Mark took his responsibilities as sponsor seriously by:

- providing help when needed and with implementation
- ensuring that the project fitted in with overall corporate level initiatives
- ensuring that senior management provided access to the relevant people and were seen to be taking the project seriously

Mark felt he should have provided more help in obtaining and sorting information and prioritizing sources, as well as having more input at stages throughout the project. With hindsight, he suggested that, in relation to criteria for choice and success, the project should address an issue which fits in with the company's business priorities and will engender support from influential people, particularly in respect of implementation.*

KEY POINT SUMMARY

- Different learning styles are evident at different stages of the project.
- The ideal of securing big chunks of time for project work is rarely achieved in practice, since the project becomes interwoven with the manager's day-to-day agenda.
- Where a manager is ready for a new job, a project separate from the job can provide a springboard for the move.
- Project responsibility is vested in the project owner, with the sponsor being available and ready to respond when needed.

---

* This project was used by Sundridge Park to produce a video as guidance for managers on the Younger Manager Programme (Module 1). It formed the basis of a Project Guide, reproduced in the Appendix to this chapter.

APPENDIX: THE PACIFIC RIM PROJECT

These notes are designed to supplement the video you have seen, tracking one person's journey though his project. The segments mirror those presented in the programme and contain generic points, which are applicable to any understanding of this nature. This is intended to act as an *aide mémoire* so that your project will prove useful, thorough and comprehensive.

The aims and objectives are to:

- Implement the learning from Module one of the Younger Manager Programme.
- Think creatively to enhance or change an aspect of your work.
- Collate and analyse information and review it critically.
- Use formal tools of analysis.
- Make clear recommendations.
- Gain greater understanding of your function, the relationships between functions and the business of your organization.
- Develop interpersonal skills and expand your network of relationships.
- Adopt new points of view.

OUTCOMES

Provide tangible benefits to you, your project sponsor and your organization.

TIMESCALE

Your project will be deemed successful by your organization if you succeed in 'selling' it. It may therefore not end with your presentation; implementing your recommendations will require your active involvement.

CHOOSING A PROJECT

There are criteria which you should have adhered to in selecting your project. They have been chosen to help you implement the learning from Module 1 and to ensure that the exercise enhances your own personal development and is deemed to be valuable by your organization:

- Check that you have chosen an area where there is a need for improvement or problem in search of a solution; it may form part of your ongoing work.
- Check that your ideas are in line with your company culture.
- Be careful to check assumptions when you are defining the problem.
- Ensure that you will need to extend the management skills you have been using.
- Involve other people.
- The subject chosen should entail both information gathering and analysis thereof; it should not be a desk type study.
- Suggest recommendations which could involve implementation.

ACTION

- List possible areas for a project.
- Having met with your project sponsor what was the outcome of your discussions?
- What are the objectives of the project?
- What outcomes do you hope to achieve?
    - for yourself?
    - for your division/department?
- What will be the likely constraints (for example you could consider people resistance, resource limitations, a dearth of information, unsympathetic company culture)?
- How could you overcome them?
- Who is likely to be involved?

POSSIBLE PITFALLS

You may find that your ideas are all-encompassing; narrow your focus to make your task achievable.

Take care to ensure that the subject you select is sufficiently important so that any conflicts of priority between your work and your project are minimized. Managing and resourcing your project alongside your own work objectives needs to be clarified.

Try to ensure that the subject you select is manageable in terms of scope and is within the bounds of a solution.

SPIN-OFFS

- A greater clarification of the areas which need improvement or change.
- Ability to adopt an approach to managing change albeit in a discrete area which has worked.

PREPARATION

Thorough preparation, planning and a means of monitoring your progress are instrumental to the success of your project.

ACTION

- Have you identified what information you need to gather?
- Where can you get it?
- What tools or criteria will you use to assess/evaluate the information?
- Who should be involved?
- How should you present yourself and your project to get their help and contributions?
  - within your organization
  - outside contacts
- What resources will you need?
- What interpersonal skills may you need to use, e.g. interviewing, influencing and persuading?
- What techniques or tools may you use, e.g. creative thinking, problem-solving methods.
- What benchmarks will you use to measure your progress?
- Test periodically that both you and the other party have a common interpretation of requests and agreements.
- Have you clarified the project end point for the Sundridge Park presentation: this may be different from the end point of the project.

POSSIBLE PITFALLS

- Time needed for planning is usually underestimated.
- Plans rarely work out in practice; build in time to cope with contingencies.

- It is common to underestimate the amount of detail that will be required.

SPIN-OFFS

Your relationship with colleagues could be strengthened through a better common understanding of divisional/unit objectives.

RESEARCH

You have now reached the analytical stage which could prove the most demanding and time consuming. It is at this point that the impact of your environment both politically and culturally will come to the fore and you will have to weigh up the risks.

Having collected the data you will have to ascertain whether what you have is sufficient and decide on a tool to carry out formal analysis, such as SWOT analysis.

ACTION

- Do I have all the relevant information?
- Have I made any omissions? What are they?
- Have I investigated thoroughly anything which may have been done in this area and the past solutions/recommendations?
- What new insights have I gained on the issue and my organization?
- Have there been any critical incidents where it would be advisable for me to review the goals of my project?
- If appropriate, how can I modify my project without compromising the outcome?

POSSIBLE PITFALLS

Beware of being too rigid. It is important to be open to new events and information which may mean modifying your preconceived ideas. Be flexible in face of change.

Try not to become demotivated. Your sponsor is likely to be most critical at this stage. Their suggestions may ultimately enhance not only your project but also your self-development.

Do not be surprised when you find that your normal work priorities conflict with your project.

SPIN-OFFS

There could be unforeseen opportunities, try to spot them and use them to advantage.

You will have the opportunity to increase your profile within your organization and extend your network.

PREPARING THE REPORT

Having collated, assessed and evaluated the information you now need to synthesize it. Think about strong and viable recommendations. At this stage it is important to seek assistance from your boss/sponsor to ensure that the report you present is in the form and language which will inspire agreement and support.

ACTION

- Is your analysis sufficiently broad and deep?
- How are the results different from what you have anticipated?
- How will you modify your pre-conceived thoughts to maximize the viability of your recommendations?
- Are your recommendations sufficiently robust to withstand rejection?
- How will they be implemented?
- What will the tangible benefits be to the department/division/organization?
- Review: Could you have used other tools which would have enhanced the validity of your findings?

POSSIBLE PITFALLS

Beware of leaving any gaps to avoid presenting an incomplete case.

Allow plenty of time to write several versions of the report so that the language you use is within the framework of your company culture.

You may be assuming too much prior knowledge and comprehension from the recipients of the report. View the report from their perspective.

SPIN-OFFS

- Practice at report writing will improve those skills.
- You will develop a greater understanding of the needs of different audiences.
- Immersing yourself in this exercise will enhance your ability to think critically.

PRESENTING

At the outset of Module 2 you will be asked to present your project. The presentation will be followed by an open forum where members of the audience will have the opportunity to question you about your recommendations and learning experience. Whether or not you have any experience of 'public speaking', there will be an optional workshop in the intervening period where you will be given guidance on presentation skills and have an opportunity to practise them.

ACTION

- Introduce yourself.
- State the objective of your project.
- Explain why it was an important area to tackle and its relevance to your organization.
- Outline the information you gathered, state your sources and explain how you assessed that information.
- Communicate the benchmarks you used.
- State your recommendations.
- Explain how those recommendations have been or will be implemented.
- Outline *your* learning experience, if and how you have improved or changed, what you may do differently or how you may have altered your views.

POSSIBLE PITFALLS

- Avoid unnecessary detail to ensure that your presentation falls within the allotted time limits and that you cover the pertinent points. Try to take an objective view.

- Ensure that your presentation does not leave unfilled gaps which may undermine the strength of your findings.
- Beware of insufficient rehearsal.
- A failure to anticipate likely questions could undermine a successful presentation.

SPIN-OFFS

- You will have the opportunity to practise your presentation skills in a safe environment which will result in greater confidence.
- You will be reminded of the importance of presentations in your role as a manager.
- You will become aware of the importance of researching and evaluating your experience.

BENEFITS

Some of the benefits will be immediately obvious. More importantly, a review of the process will help you determine the skills you could adopt for future undertakings of this nature, e.g. in management of change.

ACTION

- What new skills have you learnt?
- What skills have you improved?
- How will you secure the implementation of your recommendations over the required period of time?
- What unanticipated opportunities has your project created?
- Illustrate your new network of relationships in the form of a diagram and decide on how it can be used in the future.
- Can you use your project to enhance your role?

. . . AND FINALLY

To date, projects have been completed by a significant number of people who testify the real benefits of this undertaking; benefits both to the individual and the organization. It is only by implementing what you hear and read combined with experience that you can measure your learning and be certain of its applicability. By embarking on an exercise related to your real work, you will hopefully have the rare opportunity of standing outside your immediate functional role and gaining a better understanding of both your function and your business.

6 Strategic Management at Allied Domecq

While most company experiences in project-based learning are at middle or junior management levels, there is no limit to the level at which projects can make a profound impact on individual development and business results.

The top-level strategic management programme carried out for Allied Domecq, with development provision by Sundridge Park, is an initiative which ably demonstrates the development potential of project-based learning.

Before examining in detail Allied Domecq's approach to projects and the outcomes from them, readers need a broad level of understanding about the businesses, complexity and speed of change within the organization.

ALLIED DOMECQ – THE BUSINESS

Allied Domecq is a spirits, wine and retailing company which operates in 120 countries across the world. The name will mean less to people than the names of many of its spirits brands:

Ballantine's	Laphroaig	Teachers
Tia Maria	Kahlua	Courvoisier
Lambs Navy Rum	Lemon Hart Rum	Beefeater Gin
Presidente Brandy	Sauza	La Ina Sherry
Harveys Bristol Cream	Cockburn's Port	Ballygowan
Gleneagles Water	Jean Moreau Wines	Lanson Champagne
Makers Mark	Canadian Club	

The company's retailing businesses, primarily in the UK and USA – with expanding presence in Europe through, for example, John Bull Pubs – comprise 13,000 retail units. This figure embraces 1500 wine shops (Victoria Wine, The Cellars and Haddows), 4500 pubs previously associated with such Brewery names as Tetley, Ansells, Ind Coope, Taylor Walker, and Tetley Walker but now, increasingly, becoming branded as service propositions in the UK such as Firkin, Big Steak, Wacky Warehouse, Football-Football, etc., and 7000 retail outlets for Dunkin Donuts and Baskin Robbins in the USA. In addition to these businesses, Allied Domecq retains its interest in the origins of the group – the breweries – through a joint venture in the UK market with Carlsberg the Danish brewers. Carlsberg-Tetley embraces two of the key beer brands in the joint venture name which, together with Castlemaine XXXX, Lowenbrau, Burton Ale, Skol and other beer brands brewed at one of the six breweries that the business owns in the UK, has a £1 billion turnover.

The diversity that Allied Domecq needs to manage as a business, whether because of geography, cultural differences, the maturity or the development stage of the marketplace, means that the business requires a critical mass of mobile, high calibre executives. Members of this cadre must have business acumen and the social adaptability that will enable them to relate effectively to what is happening in the business, in whatever part of the global map they operate. For Allied Domecq executives with the appropriate potential and personal circumstances, the possible career path and development opportunity provides a good rationale for employment with the company. With its scale of business and global reach, there is an infinite variety of opportunities, problems and challenges that continuously need to be taken on by people who are capable of doing what is required within the ethos of the organization.

Allied Domecq as a business has evolved to its current shape by means of many amalgamations, alliances, mergers and takeovers. In the early 1960s, three of the biggest brewers, Ind Coope, Tetley Walker and Ansells came together to form Allied Breweries. At that time the business was capitalized at £100 million. One of the major disposals Allied has made is the food and beverage business J. Lyons & Co. In the past four years, Allied has acquired or disengaged from businesses with a total value of £2.5 billion. This gives an indicator of the level of change taking place within the group.

114

Pedro Domecq is the latest in a series of acquisitions, mergers and alliances that has positioned Allied as one of the world's top three drinks businesses. In 1968, Allied Breweries acquired companies that produced Babycham, Harveys Sherries and Cockburn's Ports. Then came the move to food and non-alcoholic beverages in 1978, with the acquisition of J. Lyons and brands such as Tetley Tea, Baskin Robbins Ice Creams, Lyons Coffee, cakes and biscuits. In 1986, Allied-Lyons as it was now called, acquired 51 per cent of Hiram Walker, the Canadian drinks business founded by the Hatch family, with whom Joseph Kennedy had some dealings around the time of Prohibition. The brands included in this deal were Canadian Club, Courvoisier, Ballantine's, Kahlua and Tia Maria. Then, in 1989, Allied-Lyons acquired James Burroughs (including brands such as Beefeater Gin, Laphroaig Malt Whisky and Dunkin Donuts). In 1993, Allied-Lyons formed a joint venture with Carlsberg called Carlsberg Tetley, formed from the Danish Breweries and its own brewing arm. This followed in response to the Monopolies and Mergers Commission regulation of the beer market. The beer orders obliged Allied to dispose of close to 50 per cent of the pubs it owned at the time. The joint venture's business includes brewing and wholesaling brands such as Tetley Bitter, Carlsberg Export, Skol and Castlemaine XXXX.

In 1994, Allied-Lyons accelerated its business in international wines and spirits and retailing interests by acquiring control of Pedro Domecq. This brought major brands such as Presidente Fundador Centenario and Sauza Tequila. Allied Domecq PLC, as it was renamed in September 1994, has two main sectors in its operations besides involvement in brewing – Allied Domecq Spirits and Wine and Allied Domecq Retailing.

EXECUTIVE CAPABILITY

The change in this business, as with many similar ones, is increasing in scope, pace and intensity. The pressure to respond to continuously increasing standards of performance is evidenced by the many choices the business has made, as well as the challenges Allied Domecq continues to tackle. Operating efficiency and market leadership confront management in Allied with the necessity to rethink, evolve and innovate in relation to product and service strategies across many areas of the portfolio. There is considerable pressure to enhance the value of Allied

Domecq businesses in both the short and long terms. They need to achieve short-term performance at levels that satisfy the city, as well as achieving responsiveness and flexibility in a more competitive environment. Time will become a critical dimension of effectiveness in decision making within the business. Management will need to find new ways of processing relevant information and structuring decisions so that appropriate responses are actioned within the necessary timeframes. The judgements by executives and, therefore, the time it takes the organization to respond provide the critical influence on the relative positioning of the business and its performance. How well executives assimilate and make sense of the realities of their business environment and industry, as well as the internal challenges facing the business and how well people can 'get their act together', are key elements of the strategic capability.

Allied place a considerable value on delegating decisions to levels that understand the local business environment. The assumption that must accompany this delegation of power is that the executives involved can, and will, handle the responsibility effectively. This would be a straightforward skill development issue if the marketplace, the organizational infrastructure, competitive practices, not to mention the increase in government and other regulatory interventions, were moving at a manageable pace.

THE PROGRAMME

The formal aims of the programme originally were to:

- help participants to improve their ability to think strategically and implement their decisions effectively
- improve their knowledge and experience of the business, together with the skills and attitudes appropriate to the changing nature of the business, their roles and capability levels.

Since the first iteration of the programme, nominations have reflected the diversity of the business environments and geography of the business. In a group of 18 individuals there can be eight to 12 different nationalities, with considerable diversity in their experience, specific roles and business environments. The value the development process aims to deliver is:

- improved knowledge of Allied business
- improved network of peers

116

- enhanced capability to undertake general management and change agent roles.

The ability of Allied executives to design, develop and implement projects that help the business to implement tactical and strategic changes is a core capability that can support the business in its endeavours to evolve and change more proactively. The ability to maintain both a strategic and operational focus, i.e. to keep in view the perspective of the general manager as well as that of the functional or operational specialist, is important in managing performance effectively. As the pace at which the socio-economic, technological and political environment and context change, the processes, roles and responsibilities of executives will need to evolve at least at a similar pace. Only if this happens will the challenges posed be handled effectively: 'If you always do what you have always done you will always get what you have always got.' Change to existing ways of thinking and mindsets are inevitable. Nothing will change, however, if the behaviour of individuals does not change.

Too often the commitment to change is at a philosophical or intellectual level. It is easier to speak the words than to effect the required changes in ourselves or in our patterns of activity. So, too, with learning, as John Ruskin suggests: 'to understand is one thing . . . to act on what you know is all that matters'.

The initial programme sought to help the participants to:

- become more aware of core strategic issues and challenges facing the business
- explore their personal capability to contribute as a director of an operating company and, potentially, at higher levels within a two- to five-year period
- make a personal return on their companies' investment in their personal development by developing a proposal or project to help progress the strategic agenda.

The programme design, featured as a programme route map in Figure 6.1, is based on case materials on strategic issues, general management type discussion topics, team development initiatives, project management processes, strategic frameworks and selected psychometrics.

117

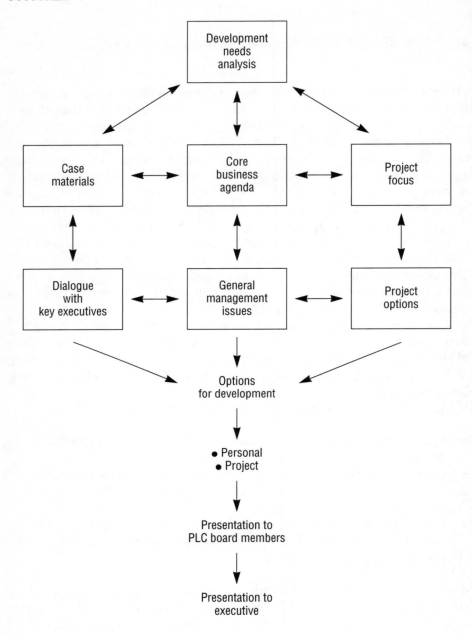

Figure 6.1 A programme route map

PROGRAMME PROCESS

Stage one of the process starts with senior executives deciding, in consultation with sponsors, who among the existing cadre of high calibre executives is likely to benefit from attendance on the programme. Participants learn of their selection from their sponsors or bosses who, as coaches, have a significant role to fulfil during the process. This role may be less ably addressed by sponsors who do not espouse the appropriate values and beliefs required, e.g. people who operate their managerial prerogative through the management and control ethos. Project owners, whose sponsors are comfortable with a coaching approach, generally experience more active support and space for developing their projects.

Stage two involves the programme director briefing participants on what is required from the development process. At this point, before attending the main module, individual participants are asked to discuss and agree their personal development objectives and outlines for a potential project.

During this stage also, the potential for extending participants' own personal network develops into an activity. The networking activities lead to improved cross-functional relationships and greater empathy across operating company boundaries. Equally, participants have the rare opportunity to exchange views on different aspects of the strategic agenda with senior executives and directors responsible for them. These exchanges help both parties to develop a better understanding of the range of views and insights available on any of the core issues facing the business.

Stage three involves concentrated periods of practical work in becoming familiar with Allied's business agenda; exchange of views with all the key directors of the businesses; concentration on personal/team development and practice in applying strategic frameworks to improve executives' perspectives of development priorities and issues for the business.

This stage also gives participants the opportunity to test their progress on projects with those individuals who will review the projects to be presented to the board.

In *stage four*, participants present and discuss their projects with Allied's PLC board members. Each individual is given an hour in total for the presentation. Board members have the opportunity to read the reports before hearing participants present their cases. Projects are reviewed against criteria which seek to grade:

- quality of the definition of the opportunity or problem
- quality of the analysis
- appropriateness and implementability of the options outlined
- effectiveness of the presentation to the reviewers.

PROJECT SELECTION CRITERIA

For a project to be an acceptable development challenge for the individual, it should fit a number of criteria, among which should be the following:

- A clear connection to the participant's current job.
- Focus on a relevant strategic opportunity, threat or problem for the business in which the manager is engaged and also consistent with corporate direction.
- Stretch for the individual beyond the current role, by crossing organization and functional boundaries and helping the individual to develop a greater understanding of less familiar activities and business functions.
- The capability of making the required return on investment needed to meet quantitative and qualitative review criteria. For example, if the project outcomes/outputs are applicable across a number of business areas, rather than confined to the area of the pilot test only, then it would be more valuable. Equally, from a financial point of view, the envisaged potential return would need to meet existing project appraisal criteria in Allied.

In addition, if the project is merely a progression on the current mindset or operational framework of the business, as opposed to being an innovative or creatively adaptive addition to new product development, customer focus, operational excellence, etc., then it would not really merit inclusion or selection. The level of stretch to the individual's development may be related, e.g. to the innovative quality of the analysis undertaken for the project.

So, the project selection criteria help to ensure a forward looking, opportunistic and strategic type of project which can help individuals redefine the business and their own role and performance standards more effectively.

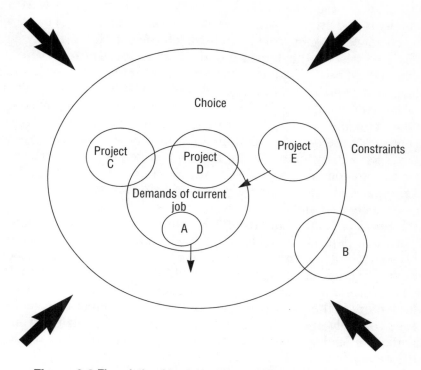

Figure 6.2 The relationship of the project to current job rates

PROJECT VISIONING

Perhaps the most difficult phase of the project management process is getting started. When trying to obtain a perspective of what, potentially, can lead to a productive avenue of exploration, difficulties abound in limiting the project owners' expectations. We have dealt with a selection of project-based learning issues above, all of which are about positioning the projects most helpfully to attract the level of support required to undertake what is neither an easy nor superficial process. If the project owners make 'sufficient' progress, they will have undergone a highly visible (especially in the eyes of senior executives) change during their education and development process. Furthermore, the individuals should be able to reflect on how they might redefine the added value of their role.

121

Figure 6.2 (see page 121), based on Rosemary Stewart's work, can help sponsors and project owners to visualize the positioning of the project and its relationship to current and future job roles in the company. The inner circle represents the demands of the current job. These are the elements which must be undertaken effectively in order to demonstrate a minimum level of acceptable performance. A project which is defined only in terms of these demands, e.g. Project A, is unlikely to gain approval unless it can show how the scope can be widened during execution. The outer circle represents the boundaries of the job which cannot be transgressed without encroaching onto the job territory of someone else. Project B is a representation of such a project, which can be done only with the willing agreement and support of the person or persons concerned.

Projects C, D and E are representations of typical projects. In each case, the projects contain an element which falls in the area labelled 'choice'. This area depicts elements of a job which are optional according to the preference of the particular job holder. Most jobs have a much wider degree of choice than may be apparent from the job description. Project C will involve a substantial element of choice, while Project D will concentrate more in the area of demand. Both are completely acceptable. Project E lies entirely in the choice area and is not directly related to current job demands. Such a project has potential for acceptance, but would require the demonstration of a link back to the participants' perception of current job demands during execution of the project.

THE PROJECT MANAGEMENT PROCESS

The project management process consists of three stages spread over eight to nine months. These stages cover selection, work-in-progress and review.

PROJECT SELECTION

Selection for the project has, to date, involved the individual proposing a project focus to the sponsor, who is normally the boss. Should the boss of the participant agree, the chief executive of the business sector would offer some guidance from a PLC board perspective. The variety of inputs at this stage can help avoid possible failure later in the process, when the time to complete is tight and a changed project is not acceptable.

The project selection stage, besides the necessity for ensuring suitability in organizational governance terms, also requires the participants to select actual opportunities to make progress in a breakthrough area. Members of the board of trading/operating companies are expected to have the capacity to define appropriate projects in the context of developing the business and, as importantly, lead these to valued outcomes. The programme concept allows executives to take projects through management to business results. Making time to do the project has been a real difficulty for executives who have had to focus hard and long at the project selection phase on defining a project that is likely to be valued and have the probability of valuable outcomes. Another issue at the project definition stage has been the lack of involvement by the sponsor in giving 'organizational' guidance as to what is valued, what has been dealt with or is in process already. The quality of networking with senior executives, relevant 'experts' and specialists, both within and outside the organization, if not conducted adequately can create a number of pressures and difficulties later in the process, not least in terms of the quality of the project focus and, consequently, the outputs.

PROJECT PROGRESS – LESSONS FROM EXPERIENCE

Each iteration of the programme brings new insights into project-based learning as a vehicle for aligning the development of individuals with the necessary changes required in both the business and the organization. In order to gain a useful perspective on managing this process, it is helpful to consider how best to link the business agenda (especially specific strategic aims) to the organization's potential for delivering outcomes to participants' projects. The links are shown in Figure 6.3.

The stronger the link between the three circles shown in the figure, the more political and active the support, e.g. the politics of sacrificing short-term for medium to long-term gains the individual is likely to attract. The value placed on the potential gain in business terms will help balance some of the counter arguments against the investment of resources, principally the participant's time on work for the project as opposed to the focus on normal day to day activities.

The belief in the prospective value added that the project can help the project owner achieve, lends a helping hand to developing the level of self-confidence required for making challenging proposals regarding the business to PLC directors. The level of debate at PLC meetings will frequently

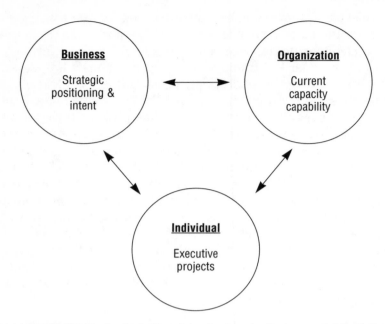

Figure 6.3 Linking the business agenda to the organization's potential for delivering outcomes to projects

focus on large-scale projects featuring, in corporate terms, much bigger numbers. So, if the relevance of a project can be demonstrated in the individual's own business area, as well as across the businesses in that sector and, perhaps, across other sectors, then it will attract a relatively high level of support, both during the project journey and at the review stage.

Ultimately, however, it is the individual's level of commitment to the work that is of central concern. Selecting people for a development experience is not easy in any large corporation. Their positioning with the business, i.e. the level of attainment achieved, the regard the business has for their ability, the reliance of business (particularly the sponsor) on the individual to deliver results, the quality of the peer and subordinate group, the level of change going on in the business around the individual, the ability of the sponsor and the individual to position the development experience appropriately are all contingencies that businesses often take for granted at their cost.

In putting an individual on a development programme, actively driving a work agenda in the individual's direction that undermines the capacity to focus on deriving benefit from the real learning challenges of the project back on the job should be avoided.

Individuals, then, have to plan in *four areas* to position themselves for an optimal productive experience, more in keeping with the potential benefit available from learning on the job through project work. These are:

- Before accepting the place, individuals will find it helpful to have detailed conversations with:
  - the boss/sponsor
  - the peer group
  - subordinates
  - family, partners, etc.

  This will enable them to arrive at an appropriate personal contract for the journey. The core network provides either the primary detraction or support to the individual entering the development process. All these influences can have a direct bearing on the individual's capacity to manage and benefit from the development opportunity. For example, subordinates can support project owners by taking on aspects of their role which, in turn, can be a development opportunity.
- The sponsor of the programme (the Chief Executive at PLC) needs to position the development experience in terms of the strategic aims of the business and the responsibility of the corporation to identify future high calibre executives. Individuals will need to link their development agenda to the business and organization development agenda by positioning themselves appropriately. In terms of what constitutes 'real value added', the selection of projects and their relevance to the business can help attract appropriate levels of support.
- Individuals rarely, if ever, complete all the work of the project journey themselves. The combination of colleagues who share a vested interest in the outcome or outputs, networks of people inside and outside the business who owe 'favours' or are willing to support the project; programme tutors, not to mention sponsors with an active interest in the participant's success; all contribute directly and indirectly to the work associated with the project. The organization of how the work gets done, the careful projection of deadlines for activities, the management and focus of concurrent activities, all require an organizational ability, in order to keep commitment at appropriate levels while maintaining relevant focus. This is a prerequisite that individuals need to manage.

Effective networks are also essential to project success. Dimensions and features of these networks need to reflect the nature of the challenges the project offers. For example, if you are challenging the conventions of current business performance processes, sanction and political 'approval' will be needed from Sector/PLC Board level. Should that not be forthcoming, a new project focus would be advisable. In theory this should always be possible. Frequently, in practice, the opportunity as well as the quality and timeliness of communications may not enable this crucial point to be clarified in good time.

- Positioning the project to meet 'felt' needs in the local sponsoring business, and to be high up on the sponsor's personal agenda as well as suitable to both the individual's role and development needs, helps offset the level of local 'interference' with the potential value of the project development experience. On a more positive aspect, the quality of the sponsorship, particularly the level of personal interest taken and latitude given, will be more in keeping with the role of a coach which the sponsor can helpfully fulfil. Frequently, desired development of high calibre people in the business is subjugated to the personal interest of the sponsor. Ignoring 'local' support and the potential contribution of an active coach to the project owner will be unhelpful. In many respects, the programme sponsor and the 'faculty' ought to establish ground rules to cater for local and special circumstances as part of the development of the 'contract' between the sponsor and the individual.

In each of these four areas, individuals can confront in advance areas of difficulty that could undermine the value of the experience and the quality of the outputs and outcomes. Having a personal project vision, and revisiting it regularly to integrate the learning from progress to date, will help individuals to have a more accurate perspective of where they are at any particular point in the development process. Project route mapping and visioning skills combine to help individuals stretch their personal ability to add value to their business and, more importantly, be more visible in delivering the contributions in the eyes of those who govern the business. These activities can help redress the imbalance in thinking styles between left and right brain activity. It is interesting to note that City criticisms of industry tend to concentrate on many of the unhelpful excesses of left brain activities undermining the more visionary, innovative thinking which leads to genuine development of products and services which, in turn, enhance shareholder value and competitive positioning of the businesses.

PROJECT REVIEW

Every project experience has its own potential in terms of personal and team learning, as well as organization/business development. What has been learned as a consequence of project work by the stakeholders (i.e. the individual, peers, subordinates, sponsor and senior executives) is as pertinent as the specific output of the project. Who is involved in reviewing the project experience and how projects are reviewed are not incidental in terms of the learning that will take place. Frequently, the temptation is to concentrate on evaluating what the value of the recommendations are and to ignore what actually has been learned about the business, the people and processes in the project journey. The choice of review mechanism and who is involved are useful questions to consider in terms of what you are required to achieve. PLC sponsorship of the evaluation process can greatly help future networking and visibility.

In Allied Domecq's case, the two-stage process involves chief executives of the sectors, i.e. PLC director equivalents, and in the second phase of evaluation the programme sponsor, the group chief executive as well as the chairman and vice chairman, i.e. the executive.

The first round of project reviews is designed to establish the quality of the focus and the analysis and relevance of the recommendations, as well as to gauge the adequacy of the presentation in corporate board level terms.

The criteria for a good presentation to this audience are not surprising. Project sponsors and reviewers expect project owners, in their presentations, to cover the main elements set out below. Each element has been expanded to provide examples of what might need to be included.

Clarify the *rationale for the choice of project*:

- relevance to the direction in which the business is moving
- strategic importance of leverage in this area
- level of transferability across businesses and sectors; impact of making progress in this area.

Articulate the essence of the analysis:

- separate assumptions from facts

127

- emphasize relevant new insights to the problem or opportunity being explored
- identify important contextual issues to be dealt with in the business (the structure, culture, etc.).

Demonstrate *options available for making progress* and clarify the *principal evaluation criteria*:

- *Suitability*:
  - deals directly with opportunities/weaknesses/threats/actual problems
  - exploits what we have going for us
  - supports corporate, sectoral and business unit level objectives/goals.
- *Feasibility*:
  - resources are available or can be created
  - market position will be influenced by outcome(s)
  - competitor responses have been taken into account
  - people have the capability and the capacity, e.g. competence and time
  - business and IT systems will support the propositions.
- *Acceptability*:
  - outcome will meet standards of return required
  - risk/benefit analysis
  - fits with trend in regulation of the business environment
  - links with visions of own business in the future.

Presentation of core project learning is a skill to which too few executives pay enough attention – not everyone is a good communicator in writing. It is most unfortunate when we combine poor performance in speech and written dimensions of our presentations. While no one would like to think that really good ideas can be lost in poor presentations, it would be helpful to remind ourselves that presenting to senior executives is not a generic exercise. Each senior executive is a product of his or her professional and life experiences. Each will have had different experiences of business cycles in different businesses as well as, perhaps, a variety of consequences from different types of decisions. It is easy to forget the isolation of the many individual business contexts that can exist in a sector or a division of the PLC. Getting to know, share, appreciate and develop a wider perspective of what is going on is a critical step towards feeling less isolated and,

128

more positively, feeling more able to identify and want to be linked to what is going on elsewhere in the business. The sense of purpose and sense of identity are critical ingredients in executive success. As Sir Christopher Hogg, current Executive Chairman of Allied Domecq has said, there are two types of failure: one of direction (or lack of it), one which is personal (cases where behaviour and personality gets in the way).

The relevant questions for the presenter are: Who am I presenting to? What are their expectations? What weighting will they give to what evaluation criteria? What are they currently 'obsessed' or preoccupied with? How well do they know the area I will be exploring? What can I take for granted? How do they perceive me?

The quality of the presentation has a much more powerful impact on the actual review than many presenters and listeners would, at first, acknowledge. The well-known primacy effect in communications can leave an enduring good or bad impression on the listening reviewer.

The value of the project-based learning process is seen, both at the review time and subsequently, in terms of what change takes place in the role of the individual, the perception of the potential the individual offers in terms of doing development projects for corporate sector level as well as, of course, what happens to the actual project itself.

CONCLUSION

As a developmental and educative process for Allied Domecq, the programme and project-based learning process has opened up new conversations, new challenges and new relationships. This particular forum has helped to forge new networks in the business. As one Mexican participant has said 'it will now take me five minutes to find out what would have taken three months to do previously'. Participants learn not only about the difficulties of the daily struggle, but also about the potential that exists for them and for others to seize and create opportunities. Participants learn that the act of commitment does not mean waiting until the support conditions or climate are favourable, but taking action that helps progress even if only in small, but initially successful, steps. Equally, participants often 'discover' a new-found pride and commitment in their business and their corporation. In a wider sense, 'growing up' in the business is about evolving your sense of identity with what needs to happen. Forging strong networks of able people across sectors and across businesses helps the corporation to integrate what it is doing at corporate and local business levels. The transference of learning can more easily take place between people who will listen to each other. The project-based learning process can challenge helpfully the complacency of current thinking.

KEY POINT SUMMARY

- For senior executives, it is essential that individual projects provide alignment of individual development with the strategic positioning of the business and the organization's capacity and capability.
- In influencing project selection, the project owner should ensure that 'real added value' is one of the chief criteria for choice in the project, since this will help to attract appropriate levels of support from stakeholders.
- At this senior level in an organization, it is unlikely that the project owner alone will carry out all the activities involved in the project. The network of stakeholders (internal and external) with vested interests is, in effect, the management.
- Often, due to the size, significance and complexity of projects at this level, exercising effective project management skills is essential.
- Occasionally, sanction and political approval from board level may be necessary where a project appears to be challenging the conventions of current business performance procedures.
- The project owner must have a personal project vision and revisit it frequently in order to integrate learning with project progress.
- In reviewing project learning, look outside the evaluation of recommendations and include what has been learned about the business, the people and the processes.
- The positioning of a project and its relationship to current and future job roles in the organization, will become clearer with the application of the model of Demands, Constraints and Choices, as researched by Rosemary Stewart.
- The learning from the project is primarily centred upon the project owner, but there is a need to recognize the learning by other stakeholders, particularly sponsors.
- CEO/board level sponsorship of the evaluation process is helpful for future networking and visibility.

- Principal evaluation criteria from a business perspective can usefully include suitability, feasibility and acceptability.
- The project owners should be clear about the sponsor/reviewers' 'expectations'; weighting given to evaluation criteria; current 'obsessions' or preoccupations; frame of reference; knowledge of the area or topic and perceptions of themselves.

7 Developing Younger Managers within ICI

Project work forms an integral part of the ICI Foundations of Business (FOB) programme developed in collaboration with Sundridge Park. This is part of the Core Development Programme in which younger managers participate, within the first two to four years of joining ICI. These managers have usually joined ICI directly after completing their university education, typically in a science discipline, and have spent their first few years gaining experience in an operational or technical role. Graham McGregor is the ICI training and development manager responsible for the FOB programme, which is one of a set of core programmes sponsored by the ICI Chemicals and Polymers Training and Organisational Development Group, managed by Colin Thompson. Other ICI businesses also participate in the core programmes. The FOB programme explores concepts and techniques of management in strategy development, marketing, finance, R&T and operations.

Programme aims are to:

- Lay foundations of a thorough understanding of business management, enabling participants to work confidently in a business-led organization.
- Show the interrelationship of functions within a business, the influence of the wider business environment and the importance of effectively integrating different functional contributions in the business strategy.
- Develop understanding of how to interpret and use financial information in making business judgements and decisions.
- Use project work to apply and reinforce learning from the programme and contribute to improving business results.

Project work has been part of the programme for several years and over 600 individual projects have been undertaken. In the earlier years of the programme, the project work centred on developing an improved general understanding of the mission, objectives and critical success factors of the particular business unit to which the participant belonged. Acquiring experience of differing functional perspectives (e.g. marketing, production, research) and the interfaces between functions also formed an important aspect of project work. In this way, project work helped participants improve their understanding of general business management issues and of how their own professional discipline can effectively contribute to business success.

A further benefit of the project work has been that it provides a common framework for participants to share their knowhow and insights concerning a diverse range of businesses within the ICI portfolio and, in so doing, recognize common issues and approaches to analysing and solving problems, which might otherwise be obscured by local technical jargon.

RECENT DEVELOPMENTS

More recently, increased priority has been given to selecting projects which concern current business issues in the changing ICI business environment. The de-merger of the company to form a new ICI and the biosciences company Zeneca, along with other company reorganizations, has provided participants with opportunities to undertake projects which allow them to explore potential new roles and familiarize themselves with new, emerging business environments. This emphasis on current issues has been undertaken in parallel with stronger involvement by sponsoring managers in the selection and review of projects, and also with an increased contribution by local ICI trainers as facilitators in the support of project activities. A summary of the process is shown in Figure 7.1. A description of the important aspects of the process follow.

THE SPONSORING PROCESS

The recommendation of appropriate projects by sponsors is a crucial factor in the success of the process and the identity of the sponsor is equally important. The sponsor may or may not be the participant's line manager, depending on the business context. The involvement of a senior manager from the Business Team of the business in which the participant

---

ICI Foundations of Business
Stages in the Project Life-Cycle

1.　Generating ideas

2.　Scoping the project
　　　– with ICI Sponsor

3.　Definition and agreement
　　　– at Sundridge Park

4.　Finalizing the 'contract'
　　　– with ICI Sponsor

5.　Undertaking the work

6.　Presenting the recommendations

7.　Implementation

8.　Measuring the outcomes

Figure 7.1 Stages in the project lifecycle

is employed is encouraged. The Business Team is the group of managers responsible for the management of a business unit, and include managers representing the various functional disciplines (e.g. marketing, manufacturing, finance). This allows the opportunity for the participant to develop contacts with senior functional managers and involve them in project activities. Extracts from the briefing note which is provided for the project sponsor follow.

This outline should also include a commentary from the participant's manager endorsing the project selection.

BRIEFING NOTE FOR PROJECT SPONSOR: DEFINING THE PROJECT

It is required that, following initial discussions with the project sponsor, the participant write a one page project outline. This outline should include the following:

- Project title:　　this may be a provisional title
- Scope:　　　　the overall purpose of the project and what it aims to do
- Outcomes:　　what the project is likely to achieve for the company and for the participant's career development

---

135

Once the project outline is completed it should be reviewed and approved by the project sponsor. A copy of the agreed project outline is to be provided to Sundridge Park before the start of the FOB programme. Participants will refine their project, using knowledge and techniques developed during the course, and produce a project plan. Following the course, the plan will be approved by the sponsor, with facilitation by ICI training staff.

Role of Project Sponsor

The project sponsor (who might not be the participant's manager) largely determines the successful outcome of a project. At the outset, there is a requirement to agree the scope and broad outcomes of the project. At this stage the initiative for selecting the project area should come from the participant, using the criteria provided to the participant as part of the 'Initial Guidelines' for determining projects. The project sponsor may suggest areas for enquiry but should avoid forcing the choice of a project.

In deciding whether to endorse the selection of a project, sponsors should pay particular attention to the scope of the proposed project and the feasibility of producing a quality outcome in the time available. The sponsor has the absolute right of veto if not satisfied that the proposal meets the characteristics of a good project.

Being a project sponsor requires a careful balance in the following areas:

- Neither being overly directive towards nor ignoring participant needs.
- Allowing freedom of action, but at the same time, providing support when needed.
- The needs of a participant as an individual compared with the needs of the company.

These balances can best be achieved by regular contact and discussion, between the participant and the sponsor or ICI training staff who facilitate project activities, during the period from project selection to follow-up activity after the project presentation.

DEFINITION AND AGREEMENT

Following discussions between the participant and the project sponsor, the participant completes a project outline pro forma, which is sent to Sundridge Park, before the start of the residential stage of the programme (as outlined in the above briefing note).

At an early point in the Sundridge Park stage of the programme, participants explore and expand their ideas for their project in a workshop session. This session makes use of the database of past projects undertaken by previous participants, using a PC-based system to identify earlier projects of potential relevance and also to identify the names of individuals who may have related interests.

During the Sundridge stage, participants develop their project ideas further and can apply learning from the sessions within the programme in order to refine their approach. For example, SWOT (Strengths, Weaknesses, Opportunities, Threats) and Portfolio analysis may be incorporated for business strategy or marketing-orientated aspects, and measures such as RONA (Return on Net Assets) may be included to highlight financial performance issues.

Towards the end of the Sundridge stage, individual participants present their project plan to a group of other participants (usually four), who play the role of 'Business Team' members of the participant's business. This affords dual benefits in that the participant project owner receives feedback and contributions for the other participants concerning the project. In addition, the 'Business Team' participants are given the opportunity to test their skills at formulating questions and probing issues at the level appropriate to the management of an ICI business. They receive feedback and guidance as the session progresses through the presentations.

THE CONTRIBUTION OF TECHNOLOGY

Technology has contributed to the management of the projects process. A projects database has been created at Sundridge Park using PC software. This enables a record of each individual project to be maintained and accessed by participants via PCs at the stage in the programme where they are refining the scope and approach to be taken within their projects. A keyword search facility enables participants to identify earlier projects and to make contact with the colleagues who undertook the earlier projects. In this way networks of individuals with common or related interests can be established. (Appendix 1 on page 149 contains details concerning the use of technology and the analysis of project outcomes.)

SELECTED PROJECT EXAMPLES

Two examples of projects from the FOB programme are outlined in the following sections.

ICI PROJECT CASE STUDY

Project Title

The process of taking a new analytical procedure from R&T to the plants at XYZ Works

Project Owner

Trevor Morris, ICI Acrylics

This is an excellent illustration of how project work can develop understanding of:

- cross-functional working
- customer focus
- financial performance measures
- teamworking.

The content and style of the report also highlights the dual benefits of tangible business results and personal learning which a project can provide. The project report is written as a personal log in a well-142

structured, easy to follow style. The following extracts from Trevor's report highlight the key issues and outcomes. In the extracts, some location names and other information has been modified for reasons of commercial sensitivity.

Project Objective

This project was undertaken as part of the ICI Foundations of Business programme attended in September 1994. This project has two aims in fact. The first is to take a new analytical procedure which

138

is being developed here in the AB research labs, complete the development and transfer the technique to the plant labs at XYZ Works. Here it may be used beneficially to improve information about how the process is working and to optimize it. The second aim, which is the more important one for this project, is to analyse the process by which the transfer of technology is achieved. This will involve talking to various sets of people who have an interest in the outcome of the project and obtaining their views on how best to achieve it and what is most important.

This report is prepared in the style of a personal log. The learning is contained in the feedback obtained from the individuals concerned and in the events that occurred. I thank all those people who offered their help and advice during this project and, where possible, I have mentioned them by name. The supporting memorandum for the purchase of the HPLC system is appended to this report and contains all the financial information supporting the justification of this project.

Early in the project, Trevor's report illustrates the importance of thinking about the people who need to be persuaded of the value of the project, particularly from the plant operator's perspective.

Selling the Idea

The first discussion I had was with my project sponsor, Mike Sellers, who is responsible for our group's activities. He suggested that the first set of people I should speak to and gain the commitment of were the plant managers and above them the operations managers.

A presentation was made at our quarterly production/tech. dev. meeting. In preparation for this Mike suggested that I produce a Gantt diagram showing all the key processes required in the project with a timeframe. The project was sold on two main points. Firstly saving in analytical resource over the current techniques (relatively small in financial terms) and, secondly, in terms of improved efficiency savings. One per cent efficiency saving on one of our plants would give NN tes/yr extra production worth £XX,000. This, it was explained, was to be brought about by providing better and more frequent information about how the YY stage was performing.

Reaction to Proposals and Feedback

I went into the meeting thinking that the second of the two points would be the most enticing. However, there was considerable scepticism about the ability of the project to deliver real efficiency savings. The view was expressed by the production manager that the analytical method in itself could not deliver efficiency savings, but that it could only monitor more effectively efficiency losses. He also made the point that such a method had been tried in the past but that no one had paid any attention to the data and that there had been no mechanism for using the data to improve performance.

He, therefore, suggested that I made sure, once the analytical method was operational on site, that the plant operators on site were intimately involved in the development of plant performance models using the data, which they could use to improve the plant's performance. This would avoid the 'men in white coats' syndrome, where some new technique is imposed on the plant operatives by R&T which they have had no part in developing and therefore have no commitment to making it work.

In contrast to the scepticism about the benefits, most people were quite happy about the analytical resource saving. I think this was because these were much easier to measure. The labs manager was mainly interested in these savings as he was under considerable pressure to cut his budget. The plant managers were keen on the idea of better information about efficiency, but were concerned when I mentioned that the actual efficiency was almost certainly being overstated under the present technique. This is an understandable reaction as a sudden drop in the measured efficiency of their plants would cause them trouble.

I think this last point is an important one because it is very difficult to set in place a process of continuous improvement when people are worried about being shouted at if something does not work out as planned.

Review of Tactics

I thought the point about getting the plant operators involved was a good one. So I decided to talk to my colleague Wendy about how we might approach this. She works more closely with the plant operatives than I do. She suggested not to involve them until we had a

140

working technique that they could then set down and decide how best to use. This was because she thought that the best way of engaging their interest would be to demonstrate the new technique and its capabilities and then let them think about how they might use it (with some direction from ourselves). More importantly, if the technique was not fully working, it would give the less enthusiastic operators the excuse to dump it as 'yet another unfeasible idea from R&T'.

This last point was made to me on more than one occasion. I, therefore, became convinced that the single most important factor in the success of the project would be the robustness of the technique itself.

Wendy then suggested that we talk to each of the operations managers on an individual basis to answer any concerns they may have. These two meetings went well with both in favour of the project and its aims (provided the funding was coming from elsewhere). We decided to have follow-up meetings when we were ready to transfer the equipment to the plant site.

Difficulties and Obstacles Encountered – Project Sanction

The first area of difficulty encountered was in writing the supporting memorandum and expenditure request for the eventual purchase of the system. Again, the problem is with the vexed question of financial justification. The basic difficulty was that the most easily quantified savings were in the area of reduced analytical spend but these were really too small to justify the expenditure.

The really big savings to be made were in the area of increased efficiency saving, but while it was easy to quantify the value of a certain saving it was more difficult to quantify the actual efficiency gain possible. Initially, this was put at 1 per cent, giving a £XX,000 saving. However, this was considered a dangerously large sum of money to 'promise' as a saving. After much consideration, it was decided that the easiest thing to promise was a reduction in the variability in the efficiency. This should be possible to improve because, having continuous monitoring of the efficiency, it should allow for more frequent optimization. A 0.1 per cent sustained improvement in the efficiency was valued at £ZZ,000 for the budget production underlining the very small improvement needed to pay for the machine.

The message from this episode was to understand the sensitivities of senior managers before going for sanction. Quantifying the savings can be difficult because they have not been made yet whereas quantifying the cost is generally very easy.

The 'Summary and Recommendations' included in Trevor's report provide some very valuable guidelines for anyone concerned with introducing a new process into a plant environment.

Summary and Recommendations

The following is a suggested 10-point plan for developing and introducing new ideas into a plant environment based on feedback and experience to date with this project:

i. Think in advance about all the things that will be needed to make the project happen and try to draw up a list of critical activities that must occur. A Gantt diagram will help decide what order activities can be carried out and whether they can be done in parallel to save time.

ii. Talk early to plant customers in order to ensure that their view of the benefits is the same as yours. Also they may make points about implementation which have not been considered. Remember to keep them informed about important events.

iii. When selling the idea, consider the viewpoint of the person you are selling it to. They may have very different priorities and goals to yours. They are more likely to be amenable if it fits in with their overall objectives.

iv. When asking for capital, think very carefully about the benefits that can actually be delivered rather than potential benefits. These only need to be large enough to pay back the capital in three to six months. The more money that is requested, the more certainty that is required about the benefits.

v. Do not just consider the customers, the suppliers of services and equipment can also cause the project implementation to go off the rails. Act quickly to correct problems with suppliers, as these can quickly get out of control.

142

vi. If problems do hit, inform all the relevant people as quickly as possible, preferably telling them what you are doing to sort them out and by when.

vii. Do not, under any circumstances, try to introduce an idea onto a plant that has not been properly tried and tested first in the controlled research environment. It is better to delay than for the idea to gain a bad name in which case its future implementation will take many times longer.

viii. Do not feel that all the implementation work has to be done by research personnel. It is much better that the final plant implementation is done as a partnership with suitably committed individuals from production. Their commitment will be greater if they have had a part in developing the idea.

ix. Do not necessarily expect instant success. The implementation process will require considerable after care and support from research personnel to ensure a continuing good result.

x. Finally, when success is achieved, remember to tell people about it in quantifiable terms. This increases credibility and makes it easier next time around to get support.

Trevor's project illustrates the benefit of developing good cross-functional business understanding in managers at an early stage, a prime aim of the FOB programme. In this case, in taking an initiative from the research to the operation setting, Trevor emphasizes the benefits of achieving customer understanding and support early in the process. Also, financial data relating to performance improvement must be sufficient, realistic and presented in a way that identifies relevant and believable benefits.

ICI PROJECT CASE STUDY

Project Title
Review of ABC Balance Requirements

Project Owner

Janet Wright, ICI Chemicals and Polymers

The background to this project concerns the optimization of the supply of a commonly used basic chemical, designated ABC for purposes of the

143

case study. Many of the plants in the site concerned produce or absorb ABC and historically it had proven difficult to balance the site ABC supply, to maximize the use of resources and minimize waste.

Janet's role was as trainee account manager within the Information Systems Group. The project provided her with the opportunity of acquiring a broader understanding of business requirements and interfaces between her major internal customers on the site. It resulted in tangible operational benefits in the form of improved communications, reduction in man hours and improvement in ABC costs.

In her report, Janet summarized the process she used in undertaking the project as follows:

- Identification of all members of the ABC Balance weekly process.
- Attendance at a number of the weekly Friday meetings.
- Discussions with each member concentrating on those involved in the weekly Friday meetings asking them to define exactly what they were involved in, what data they had access to and what data they felt they needed in order to make more informed decisions.
- Flow charting of the weekly process which gained agreement from all parties. These have now been included in the overall process flow charts of the ABC Business.
- Analysis of the data to identify those areas where improvements could be made.
- Discussions with key members to confirm conclusions/recommendations.
- Informal presentation of conclusions/recommendations to selected members of the Business Group.
- Customer acceptance of recommendations.
- Project accepted by IT Group to implement the recommendations.

Some of the findings in the report illustrate how a project can generate the opportunity to step back from the day-to-day operational pressures, under which production staff operate, highlighting how 'ownership' and time constraints can lead to deterioration in communication and decision-making processes, even where the basic operational review process is good. Janet's report continues:

144

It had always been recognized by the production staff that the ABC Balance was not being run as effectively as it possibly could be. Unfortunately, in the past, any investigation into the ABC Balance had been initiated by the production staff and there had been difficulties with 'all-user' ownership and getting access to customer knowledge.

After examining the process and looking at the data requirements and current data available, it became clear that although the actual process of the weekly balance was in fact good, the actual data utilization was poor thus making the process itself look inadequate.

A significant amount of purchase for resale happens each week and at present this is not included in the weekly process. By not including this data, any analysis of sales predictions versus actual or plant performance against planned targets is confusing and time consuming, as often the real variances are caused by the purchase for resale arrangements. Trying to identify ways of improving the forecasting is therefore difficult as the true facts are often hidden and can often be ignored due to time constraints at the weekly meeting.

In her review of key learning points, Janet succinctly describes how a project can highlight the unseen boundaries between business groups and functions and also refers to her use of techniques from the FOB programme (critical success factors (CSF) and SWOT analysis) in pursuance of her project. She continues:

There can be unrecognized boundaries between the business groups and the production areas. This can mean that vital data is not shared and improvement opportunities can be missed. Projects initiated by one function are not necessarily limited to that function and usually cross a number of functions within the business. It is important therefore to consider all functions when examining any aspect of a business.

Often due to the integration of products on a site, there can be a number of businesses interested in a specific project and these must be identified and consulted.

Improvements identified by one function within a business area may be seen as problems for another group. If there is only one business group involved then the improvements must be seen as contributions to the overall success of that business. When a number of business groups are involved then the benefits identified must be seen to contribute to the critical success factors of the company as a whole, even if this causes difficulties for the specific business areas.

In order to identify true weaknesses in an area it is important to use the SWOT analysis technique as not only does this help to identify those areas which are weak, it also identifies strengths which can be used as reassurances that all is not bad. By identifying threats to the business it also helps to target effort into areas which are under your control.

BENEFITS OBTAINED

In her post project review questionnaire, Janet identified the following learning benefits:

- Better understanding of wider business interests and the key driving forces.
- Realization that I can help poor communication processes between business functions by acting as a link between them.
- Utilization of certain techniques, e.g. SWOT analysis.

The sponsor of the project, the plant manager of the site concerned, commented as follows concerning the benefits obtained from the project.

The 'real' customers of the ABC Balance were identified and an overall consensus of a complicated ABC Business was obtained. Misguided historical views were ignored. Projects in the past have failed because they were too ambitious and claimed unrealistic benefits. This project narrowed the benefits down into realistic ones.

Previous ABC Balance projects had little success because of unrealistic benefits, no business support – and some people saw it as a 'hobby horse'. These difficulties had to be overcome when yet another person started yet another project.

146

CONCLUSION

Project activities are seen as providing twin-track benefits, both in terms of applying and reinforcing the learning for the individual and also in providing tangible benefits for the organization. The tangible benefits can indeed be significant. In the setting of the high cost technological environment within which ICI operates, it is not unusual for project initiatives to result in significant savings, measurable in tens or hundreds of thousands of pounds. The less tangible, individual benefits of projects are of course equally important. The increased understanding and confidence that individuals gain from project work will continue to provide benefit to the organization on many occasions throughout their employment with the company.

KEY POINT SUMMARY

- Projects are an excellent means of developing cross-functional business understanding at an early stage in a manager's career. This may be particularly important in an advanced, high-technology business where specialist roles and functional perspectives can all too easily dominate everyday activities.
- During time of great change, such as merger or demerger of large organizations, projects provide a route whereby managers can explore different, new working opportunities and test out their interest and abilities relative to a new context. This process can help both the individual and the organization adapt more readily to new requirements.
- A database of past projects, using readily available PC systems, can supply information to assist a new project initiative at its commencement, and also to support networking between project owners where a common interest exists. Such systems may also provide a means for capturing organizational learning.
- A manager undertaking a project will not recognize the personal development achieved through the project to the same extent as will the project sponsor. Developmental outcomes should be assessed from the perspective of third parties, such as the sponsor, line manager, peer group, as well as that of the project owner.

- In large, multi-site, departmentally organized businesses such as those found in manufacturing industries, projects provide an opportunity for the needs of the 'internal customer' to be examined from a neutral perspective. The project allows the project owner and the parties involved to step back from day-to-day operational requirements and departmental targets, as well as to determine a solution to a problem in line with the needs of the whole business.

APPENDIX 1: USING TECHNOLOGY TO ANALYSE OUTCOMES

Figure 7.2 illustrates an example of the keyword search facility being used to identify projects relating to catalyst themes and Figure 7.3 shows the related screen identifying the owner of the project which was highlighted during the search. A copy of each project report is available at Sundridge Park to participants in the programme, enabling them initially to examine the relevance of the earlier project to their own area of interest. Direct contact between the earlier and the current project owners can then follow if desired.

PROJECT OUTCOMES

The tangible outcomes and the learning arising from projects is followed up by requesting each participant to supply a copy of their project report on completion and also by asking the project owner and the project sponsor each to complete a questionnaire concerning the status and outcomes from the project.

The 'Questionnaire to Project Owner' includes items such as:

- Which business function were you working in when you undertook the project (finance, operations, etc.)?

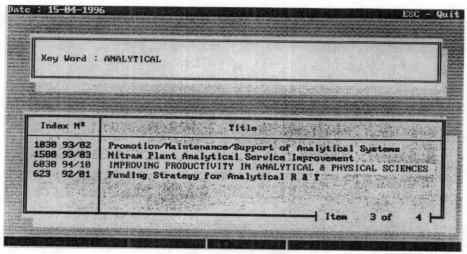

Figure 7.2 Keyword: Search
Source: Sundridge Park

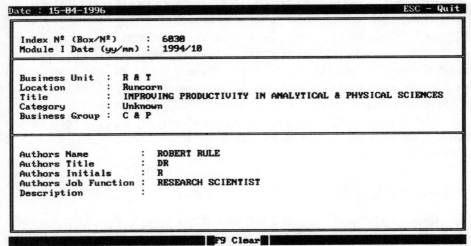

**Figure 7.3 Screen identifying owner of project
Source: Sundridge Park**

- Which other business functions did your project involve you in?
- How useful in your opinion, has the project been in:
    - developing yourself?
    - developing other people?
    - achieving business objectives?
    - hastening needed change?
- What examples are there of
    - learning benefits?
    - tangible benefits to the business, quantified where possible?

The 'Questionnaire to the Project Sponsor' is concerned with the benefits, difficulties and the process of using projects as a developmental means. It also includes an item:

- How useful, in your opinion, has the project been in:
    - developing him/her?
    - achieving business objectives?
    - hastening needed change?

The responses to this item can thus be compared with the responses to the similar item in the 'Questionnaire to Project Owner'. Scoring for this item in both questionnaires uses the following ratings:

150

- extremely useful
- very useful
- moderately useful
- of little use
- of no use

In general, project sponsors tend to rate the 'developing him/her' aspect at a higher level than the equivalent response from the project owner. Thus, as one might expect, the developmental benefit to the project owner is initially more apparent to the sponsor than it is to the individual undertaking the project.

Figures 7.4 to 7.10 illustrate the response to the 'project usefulness' questions, from both the project owner and the project sponsor perspectives.

Key to project usefulness charts (Figures 7.4–7.10)

N	No use	V	Very useful
L	Little use	E	Extremely useful
M	Moderately useful		

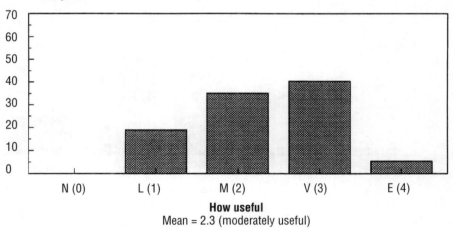

Figure 7.4 Developing self – project owner

% Response

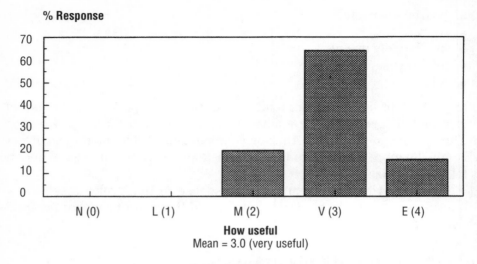

How useful
Mean = 3.0 (very useful)

Figure 7.5 Developing him/her – project sponsor

% Response

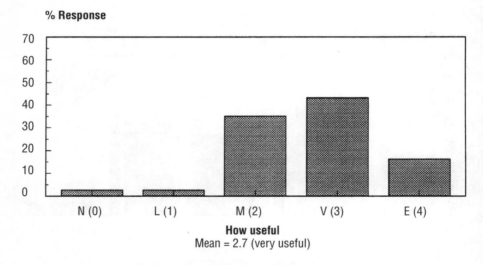

How useful
Mean = 2.7 (very useful)

Figure 7.6 Achieving business objectives – project owner

% Response

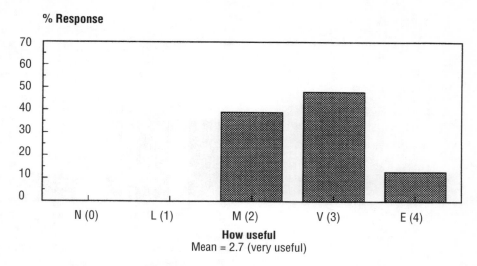

How useful
Mean = 2.7 (very useful)

Figure 7.7 Achieving business objectives – project sponsor

% Response

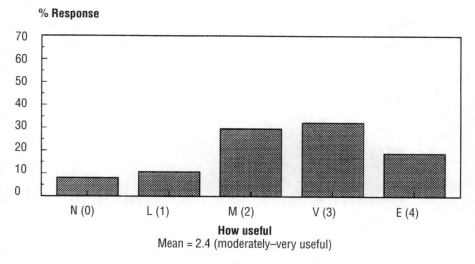

How useful
Mean = 2.4 (moderately–very useful)

Figure 7.8 Hastening business change – project owner

153

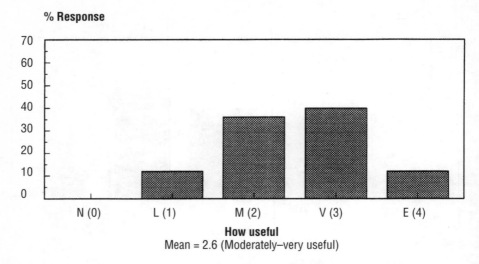

% Response

How useful
Mean = 2.6 (Moderately–very useful)

Figure 7.9 Hastening business change – project sponsor

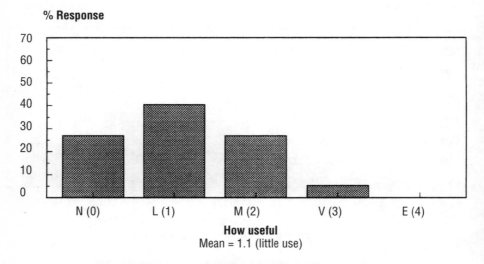

% Response

How useful
Mean = 1.1 (little use)

Figure 7.10 Developing other people – project owner

Apart from the difference concerning 'developing staff' and 'developing him/her', project owner and sponsor appear to be in broad agreement concerning the usefulness of the projects in 'achieving business objectives' and 'hastening needed change'.

As may be seen from the chart, project owners generally do not appear to value projects as useful for 'developing other people'. However, as there are no data available from the 'other people' perspective with which this might be compared, we have no means of examining the developmental impact of projects on 'others'.

The following summary provides sample responses from project owners about the learning benefits and what they would do differently if undertaking another project.

Similarly, the summary of sample responses from project sponsors/line managers describes the learning there was for them in the management of the process.

APPENDIX 2: EXTRACTS FROM QUESTIONNAIRE TO PROJECT OWNER

EXAMPLES OF LEARNING BENEFITS

- Exposure to senior business managers; tailoring presentation and reports to meet their needs and influence their thinking.
- Better understanding of wider business interests and the key driving forces.
- Understanding of how I relate to others in the team.
- Greater understanding of the needs of the end customer.
- Understanding of net present values, ROI (return on investment).
- Experience of viewing things with a global strategy.
- Best method of written presentation to achieve commitment from senior managers.
- Understanding how business teams work.
- Networking in the data collection stage of the project.
- I have learned a lot about organization culture.
- Insight into performance measurement in service organization.

If you were undertaking another project what (with the benefit of hindsight) would you do differently?

- Select one which required more business involvement.
- Aim at more business related project.
- Choose a project with direct cost benefit to the business.
- Keep the sponsor better informed of progress at the very early stages.
- I would spend more time before the course with the project sponsor.
- Link more strongly with other business functions and explain the project and benefit.
- Nothing. The course was very timely, and provided me with the 'tools' (e.g. marketing mix, SWOT analysis) which were extremely helpful.
- Carry out the project in a real business, not an internal service organization.
- Get ownership and definition up front.

EXTRACTS FROM QUESTIONNAIRE TO PROJECT SPONSOR/LINE MANAGER

What learning has there been for you in the management of the process?

- Set one's sights to develop and push the person to achieve higher goals.
- The value of defined, documented scope and formal review involving people other than the sponsor and project owner.
- Get a good sponsor who needs the project completed successfully to support his organizational objectives.
- Pre-preparation, support and all the follow-up has made it far more worthwhile than the 'one slot', away for a week detached course.
- Opinions are readily available; data is not so available.
- Delegate, but back up, coach, advise.
- The usefulness of separating out a specific issue from the business strategy and assigning it to a single person with a clear remit.
- A means of interacting with the project owner, contributing to his personal development.
- Another example of our people's ability to deal with complex projects and drive toward successful outcomes.

8 In-Company Programmes

VOLVO CAR UK*

The Younger Manager Programme at Sundridge Park has been the basis for the development of a wide range of in-company programmes with a project-based learning element. The first of these which, arguably, had a scene setting or model influence, was with Volvo Concessionaires, at the time (1989), the main profit contributor to the parent company Lex Service Plc. Since then the relationship with Lex has been severed, the Company now being Volvo Car UK. It was a top priority to strengthen management education, training and development, particularly at junior and middle levels of management, which ultimately led to the tailored in-company version of the Younger Manager Programme.[1]

The needs analysis process was rigorous, including the use of repertory grid interviews and a work profiling questionnaire (Saville and Holdsworth) to define core generic competencies. This analysis was further enhanced through findings from assessment centres (focusing on potential and career development) and feedback from the appraisal process. Subsequently, the company's employee development group (a group of senior line managers responsible for sponsoring employee development) concluded that there was a need for the development of a core competence base.

It was at this stage that the company sought a partner with whom to develop a core programme for a junior/middle management population of around 120 people.

A trial run of Sundridge's Younger Manager Programme was based on:

* This account is largely based on the article Project Based Management Development 'The Volvo Story' by J. Branch and B. Smith

159

- review of open programmes on offer in the UK
- apparent willingness to tailor to company needs
- track record and cost
- perceived culture of client service (untested!)
- anecdotal references from other clients and the attendance of two managers on the Open Programme (guinea pigs) with subsequent feedback.

The trial run led to the company exploring further the tailored programme option, and, in so doing, the company was keen to:

- obtain senior management's ownership
- encourage self-managed development, i.e. culture shift
- ensure maximum value in terms of transfer
- emphasize core managerial competencies.

At the initial contracting stage, the offer of a genuinely tailored service was valued by the company. Capability of the provider was seen as not just academic excellence but a willingness to take time to understand the client and deliver what was wanted.

The next stage was to hold a meeting to develop the tailoring process. This included the chairman of the employee development group (an operations manager) and the personnel manager.

Needs which were not included in the standard Younger Manager Programme were identified. In addition, there were certain topics like interviewing skills which were excluded, since managers had received such training on previous Volvo Concessionaires (VOCS) courses. In contrast, the priority given to self-awareness and self-development on the Open Programme needed strengthening. A more detailed tailoring process was set up at this meeting at which members of the Sundridge Park team arranged to contact directors and senior managers of the main business functions to explore needs in more depth. The programme was also checked against the VOCS competence model.

A significant, if surprising, outcome of this meeting was a top-level commitment to senior management involvement. The chairman of the employee development group proposed that directors and senior managers should attend a senior management appreciation event, prior to the launch of the management skills programme. This would give them sufficient understanding of the aims, content and training methods to reinforce the learning, and help managers to put it into effect on their return to work. Another aspect of this involvement would include identification of possible projects and a willingness to sponsor projects. It was further proposed that each programme should be introduced by a director in order to reinforce the company's commitment.

The outcomes of these subsequent meetings yielded needs which could have warranted a three- or four-week programme. The management discipline of making critical and effective choices was severely tested! The cost of this tailoring stage was of the order of £10,000. At the time it seemed heavy, but it turned out to be a mere 4 per cent of the total programme delivery.

LAUNCHING THE PROGRAMME

Once the tailoring process had been completed, the team moved on to programme design and then into launching the programme. Dates were scheduled so that directors and senior managers attended their one and a half day appreciation events, before their people attend the first week of the modular management skills programme, the first of which began in January 1990.

The senior management appreciation events were designed to provide a sample of a few essential sessions plus an outline of other sessions, with some choices available. They secured initial ownership by senior managers for the learning of managers who were to attend the management skills programme. This was consolidated by using the appreciation events for senior managers to propose project topics against agreed criteria, which meant that some directors and senior managers were identified early as project sponsors. This idea of an appreciation event for senior managers as project sponsors has been replicated with other companies.

Knowledge of the aims and content of the management skills programme enabled these directors and senior managers to agree with their own managers specific objectives for their programmes. These objectives were recorded in a Training Development Link booklet (a tailored version of that used on the Younger Manager Programme), and provided a form of learning record at and beyond the particular stages of the programme.

PROJECTS

The task of defining criteria for worthwhile benefits was approached with a sense of 'bigness', i.e. big learning outputs and big learning benefits, including bottom line benefits.

Group projects, being a significant element of the programme design, benefited from top-level commitment and involvement. Project sponsors and bosses took on mentor and coaching roles. Ultimately, they became assessors of project outputs and, thereby, of elements of their managers' performance and learning.

While projects were identified and offered to the programme, participants' choices were made based on a mix of criteria including:

- interest and perceived results
- functional mix of disciplines
- balance of team role preferences and styles
- logistics of project group meetings.

The process took place on the first module and occasionally included contact with sponsors to seek clarification, or possible modification, of project aims. This selection of projects and of team membership established real ownership for the projects.

The intermediate workshop provided an opportunity to share progress, to seek further help and to look towards the delivery of the project. Since the projects were status-acquiring opportunities, presentation skills became a main element of the workshop.

On the second module, the project presentations were attended by sponsors, bosses and personnel and management training specialists. On some programmes, as many as 20 guests attended – a clear indicator of top management commitment. Presentations are a team activity, as are the handling of questions from guests. The professionalism of the presentations is enhanced by the quality of the project reports produced; several recommendations have been actioned. One group was invited to repeat its presentation to the board of directors.

INGREDIENTS OF SUCCESS

A clear set of ingredients has contributed to the success of the Volvo–Sundridge Park partnership.

Ambassadorial selling

Where members of the client company can sell on behalf of the training organization, then it makes it an easy process. But of course, that selling will not happen unless high quality in design and delivery is evident.

Investment in diagnosis and tailoring

As in many training interventions, if you get the diagnosis and tailoring right then you are in a strong position to meet the client's needs fully. This substantive initial investment yielded results, particularly in gaining a true understanding of the needs of managers.

A strong client team

The concept of a dedicated core team, within which any one of three people could and did manage the programme, was critical to success.

Managers' desire to learn

This made managing and contributing to programmes a great pleasure. Managers had very clearly not been sent; they had been selected and wanted to be there. Also, it was very rewarding when six months later it was possible to perceive some growth and development in individuals.

Programme design

Inherent strength in the design of the original Younger Manager Programme was crucial. Its modular nature, the project element which yields organizational and personal benefits, as well as the training link booklets which ensure a planned approach by participant and manager, all combined to underline the importance of self-managed learning to the success of each person's training experience.

Top-level commitment

Senior management involvement in the programme throughout the company took the form of:

- The attendance of all directors and most senior managers on appreciation events or 'tasters'.
- The sponsoring and mentoring of projects by senior managers.
- Consistently high *attendance* levels at key points on each programme.

The tailoring process

The pairing of senior managers and directors with Sundridge Park staff, in tailoring the programme, contributed to quality.

The use of company-specific case studies designed by managers

Company-specific case studies raised the face validity of the programme and provided an illustration of how the learning can be transferred to 'real' problems. Examples included product launch issues, dealership finance problems and customer service cases.

PROVIDER'S RESPONSE

The partnership was undoubtedly fostered by the quick response of Sundridge Park to VOCS needs. Examples included:

- the success of the tailoring
- the speed of implementation of the programme
- the publication of a programme brochure for VOCS
- the design and delivery of senior manager appreciation events.

BENEFITS

The programme produced the following real benefits:

1. There were improved performance appraisal ratings among those who attended the programme, plus a greater willingness to begin to regard job mobility (lateral moves) as a development opportunity.
2. A number of projects were researched and recommendations accepted and/or implemented, producing *tangible* benefits. Examples included:

   - Better co-ordinated approach to head office secretarial utilization and development, resulting in savings of £20,000 per annum.

164

- Establishment of a set of criteria to improve the selection of potential Volvo dealers and hence minimize risk of failure.
- A proposal to pursue a new sponsorship opportunity – the collation of diverse competitor information to support salesand marketing (an external consultancy quoted £10,000 for the project).
- Reductions in overhead costs amounting to £25,000 per annum plus an ongoing investigation into further savings by a multi-discipline cost reduction team.
- A proposal (taken up by the employee development group) to foster a culture more supportive of innovation.

3. A post-project review suggested strongly that these tangible benefits derived directly from the success of the programme in meeting its objectives to:

    - increase the levels of knowledge and understanding of management principles in the context of VOCS competencies
    - increase participants' self-knowledge and understanding
    - enhance participants' skills in utilizing the learning which they have acquired.

4. A further step towards building a culture based upon self-awareness and individual ownership of personal development among managers, away from a compliant, prescriptive permission-seeking culture.

5. Development and practice in mentoring/sponsoring among the senior management team.

Incidentally, a review undertaken by one participant following attendance on the programme led to the redefinition of her role and VOCS' approach to managing cash. The finance director estimated that the potential savings to VOCS, when revised systems were fully operational, would be very considerable.

LEARNING POINTS

The following is a 'warts and all' list of learning points based on a cross-section of comments from the 'composite participant':

- The link to competencies, while clear in the initial programme tailoring, has been less obvious to participants. The opportunity to promote management competencies through training has therefore not been fully achieved.

- The comments on transferability have been consistently positive. Undoubtedly the project has been an influence here, but so too has the high-reality business simulation, case studies and the practical nature of much of the programme input.
- Time has been a problem. We still strive to achieve the right balance between providing substance in course content and allowing sufficient time for reflection. Generally, the pace may still be a little too demanding.

   In terms of content, marketing presented an early difficulty. One participant commented that he never expected to find the finance session more fun than marketing!
- The Sundridge Park facilities are consistently commented on positively, the only problem being too little time to enjoy them.
- The documentation linking the programme back into the workplace has been positively received in terms of stimulating good quality discussion with participants' managers and supporting learning transfer. However, continued utilization of this link document in the latter stages of the programme has fallen off.
- Frequency of programmes can result in project over saturation and diminish the profile of some excellent work. Spacing between each programme is important and, with the benefit of hindsight, the five programmes should have been spread over a longer period.
- Cost must be an issue for companies currently trying to squeeze maximum returns from diminished budgets. The partnership approach, using company HR managers or line managers to deliver some elements of the programme, might offer a way to trim consultant costs in future.
- What about my boss? While senior management involvement and understanding has been a feature, by no means all participants report to a senior manager. Less successful was the development of understanding and commitment among the broad middle management tier. This did, on occasions, lead to dissatisfaction among some participants with the leadership they experienced from their immediate bosses. Equally, some of this group of middle managers were frustrated that they lacked a detailed understanding of the programme and its aims, objectives and methods. Future programmes addressed this issue.

- While valuable as experiential learning opportunities, the projects have not always been demonstrably implemented, although they were often influential on organizational thinking. Sponsors have not always been clear about their roles in feeding back to project groups, who have thus been left unclear of the rationale for acceptance or rejection.

Follow-up initiatives were carried out with past programme participants including:

- The publication of a participants' 'user manual' as a practical tool to promote the use of models and techniques covered during the programme.
- On-site one day workshops, with participants offered the chance to apply learnt techniques to solve real problems in action learning sets.
- Circulation of a complete list of projects to all managers, available from a central library, to ensure the maximum utilization of the research and proposals throughout the company.
- Formal accreditation of the programme towards national management qualifications.

This accreditation was carried out using the Graduate Business School of the University of Strathclyde as the accreditation body.

All of the above are regarded as important in extracting the maximum effectiveness from the investment of time and money in this important management development initiative.

VOCS chief executive, Stephen Dixon, commented:

> Volvo Concessionaires has long recognized that its success is dependent, in large part, on its people. Hence training and development has been seen as a significant investment for many years. However, the management skills programme has, for the first time, provided a comprehensive, solid, practical foundation upon which our managers can now build their personal development programmes.

The initial vision of 120 managers attending the programme was scaled down to about 70 over a two-year period. This was due to the impact of the recession. But the programme was reviewed and repeated in 1994.

The following Volvo criteria were articulated emphasizing that projects should:

- be linked to a strategic opportunity for Volvo Car, i.e. strategic issue relevant to both the present and the future

- cross boundaries – functions, departments and units
- be personally stretching and a basis for growing the job along an important dimension
- be a possible route for future career development
- provide a potential return on investment, with a mixture of quantitative and qualitative measures
- be innovative with a balance of analysis and creativity, but breaking new ground
- be of an appropriate scale so as to provide scope for quality work, i.e. not so large as to result in lack of time for adequate exploration of issues involved.

In the interim, Sundridge Park was involved with two other training providers as part of a Consortium Alliance for Learning[2] in a development programme for the Senior Manager Group (those reporting in to the director group). This was a modular programme and, again, included four projects linking with Volvo Car's new Strategic Intent. Also, as with the Middle Manager Programmes, there was an appreciation event, this time for the director team, most of whom were sponsors for the strategic projects. A significant aspect of the Strategic Intent initiative was gearing up for the Renault/Volvo merger – the merger that never happened.

One thing is clear: use of projects and valuing the learning from them is an embedded part of the Volvo culture and philosophy.

GESTETNER

Another current in-company initiative using group projects, this time within Gestetner, is described next.

The Sundridge Park programme is modular and project linked. It is designed to be an integral part of the overall development programme called Athena, which is spread over six months. The participants are pan-European managers from a multinational company, with proven potential and from a mix of functional disciplines.

The structure of the programme enables participants to address effective self-management covering awareness of self, one-to-one and team relationships, using key management processes and principles. They are also asked to investigate their leadership abilities including the develop-

168

ment of themselves and others.

The skills transferred are demonstrated through delivery of practical, real-time projects and in the completion of a high reality simulation which consolidates and reinforces earlier learning.

Course objectives ensure that by the end of the programme, participants will:

- have a sound framework of best management practice against which to measure their earlier experiences or perceptions
- have acquired the knowledge and skills to face future challenges and opportunities with greater confidence
- be equipped with the relevant knowledge, skills and attitudes to plan their own career development within the total development programme of their own organization
- have completed a clearly defined project within Gestetner, using the skills and knowledge derived from the Sundridge Park programme
- have carried out a high reality business simulation which converts part learning into whole learning and demonstrates to participants the consequences of decisions made in one business function impacting on others.

The content of the first module, while providing stand-alone topics with learning objectives, also helps participants to carry out the group projects. Topics include: Team Leadership, Teamworking, Planning and Controlling, Creative Thinking in Problem Solving, Time Management, Self Awareness/Assessment, Networks of Relationships, Influence, Persuasion and Negotiation and Presentation Skills.

During this module, a process of team formation is achieved in respect of projects offered to the programme by sponsors. An early session explores Interests, Expertise, Commitment, Motivation as part of team formation, together with a team SWOT analysis leading to initial Project Planning. A later session builds towards an outline plan of Action and Planning for Project launch. This is shared through a presentation with the project sponsors, who offer constructive critical feedback. The scene is then set at the end of the module for re-entry to the work environment and to commence putting the project plan into action.

As with other modular programmes there is an intermediate project workshop to review progress and start planning for the presentations (which are carried out at the end of the six-month period).

Review of the project element of the programme through discussions with company HR staff, Roger Headey, Personnel Co-ordinator and Tony Milne, European Training Manager, highlighted the following:

Selection of Project Groups

The selection of project groups was done with little knowledge of the individuals and without consideration of personal profiles. In one group this resulted in all members being high shapers (Belbin[3,4]) and not yielding to a project leader. However, in the subsequent year, teams have selected themselves.

Sponsors

Allocation was on the basis of having a business interest in the project output, but the role and responsibilities of sponsors was not made particularly clear. There was a need identified to have clearer terms of reference and at the start of the project to review, reflect and rethink, before launching out on a particular route. It was recognized that it can cause difficulty if the sponsor is a level too high in the organization. The project output needs to be particularly important to the sponsor as well as the sponsor being close enough to have some impact on the project.

The sponsor will usually have an idea of the output and the direction/ avenues for the project group to pursue. But it is important that the sponsor does not give a definitive 'this is the right or wrong answer'. It is also important for group members to manage the relationship between the sponsor and other relevant people.

Project understanding

Project understanding can be a problem with seven to 10 multinational managers on a new project. A lack of clear focus at the start of the project with corresponding allocation of tasks, can result in a mediocre output where essential information has not been drawn in, resulting in a somewhat embarrassing presentation. Ultimately, it is essential for a project team to agree a common goal and strategy – what they want to achieve, and how.

Characteristics of good sponsors

The characteristics of good sponsors include having a sense of responsibility for the project, with direct involvement – keeping close to it but with hands off. A combination of showing a lead and questioning the thinking of group members has been typical, particularly in getting them to question their own assumptions.

Sponsors have also brought in others, where appropriate, to assess progress as part of their need to take ownership for the quality of the output.

Group involvement

With a wide geographical mix involving several different countries, it has been difficult to secure and maintain equal member participation. What has usually happened is that two or three people (out of a group of five or six) have driven the project and made it happen from Chiltern Street. In addition, resources and time, especially in a mini-group, have been easier to secure from head office.

Benefits

For members who have come from the subsidiaries, there have been clear benefits in improving career prospects through building a network of relationships. As Roger Headey said, 'the project is the strongest builder of networks'. Those located in head office can easily become recognized by head office staff who, because of proximity, are likely to know what is going on in projects. 'A big benefit is that we get to see those who can achieve and perform. Also, they are seen operating in a multicultural environment' commented Roger Headey. Tony Milne added, 'They have gained enormous value out of working together. The network of contacts established still thrives. It has been an important first experience of inter-disciplinary working and group working.'

An acknowledged benefit has been the genuine added value from understanding business better. Another, unexpected, benefit has been the challenging of preconceived views (current wisdom). This has been particularly evident in projects with a financial/insurance focus across Europe. This is one example of learning for sponsors derived from projects. A further benefit in working with others has been knowing/understanding more about people management. 'A benefit which augers well for the future is learning to get people to do things where they don't have the authority', said Roger. Clearly this is of importance in the matrix organization structure within the company.

FROM START TO RECOMMENDATIONS TO IMPLEMENTATION

Over the three years of the programme, the end points of projects have moved through recommendations (the early end point) to implementation. On earlier projects, there have been concerns about nothing happening following the recommendations stage.

Again in the early stages, the company's perception of the project was as a vehicle for delivering learning by delivering results (recommendations) whereas the Sundridge perception was biased more towards the learning. The move by the company more towards implementation is narrowing the gap, such that learning by doing and taking real action is becoming the new norm.

One learning point has been that if the group does the right things at the start, early progress can be motivational. This applied in the 'Paper' project where lots of contacts were made in visiting a paper mill at the start of the project. The paper industry then provided a continuous stream of advice, information and paper.

Another success was the 'Client Management' project where the objective was to define the exact information and format for client information to be held on a database. This was an example of a project which was tangible, where it was possible to see a result.

The duration of a project has typically been six to eight months, from initial conception through to presentation of outcomes. It is thought that this may appear to the participants too long and that efforts might be more concentrated if the timescale was shorter, i.e. people can easily put off work on the project. This has been the case where there has been a strong surge in the last few weeks, which may indicate a need for improved project management skills. However, it is seen by those in the company as reflecting the reality of working in a challenging business environment. But it is acknowledged how important it is to plan for time to be spent together by group members.

In monitoring progress in the early stages of a project, it is difficult to predict or identify signals indicating whether the project will be a success or not. Such indicators could be particularly important to the sponsor who needs to monitor aggressively, while not necessarily directing, the work.

In one project which was not considered successful, there was confusion among members as to what the objective was or should be, as well as no clear leadership. However, other projects have exhibited these same characteristics and still delivered. These represent possible indicators to be picked up at an early stage. Despite having a 'task' output which was not seen as successful, the members claimed the learning output of a network of colleagues where relationships were of openness, trust and friendship – not something to be undervalued.

GROUP MEMBER PERSPECTIVES

An opportunity was also taken to discuss project experiences with available group members.

For one project, 'Colour Copying Market in Europe' with the objective of doubling market share of colour copiers, a lack of clarity about the objective within the group and with the sponsor was the biggest issue/concern. This made motivation difficult. In addition, the objective was seen as unrealistic, and failure was acknowledged by not going outside the company for knowledge/experience – a self-imposed constraint as the choices were there.

Group working left a lot to be desired. As members commented,

> 'We were in the storming phase for three months and position jockeying was continual.' 'We had two panics along the way and only came together towards the end of the project.' 'We thought we'd been set up to see how we'd react!'
> 'In being a multi-discipline group consisting of five shapers/leaders we had a lot of arguing, compromising and being diplomatic; this probably led to a mediocre output. A learning point – need for planning and don't panic.'

The 'process' in the group was poor – there had to be a lot of bringing in. Not all members came on board until the last two months when the pressure of an approaching deadline became acute. Recommendations were not implemented since it was seen as part of a larger IT project.

The perceived benefits were teamworking and having to deliver to deadlines. The use of brainstorming was valued, but it was also recognized that it was difficult to stop people from evaluating too quickly.

A further project had as an objective deciding how to use *customer satisfaction survey* results. Essentially, the outputs from the customer satisfaction survey aimed at benchmarking performance against key competitors, requiring liaisons with European subsidiaries.

The 'area' of the project was a good choice since it was something different and new to nearly all the members, but the project itself was too easy. There was a need for something more tangible. The sponsor outlined the problem and kept the group on the path without being directive.

173

He was looking for creativity, but we did not identify much that was new or ground breaking. Instead, we provided more evidence for the sponsor's message – that customer satisfaction surveys are critical to the business. In carrying out the project some members concentrated on the research and others on the report, bringing together the two strands at the end for the presentation. Much of the work was done by only a few individuals.

The main learning points from this project were being more aware of customer perspectives and understanding 'what customer satisfaction is'.

With hindsight, we would try to be more creative and concentrate more on figures, to put a value on opportunities gained by using such surveys and business lost when they are not used.

A 'sales productivity' project focused on how to improve productivity within which the role of first-line sales supervisor was seen as crucial. Questions included were:

- What do sales supervisors see as the main performance measures?
- How do sales supervisors use these performance measures?

The end result of the project was perceived as an operating handbook for the first-line sales supervisors.

There were six members in the group. Their abilities, interest and workloads were different. There was a project leader who related closely to joint sponsors. The project leader purposely looked for sponsor direction so that the output would be useable.

It was perceived by the group members that the sponsors changed their minds about the end product and they had expertise to offer in refining tools, i.e. booklets. Early on, there was considerable misunderstanding of what the project was aiming to achieve.

The project was an ideas-based one, not a research-based project, so it was more important for members to be together. There were problems in managing at a distance and fitting people into roles.

Learning points here involved managing a diverse team and selling within the organization. For the leader it helped to build business confidence and to be recognized for other talents (first discipline is law). It also built relationships with sponsors which has been career advantageous.

CURRENT INITIATIVE

Based on a review of the project element of the programme, project management techniques have been introduced, including the preparation of project plans with main events or stages and control points.

The project plan has to be approved prior to the launch of the project. It is considered that the inclusion of more 'hard' skills will ultimately enhance the quality of project outputs.

LLOYDS BANK INSURANCE SERVICES (LBIS)

THE PROGRAMME APPROACH

In contrast to the two preceding cases the Lloyds Bank Insurance Services Division brings a different marketing perspective.

An innovative three-level project-based learning programme was completed by the marketing group in collaboration with Sundridge Park during 1994/95.[5] This was a key element in a development process spread over eighteen months.

The marketing group, comprising 60 people, covers product design, pricing and manufacture in co-ordinating risk bearing suppliers of components, full promotion and distribution via multiple channels, market research, customer service and product support by specialists in expert niches. Distribution itself comprises the bank branch infrastructure, a 'direct' operation (Lloyds Bank Insurance Direct), and third party alliances under a variety of brands. In essence, the Marketing Group drives the business.

The main concerns that started the initiative were:

- managing growth and change in a competitive marketplace
- a comparatively young team with little formal development
- strains on teamwork across multiple marketing disciplines
- a wish for better integration and understanding of 'functional' areas
- a determination to be even faster to market with new products.

The target audience was streamed into three levels consisting of three × three-day modules. These were all delivered over a period of a month. The streams were:

- Directors
- Middle managers
- Junior managers (in two sub-streams)

175

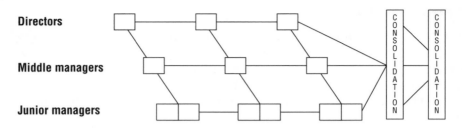

Figure 8.1 Sponsoring and mentoring model

In each case, the level above sponsored and mentored projects for the next level down. This did not merely follow normal lines of managerial reporting. It required cross-functional co-ordination. After the sets of modules for the individual streams, two consolidation events brought the entire team together for joint presentations and issues workshops. The model is shown in Figure 8.1.

Discussion with the Managing Director, Colin Sampson, the Marketing Director, Keith Gibbs and the other directors enabled the content to be scoped through an iterative process. Brief workshops for other groups brought issues and concerns to the surface and subjected ideas to a reality test. The participants needed to own the process and to have real input. They were enthusiastic for the idea of development and relieved that it would not be a mere 'sheep dip'. A consideration was to ensure direct learning transfer from modules into the work place.

Pre-design diagnosis and feedback indicated a strong results-driven approach, i.e. to get things done to tight timescales which had led people to concentrate on functional behaviours, with high 'task' orientation and with little regard for 'process'.

The commitment of all of the marketing directors in helping to make it happen was a criterion for success. They were involved in two main ways:

- They went through, and were seen to be going through, modules themselves – a clear signal that all have development needs.
- They were to be directly involved in specifying projects for group work. This included 'formal' review involvement in other modules as well as coaching and mentoring on the job. It ensured that other directors, Managing Director, Finance Director and HR Director were seen to be involved in and strongly supporting the initiative. This was both highly symbolic for most of participants and provided

176

real and practical involvement in several modules, especially those relating to projects. It made clear that tangible results were expected.

This approach led to a stronger emphasis on behavioural areas and less on the specific functional skills.

There were two types of projects. One, for middle managers, centering on a 'task' issue defined by Directors on their first module. The other, for junior managers, was more learning-orientated, centering on specific marketing disciplines. Each was to be undertaken by small (three to six) groups of participants at the same 'level' and sponsored/mentored by an individual from the next level up.

MIDDLE MANAGER PROJECTS

Between the first and second modules, groups would plan their approach, research the area, complete a problem analysis and scope some alternative courses of action. At the start of the second module they presented their findings to the directors and 'gained permission' to proceed.

The balance of the second module concentrated on project management skills, through a computer-based simulation. The simulation required application of 'tools and techniques' *and* a high level of people skills for both the planning and implementation process.

At the end of the third module, they presented their progress to date, with written report documents, to their directors. Again, requests for resources, budget or permission to take things further were debated in plenary. At the final consolidation event, all projects and results from implementation were presented to the entire group.

The projects carried out focused on several strategic issues:

- recommended product development process
- increasing customer loyalty
- customer information/database development
- opportunities in new routes to market
- repositioning market in the value chain.

They had the dual benefit of producing tangible 'task' as well as learning outcomes. They also required participants to stretch beyond their normal functional area in marketing to bring about a change, or contribute towards one.

177

Support from sponsors was given when asked for. The sponsors had been asked to operate in Hersey and Blanchard[6] S4 leadership style ('delegating') to encourage stretch by the groups themselves.

Crucially, the group members had to plan and operate their projects as an assignment above their normal workloads. They were not given 'protected time'. As a result they had to work smarter and not just harder. This created some initial difficulty as they juggled priorities, delegated more to their colleagues (which of course helped stretch them!) and struggled to create joint 'windows' in already crowded schedules. As the organization was already quite flat and lean, this was more than merely taking up slack.

As the projects progressed they became levers for changing the business. This became dramatically apparent at the second module when the directors received presentations and authorized implementation of the plans, with various changes and modifications in debate.

This was a vital stage and a turning point. Up to then, the middle managers were not fully convinced that the talk of support and 'improvement' was real. In their presentations they earned the right to proceed. Moreover, some of the directors had not been fully convinced either (as they admitted later). The projects formed a basis for changing perceptions. As a consequence 'middle' managers were starting to operate in a broader cross-functional dimension; a dimension in which their directors expected them to work but had seen little prior evidence. The projects provided the vehicle by which to prove greater capability and the capacity to work at a more strategic level. This was another example of the old law, 'power is never given, always taken'.

JUNIOR MANAGER PROJECTS

Junior managers were the largest group (30) and were split into two streams, cross-functionally. The nature of their managerial function was largely external; managing interfaces with, for example, the branch banking network. They were the first line of direct communication. They had a strong internal focus, spending most of their time at HQ with the danger of an HQ 'group think' mentality.

In order to seize the high ground in terms of specific marketing disciplines, they were set the challenge of becoming centres of excellence for a range of topics. This was to involve them in external work to identify and learn from best practice and theory in a variety of areas. Each area was championed by a more senior manager. The areas selected were:

178

- direct marketing
- advanced segmentation
- brands
- market research
- relationship marketing
- technology horizons.

As a resource to project groups, the book *Forensic Marketing*, by Gavin Barrett,[7] was offered. It contained chapters, by leading practitioners, on the range of topics involved. Calculating how to become 'the centre of excellence' in an area was part of the initial challenge.

In the second module, a series of 'masterclasses' were organized with experts, many of whom had contributed chapters to *Forensic Marketing*. Self-managed learning was encouraged in the topic areas.

A 'marketing fair' was held in the last consolidation module where each group ran a stall displaying the wares of the particular specialism. It was a noisy, joyous and creative affair. Members of all three levels circulated, questioned, debated and learnt.

PROJECT OUTCOMES

These learning projects formed close networks across previously disparate marketing functions, broadened the expertise base and created an externally-orientated knowledge-seeking orientation. Unlike their senior managers' projects, the results are not quantifiable in the short run. However, they have broken down some internal barriers. Communication between functions is seen to be better and more co-operative. These learning groups are still in place and continue to search for best practice among a number of external companies. It is not exactly benchmarking in the technical sense, but it is moving towards that on an 'informal' basis. Both types of projects have contributed to the marketing operation working smarter.

'The Recommended Product Development Process' is described in more detail to illustrate what was entailed in project activity. The aim of this particular project was: 'To review the whole product development process in LBIS and make recommendations for achieving significant performance improvements, with particular reference to time to market, competitiveness, profitability and risk.'

It was undertaken by three managers from differing areas. A Senior Product Manager, Diane Barksfield, teamed with David Fiske, Customer

Services Manager and Ken Isherwood, manager within a specialist LBIS Insurance Unit. The three chose this project for different reasons. For Diane it was an area of strong personal interest, directly related to her existing role; for David it provided the opportunities to operate in a different area to gain broader perspectives; for Ken it was to broaden his network of contacts by being involved in a project that ran through most functional areas.

The project sponsor was George Baty, Director of Customer and Technical Service. He considered his role to be a supportive and interested one, but held at a distance to ensure the managers involved created their own space and learning stretch. This has proved a fairly typical approach of sponsors, giving the initiative clearly to the project group.

The group commented that he liked to be kept informed, was always available if need be, asked very helpful 'what if?' questions and unblocked the occasional barrier when asked for help.

At their first planning meeting, they made use of data on their thinking style and team role preferences, concluding that they should work well together as most bases were covered. As they were situated in different geographical locations, logistic considerations were significant. The milestone was to have a recommendation to present for approval at the second module.

The initial goals were to find out what the current process was, publish a discussion paper, research how other businesses approached the area and take soundings of views and perceptions of room for improvement.

Regular fortnightly review meetings were scheduled where progress on action points was discussed, project work was parcelled out and further actions were agreed.

At first, the issue was 'where are we now?'. Interviews with interested parties at a variety of levels were conducted. These revealed that although there was a discernible process, it was not being used in a consistent manner. Often, people and areas were being involved too late and a rework cycle caused further delay. An early conclusion reached by the team was to adopt a clean sheet approach.

From this conclusion, they sought external help and contacted BA, M&S and other insurance related businesses, both up and down stream, to provide more food for thought. Next, an outline process model was put together and refined into an initial paper. This was followed through with interested parties and amended to take account of fresh inputs.

By the second module, a well-produced business case document was presented. Permission to proceed and move to a trial phase was duly given.

The project planning and implementation tools and methods incorporated into the second module were applied to the project and found to be helpful. Moreover, the group organized a series of internal presentations and discussions to achieve buy-in at a wider level. The response was supportive, though the group had difficulty in one area. This was the search for ideal 'benchmark' timings for each part of the process (a fast track had already been incorporated).

The group wrestled with this issue for some time before accepting the need for appropriate flexibility within the process to take account of product differences. All the while, the project was broadening their personal access to other stakeholders who were buying in, a valuable learning output.

The first test on a real product was 'Hospital Cash Plan' when it was used as the basis for post case review. The group's next 'formal presentation' at Sundridge Park led to a press ahead mandate for the board. Further internal test work resulted which culminated in a 'spoof' launch of a 'Try to Stop Balding' insurance product. The humour helped to win hearts and minds.

As an output of the project, LBIS have a simple, easy to use process. It is written up with a colour-coded methodology and check lists. It has been approved by the internal auditors as standard quality process and been evaluated for broader application. The team feel good about it – and about themselves.

There are clear business benefits in better cross-departmental communications, higher levels of planning, ownership and involvement. LBIS have a clear structure and point of re-entry if things start to go wrong. It is no longer back to square one!

From the point of view of learning benefits, the team cited greater understanding of the business as a whole; more empathy with other areas, thus creating the conditions for enhanced communications; more confidence in tackling fresh issues and overcoming obstacles; greater self-confidence in managing upwards; enhanced planning, analysis and project management ability. Each individual's original objective in choosing this project has been largely achieved.

From a 'provider' viewpoint, this has strongly reinforced belief in the use of short modular programmes with learning links. Senior level sponsorship is essential for success. John Mills comments:

With hindsight we might have worked harder on that area and facilitated group reviews with the sponsors present. Our reviews were with the working groups themselves. While we were delighted with the visible progress towards greater integration, we now believe that even better results might have been achieved had we provided for a total group event in the beginning and middle of the process rather than just at the end. Though the logistics would, as ever, have been tricky, we believe greater process clarity could have been achieved.

GROUP PROJECTS

Each of the preceding case histories reflect experiences of groups carrying out projects. We should now consider how to ensure the optimum effectiveness of a group project.

A project group needs to become an effective team quickly. Building in a delay to the real project work by starting with some teambuilding activity is, in today's business climate, unlikely to be a cost-effective option. The group must be engaged in project work while integrating any teambuilding activities. After all, different groups are likely to have different teambuilding needs, dependent particularly on the relationships among group members.

Ultimate success can depend on the initial ownership of success criteria. Some success criteria are suggested below:

- All members will have a common understanding of the project objectives and scope. (There may be several iterations in meeting this criteria, such as removing any uncertainty.)
- The process of 'co-ordination' is carried out effectively, preferably by an agreed/nominated co-ordinator or leader.
- The co-ordination role will include:
  - seeking ideas
  - encouraging/building on ideas
  - encouraging testing of ideas and proposals
  - bringing members into the discussion
  - recapping and summarizing progress.
- During meetings members will:
  - say when they agree, rather than remain silent
  - explain why when they disagree
  - not interrupt others when they are speaking

- explain fully when identifying a difficulty or problem and seek ideas from others for overcoming it
- be sensitive to the balance of contributions from members within the group
- seek to use consensus processes in preference to voting when arriving at decisions.
- Stakeholders are clearly identified, together with their needs and potential contribution to the project.
- Members are prepared to flex personal resources to meet peaks in the project, e.g. collation and analysis of data; preparing for a group presentation.
- Members are prepared to counsel others who may not be pulling their weight.

IN-COMPANY PROJECTS – CONCLUSIONS

There is a growing body of successful experience in project-based learning. Providers are increasingly articulating what makes for success.

The Prospect Centre, with a reputation for integrating individual, team and organization development through business-based projects, describe a successful development project as a piece of work that:

- satisfies the client and other stakeholders
- achieves its aims and purposes by delivering results which change the organization in some way
- is completed in time, within budgets and to meet given success criteria
- gains others' trust and respect for the project team and the project owner.

Reasons for unsuccessful projects are:

- fighting over objectives
- no commitment to providing necessary resources
- team members lack skills
- supporters lack skills
- development needs are not recognized/addressed
- 'implementation' not part of the project brief
- 'unknowns' not anticipated or handled

- plans unrealistically ambitious
- plans not systematically laid
- no clear 'client'.

Furthermore, success in a project requires:

- timing
- gaining and sustaining commitment and support of key people/departments
- building 'implementation' into the brief
- resources
- project control by anticipation
- a systematic approach
- realistic timescales.

Ashridge has described characteristics of successful projects[8] as:

- multi-faceted problem
- real business issue owned by a senior executive
- team rather than individual project
- requires facilitation skills not just expertise
- ongoing support – in-company and external effective briefing and involvement of senior executives
- adequate time and resources
- emphasis on implementation
- management development providers prepared to pursue organizational learning benefits.

In addition, based on recent experiences, general learning points for group project participants (which might also be described as criteria or conditions for success) are:

- teamworking, especially among different cultures
- need to trust each individual; teamwork and individual responsibility
- the difficulties and benefits involved in challenging objectives and assumptions
- need to be open to learning anywhere, any time
- application of newly acquired tools and skills
- how to balance conflicting priorities
- need to spend adequate time on planning and agreeing expectations

- ensure regular contact with sponsors
- use modern methods of communication (e.g. video conferencing)
- get organized, have a team structure
- develop a network of helpers
- play to people's strengths and diversity of experience
- how to influence senior executives.

Projects are a growing element within the management development plans of an increasing number of forward looking organizations. Projects are now standard fare among the offering of the main external providers of management development programmes including, notably, Sundridge Park and Ashridge.

KEY POINT SUMMARY

- Before launching a modular project-linked programme, appreciation events for top management can be of great value in obtaining corporate ownership and commitment.
- Ownership for group projects proposed by sponsors can be obtained by participants applying their own criteria to project group formation, e.g. interest and perceived results, functional mix of disciplines, balance of team role preferences, logistics of project group meetings.
- Ingredients for success in a modular project-linked programme include ambassadorial selling; investment in diagnosis and tailoring; a strong core team for programme delivery; participants' thirst for learning; quality of programme design; top-level commitment; a strong customer responsiveness by provider.
- The frequency of project-based programmes must be considered carefully. Too many over a short period can result in project oversaturation.
- Programme participants' bosses must understand and support the programme and the learning for participants.
- Sponsors need to be clear about the scope, requirements and expectations of their roles.
- While an external management training provider can usefully offer criteria for project choice, there is greater ownership where the company develops its own criteria for choice.

- Valuing learning from projects can become an embedded part of a company's culture and philosophy.
- Sponsors can have a valuable input to the project process by ensuring project groups present their plan of action prior to the project launch.
- Sponsors need to be close enough to the project to have some impact on outcomes, i.e. not be separated from participants by a number of management levels.
- The sponsor must not give a definitive 'this is the right or wrong' answer.
- Project group members need to manage the relationship between the sponsor and other stakeholders.
- At the start of the project, the allocation of tasks to group members must be made clear.
- Sponsors can add value by questioning project participants' thinking and getting them to question their own assumptions.
- Sponsors can usefully bring in other stakeholders to assess progress on the project.
- The project can be a strong builder of networks of relationships.
- For the people development specialist, the project provides viability of individual achievement and performance.
- Networks established through projects can continue to thrive.
- Projects provide a valuable opportunity for participants to gain a greater understanding of business.
- A valuable benefit for participants without authority, especially high-fliers in a matrix organization structure, is learning how to influence people to do things.
- On a modular project-linked programme, the time period between modules must be appropriate. If too long a period, there is a danger that too much is left to the last minute and efforts are not sufficiently concentrated.
- Absolute clarity and common understanding of the project objective between participants and the sponsor is essential.
- Project participants need to avoid self-imposed constraints, e.g. failing to draw on knowledge/experience outside of the company.
- A project provides an opportunity for participants to develop relationships with sponsors, which may be advantageous to their careers.
- 'Hard' project management skills and techniques must be included during the initial planning phase, for example preparation of project plans with key events, stages and control points.

- Choice of sponsors for projects is an important decision. It can cause difficulty if the sponsor is at an organizational level too separated from the project team. Conversely, such a relationship can be effectively managed by the project team.
- Building networks of relationships, a frequent project output, can improve an individual's career prospects.
- Projects provide an important shop window for senior managers in being able to observe those who can achieve and perform.
- A learning benefit for sponsors can be the challenge made to preconceived views or current wisdom.
- An end point of recommendations, while having learning value, is modest in relation to the total learning potential which can be achieved by taking actions on those recommendations.
- Indicators of possible or likely project failure would be valuable, particularly for sponsors, who may be able to intervene helpfully.
- For group projects on modular-linked programmes, permission to proceed from sponsors, can be useful in ensuring that projects remain on track.
- While greater understanding of 'the business as a whole' is often a learning benefit, more empathy with other functions/departments can lead to improved communications.
- Group projects, when breaking new ground, can give individuals greater confidence in tackling new issues/challenges and overcoming obstacles.
- In relating well to project sponsors, individuals can increase their confidence in managing upwards.
- Progress reviews with project sponsors could be given a higher priority; such reviews are common practice with project group members.

REFERENCES

1. Branch, J. and Smith, B. (1992), 'Project Based Management Development "The Volvo Story"', *Journal of European Industrial Training*, **16**, (1), pp. 3–9.
2. Branch, J., Smith, B., Cannon, J. and Bedingham, K. (1995), 'Building a Consortium Alliance for Learning – The Volvo Experience', *Journal of European Industrial Training*, **19** (1), pp. 18–23.
3. Belbin, R.M. (1993), *Team Roles at Work*, Oxford: Butterworth-Heinemann.
4. Belbin, R.M. (1984), *Management Teams: Why They Succeed or Fail*, Oxford: Butterworth-Heinemann.

5. Mills, J., Gibbs, K. and Todd, M. (1996), 'Insuring Success Through Marketing Projects', *Industrial and Commercial Training,* **28** (3), pp. 26–31.
6. Hersey, P. and Blanchard, K.H. (1977), *Utilising Human Resources, Management of Organisation Behaviour,* 3rd edn, Englewood Cliffs, NJ: Prentice-Hall.
7. Barrett, G. (1995), *Forensic Marketing,* Maidenhead: McGraw-Hill.
8. Beddowes, P., Kirkbridge, P., Mitchell, A. and Turnbull, P. (1994), 'The Power of Projects', *Directions – The Ashbridge Journal,* July.

9 Public Sector Projects

As in the previous chapter, this chapter contains contrasting case studies – from the Inland Revenue, London Underground and the States of Guernsey Civil Service.

INLAND REVENUE

Over the past few years, public sector organizations have been subject to considerable challenge and change as a consequence of government initiatives. Value for money services to the public are being established through initiatives like Next Steps, the Citizen's Charter and competition for quality. This is requiring significant culture change for many government departments.

The Inland Revenue is just one department which is developing a more open way of operating that is being felt right through the organization and is facilitating the birth of a new culture.[1]

The Inland Revenue's response to the challenge has included setting up a change programme. This involved considerable changes in structure, systems and also delayering. In responding to the Next Steps requirements (in 1991), the Inland Revenue drew up a plan which included the development of 250 senior staff (just below director level) to provide them with the appropriate skills to spearhead the required culture change.

THE PROGRAMMES

Supporting this change initiative are two management development programmes. The first is Achieving Management Potential (AMP), a programme targeted at the most senior managers just below director level. These people, typically, will be Controllers of Executive Offices or Deputy

Controllers. This is a programme nationally run and supported by International Training Services (ITS). There are 15 to 18 participants on each programme divided into three groups of five or six.

The second is the lower level Senior Management Programme (SMP). These programmes are run on very similar lines to AMP and are also supported by ITS, but are targeted at senior management in front-line offices. A typical participant will be a Tax District Inspector in charge of a local office with, perhaps, 100–200 staff whom the Revenue consider it essential to develop. The SMP is run by individual Regional Executive Offices rather than on a national basis, usually for 30 participants in five groups of six people.

The main elements of the SMP are:

- self-managed learning
- action learning groups, tackling real work projects.

The North West Senior Management Programme is typical of such programmes, although it does possess unique features, such as giving each group a budget to encourage innovation and an outward looking approach, plus a menu of Regional Executive Office projects to provide focus and business pay back from project work.

On the North West SMP, the action learning groups were renamed Challenge and Support Groups (CSG) in that the description reflected more accurately how the groups would operate over the period of the development programme. The programme is modular as shown in Figure 9.1.

OUTCOMES

Outcomes from the Senior Management Programme run by Inland Revenue North West Executive Offices, which is typical of the others, are as follows:

- Individual styles of operating and the roles of senior managers have been reviewed and developed.
- Issues relating to the Inland Revenue North West/Greater Manchester have been identified, progressed, completed and implemented within the timescales agreed with sponsoring senior managers.
- A greater corporate approach including a managerial network has been developed.

190

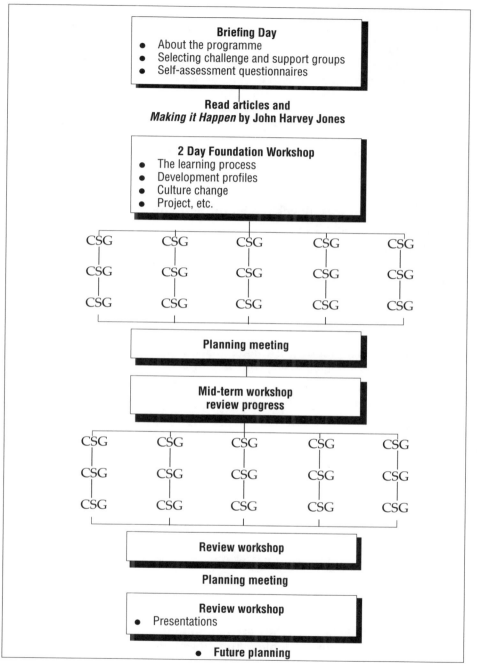

Figure 9.1 North West Senior Management Programme

191

- The benefits of effective teamworking and working collaboratively have been identified and experienced.
- Participants have developed a wider understanding and applied good practice in management and organizational development.

MEANS OF ACHIEVING OUTCOMES

The means by which the outcomes are to be achieved are set out below:

- Utilizing a range of learning opportunities, e.g. reading, projects, teamwork and Training Office events.
- Informing individual development through the use of personal profiles and other activities.
- Providing a structure to enable senior managers to pursue organizational priorities and personal development.
- Developing greater self-awareness, including the way personal style affects the way a job is carried out.
- Managing a designated budget to support activities and learning opportunities identified by the CSGs.

Much of the development work takes place in the CSGs, in particular an early focus on self-analysis/awareness and strengths/weaknesses to set the scene for challenging and supporting each other on real work issues. The CSGs identify work-related projects, using as a guide the Four Cs (four main drives for change) from the department's 'Organization and Structure' review published in late 1991. These are as follows:

1. *Customer service.* The department recognized that significant improvements were required to position the Inland Revenue as a standard-setter in meeting customer expectations for comparison with the public sector and elsewhere.
2. *Compliance.* This reminds the department of the continuing need to find better ways of helping and getting the public to comply with tax laws, thereby building public confidence in the way the tax system is administered.
3. *Cost efficiency.* Continuing to do the job with fewer resources.
4. *Caring for staff.* This underpins points 1–3, for the department believes that if staff feel they are committed, skilled and appreciated, they are more likely to achieve the other three.

192

THE PROJECTS

The following are examples of projects undertaken on the early programmes.

One AMP project, for instance, tackled all of the Four Cs. It involved making one of the Tax Advice Centres a pilot one-stop shop where customers can have all of their tax problems resolved without being referred to staff in other offices. This project impacted a large area of department activity, from raising the need to broaden staff knowledge at the relevant tax centre, to making much more customer detail available on the on-site computer. The project has worked so well that other tax centres are following its lead.

Another AMP group looked at how the department would need to change its approach to taxpayers when self-assessment for the self-employed is introduced. They studied tax systems operated in other countries with self-assessment regimes as the basis for their work and came up with some surprising recommendations for the board's consideration.

Group member Alan Harley, deputy controller London, explained:

'During the project, we underwent a gigantic shift in our thinking. Our colleagues will probably say we have gone crazy, but we believe that by the year 2000, if the public are not accurately completing their returns, then we should share the blame for not helping them get it right.

Instead of taking a solely adversarial stance with the public and challenging their returns, the group members believe department staff will have to put more effort into helping taxpayers understand their obligations and, hence, enable them to get their computations right.'

For Alan, the project gave him a huge sense of freedom. 'It gave us the opportunity to try something new without being told what to do', he explained. He also feels that the team aspect of the work was very important, 'I hadn't worked in a team in quite that way before. As a team that is working well,' he added, 'you are much stronger than a group of individuals and are able to get things done'.

Like a number of other AMP participants, Alan was so enthused by his AMP experiences that he introduced an adaptation of the programme to 30 of his senior staff. 'I felt I got such benefit out of the programme that I had to hand it on to someone else', he said.

Looking at internal relationships, another group addressed the apparent gulf separating the technicians in head office who provide advice on the application of tax law, from the staff in the networks who have to put it into practice. 'We wanted to see if we really were working on the same

193

side and what could be done about it', recalled John Hudson, District Inspector.

The group investigated the needs and expectations of both parties and made recommendations on how to bring the two closer together. 'They held diametrically opposed views,' John recalled, 'with neither seeing the other as a customer.' Based on 'plain common sense', the group's recommendation involved such things as making the manuals the technicians prepare more user friendly and were well received at board level.

More recently (March 1995), one of the authors was invited to join a Senior Management Programme Final Review Workshop as a member of an evaluation team, where the purpose is to confirm what has been achieved and, through peer review, to plan future development action. It also involves making a presentation to the project sponsor and other groups on the programme.

To indicate the range, depth and quality of projects carried out, we have summarized perceptions of the following three projects.

- Improving customer service and compliance
- Merger: for better or worse
- Teamworking

IMPROVING CUSTOMER SERVICE AND COMPLIANCE

The project team carried out a wide ranging review of changes taking place in the department in order to identify how resources may be released and how they might be used to improve customer service and compliance.

A number of initiatives were proposed for compliance: accounts investigations; employee compliance areas; and combining taxes and collection expertise. Such initiatives included reallocating resources, streamlining systems and processes to make better use of people's strengths and of technology, as well as developing specialist expertise where appropriate.

To improve customer service, a range of practical ideas was proposed, particularly in the development or establishment of roles which were seen to be vital to strategic changes, either planned or in process.

All these initiatives lock into the department's top priorities of improving service and performance, while simultaneously bringing in the change programme and reducing costs.

194

Learning outcomes

While the success of the project will be measured, to some extent, by the acceptance of the various proposals, team members reported several successful learning outcomes. These included the following:

- Better understanding of how the department works, how roles fit together.
- The importance in learning from both successes and failures.
- The complexities involved in managing change (particularly from benchmarking activities).
- Learning is continuous and takes place throughout a project, not just at the end.
- It is important to play to the strengths of individuals within the team.
- Leadership and facilitation can happen naturally within a group and does not necessarily need to be formalized.

MERGER: FOR BETTER OR WORSE

Mergers are commonplace, but perhaps preparation for mergers is less common. Less common still are preparations which explore the outcomes of previously merged organizations. One project team was set up to explore the challenges and opportunities facing the management of a new combined Regional Executive Office, formed from the existing Greater Manchester and North West Executive Offices. The purpose was how to make it work by drawing on experience elsewhere.

Mergers are, of course, the single most important major change which can impact on any organization, and diminishing numbers of organizations are able to claim that they have never experienced such a change.

Mergers between organizations can be the most dramatic and, for many, traumatic experiences, particularly in seeking, and often in not succeeding, to merge different cultures. But even within organizations, merging of divisions, departments, functions and experiences can often mirror those of mergers at a more macro level.

Based on agreement with the sponsor, the team adopted a pragmatic approach, paying particular attention to three specific areas:

- The likely impact on morale
- Opportunities arising from economies of scale
- Communication between the executive office and network offices.

195

The morale and opportunities issues were tackled by drawing on the experiences of other organizations – two consultancies, where finance was a mainstream activity, one Health Authority and a Revenue Regional Executive Office. For communication issues, opinions/views on best practice/pitfalls to avoid was gathered internally.

The information gleaned from the first line of inquiry (morale/opportunities) could go a long way to providing a checklist of good practice for organizations about to become involved in a merger – an example for the project group of learning which may have widespread general application.

Merged organizations – communications checklist

The team's suggested communications checklist is set out below.

- The merger should be used as an opportunity to give a clear lead and new sense of direction to the front-line staff.
- Staff should be appointed to senior positions on the basis of their suitability for the post, irrespective of their present geographical location.
- Only one culture should be allowed to prevail from the first day of the newly merged organization. This culture should incorporate the best practices from the pre-merger organizations.
- The period of uncertainty between the announcement of the merger and the appointment of key staff should be as short as possible.
- Deadlines should be used as a tool to drive forward the merger process and bring home to staff that the changes are real and cannot be ignored.
  Staff should be told the whole story, good and bad, as soon as the main decisions have been taken. This would include:
  - any decision to cut or redeploy staff
  - the location of the merged operation's head office
  - the identity of the new leader.
- A review group should be set up, 18–20 months after the event, to assess progress against the original goals for the merger and to recommend any changes needed to reinvigorate the process.

The communication surveys served to provide an impetus to improved communication (written and oral). If the merger was to be successful, the importance of effective communication at all levels, both pre- and post-merger, was underlined.

196

For any project to be successful, outputs must be sufficiently substantive so as to be valued by the relevant people, not least the sponsor. While outputs from this project may seem less glamorous than others, the provision of merger checklists and templates for effective communication should prove to be of ultimate value to others in the Revenue experiencing such change processes.

As with other groups, it was clear that the opportunity for teamworking in carrying out the project was highly valued.

TEAMWORKING

Some projects can centre on core processes for doing work. To function as a project team while investigating the subject of teamworking is a novel form of integrated learning.

TERMS OF REFERENCE

The project team clearly set out its terms of reference as follows.
To explore the implications and applications of teamworking by:

- establishing a comprehensive definition of teamworking
- evaluating the feasibility and value of the teamworking concept and within this evaluation:
  - identifying best working practices
  - outlining any difficulties/drawbacks
- considering the application of the teamworking concept within the Inland Revenue business and:
  - identifying best areas for practical application
  - testing the applications in sample areas
  - making recommendations for Teamworking in the Inland Revenue North West (IRNW).

These were set against a backcloth of considerable change which the Revenue is experiencing through delayering and rightsizing, with attendant changes in systems, structures and working methods. Defining and scoping the parameters for the project clearly identified the value of carrying out benchmarking, from which activity considerable learning benefits were gained.

The frequently cited dilemma or paradox in teamworking soon arose, namely that before teamworking can be properly introduced, culture change training is required. But can a teamworking intervention be used to spearhead such a culture change? Catch-22? Maybe. However, a sufficient critical mass of teamworking, through teamworking projects, can help to change the culture. In establishing project groups to bring about learning and change, the Revenue may be creating groups which will be ambassadors of cultural change.

While functioning as a temporary team on a teamworking project, the team members now describe themselves as having confidence in each other, together with mutual respect and trust. They listen more, talk less and, in so doing, communicate more effectively – a useful profile for an ambassadorial team!

RECOMMENDATIONS

In true ambassadorial style, the team made the following recommendations:

- There should be a project set up to introduce teamworking as part of the Revenue's programme of continuous improvement.
- The Senior Management Team should demonstrate future support for the teamworking concept – providing scope for role modelling, maybe!
- A programme should be introduced to develop managers into facilitators/team leaders, but with a prior selection process to ensure suitability for such development.
- Personnel should carry out a 'resources investigation' role to ascertain best practice and value which could be brought to teamworking, through the use of psychometric and other related diagnostic instruments.
- Successful teams should be recognized and appropriately rewarded, by exploring ways of rewarding via performance management and a special bonus scheme. There should also be flexibility for rewarding team performance locally.
- A task team should establish industry best practice in motivation and non-monetary rewards with a view to introducing similar systems.

ACTIONS

In order to convert some of these recommendations into actions, some first steps as part of 'the way forward' have been taken in embarking upon a number of teamworking ventures. Four examples are:

198

- One group of local tax offices in the North West has experimented with different types of group structures and different functions allocated to individuals. One of these three groups, called 'alternative groups', operates on traditional lines, and acts as a control group for subsequent comparative valuation. The changes within the other two alternative groups include bi-monthly rotation of key tasks, with group leaders focusing on the team leader/facilitator role without dealing with submissions. (In the traditional group the group leader deals with submissions.)
- Another experiment is proposed, with a fourth alternative group adopting a 'team' approach where empowerment will be a key feature in that the team leader/facilitator will be selected by the team and will take on the sole role of coach/developer. Role rotation of members (12) will be on a two-week cycle or longer, and the team will have the power to override structure as appropriate. There will be a main team goal of answering all public correspondence within three days.
- A Blackpool Tax District has been moving towards an empowerment/teamworking culture recently. The project initiative is now being expanded to launching workshops (including all managers and staff) to develop an empowerment/teamworking culture. Issues covering organization and structure will be open for consideration and possible change – clearly scope for developing a new model in ways of working.
- In Liverpool for the New Office Structure (NOS) initiative, a series of team-building activities are in process in rationalizing eight tax and two collection offices into one taxpayer service office and two taxpayer district offices. These activities are based on initial discussion about the direction, purpose and values under which the new offices will operate and will include culture change, empowerment and teamworking.

In the lead-up to NOS, several task teams were formed with staff from different levels and functions. The basic elements of a team were present in all task teams, with all projects completed successfully. This experience has helped to establish the principle of using short-term task teams in taking on and managing change – a start towards a teamworking culture.

As a consequence of the project team's recommendations for teamworking in IRNW, the Controller North West, who acted as their sponsor,

199

commissioned the team to produce a Teamwork Best Practice guide for use by all offices in IRNW which has recently been issued. As the IRNW Executive Office rolled out their teamwork programme, the teamwork report and guide was used by trainers to explain the importance of teamwork throughout the region.

Again, following the Final Review Workshop, the empowerment and teamworking initiative in the Blackpool Tax District was carried forward through an 'away day' where the Tax District Inspector, who was a member of the project team, supported by the other team members, acted as facilitators with the Blackpool staff. This was particularly successful in revealing change awareness at shopfloor level.

The project teams on teamworking have illustrated how vital teamworking is to any project output and, more importantly, how small beginnings in teamworking can open the door to developing a teamworking culture. There are now many examples of the new change culture, and awareness of what it means for people in the organization, being cascaded down to lower levels by senior managers who have experienced the SMP.

COMMENTS ON PROJECT PRESENTATIONS

In reflecting on the Final Review Workshop, the author in attendance offered the following comments:

- Projects are clearly vehicles for learning and change. Once a project is initiated, expectations are raised for the project group members, sponsor and other key people. People will know the project is happening, it will be in the spotlight, so members will be both visible and vulnerable (i.e. in the event of failure).
- Balance between bottom line and learning benefits needs to be appropriate. In our experience, over several years of project-based learning, there has been a shift from the main focus being on learning benefits to a more equal balance of both types of benefits.
- Valuing experiences in teamworking, through carrying out projects, mirrors wider developments wherein teamworking is gaining greater prominence in how tasks are achieved. It is usual for teams to be temporary, and individuals may have membership of more than one team at any one time. Valuing diversity in team membership is another key requirement.

200

- Introducing teamworking is not without problems. It needs a culture which is supportive but, on the other hand, a sufficient critical mass of teamworking, such as that acquired through teamworking projects, which can help to change the culture. Perhaps the project groups can become ambassadors of culture change.
- The essence of action learning is that people learn far more through taking action than in making recommendations for action. The possible follow-up through to implementation by the project groups could help in closing the learning loop. In addition, the stated intent by some groups to continue functioning with an emphasis on their own learning and development could be a significant activity i.e. the establishing of self-development groups.
- The visits to other organizations as benchmarking activities within projects was particularly successful, i.e. the readiness of other organizations to share experiences and learning. This sort of activity could be worth pursuing further and, importantly, could provide a stimulus for change within the Revenue.
- Clearly, the theme of managing change came through strongly, which is of course a vital requirement for organizations now and in the future. It is common to hear phrases like 'nothing is permanent except change' – a quote attributed to Heraclitus – 600BC. But too much change, too fast, on too many fronts will be 'indigestible'.
- Another significant output mentioned by one or two groups related to networks of relationships. We have found in our work that a characteristic which distinguished very effective managers from less effective managers is the skill with which they build, manage and handle their networks of relationships. The projects provide immense scope for this.
- The projects have also provided individuals with opportunities to take more responsibility for their own learning and development, again a trend which we are witnessing and encouraging in organizations.
- Projects need to be valued by sponsors; outputs need to be important to them. The sponsor's role and activities can cover a wide range, including coach, mentor, critic, supporter, assessor, sign-poster, door-opener and devil's advocate. The role relationship with the project group needs to be such that the sponsor is 'on tap' but not 'on top'.

LONDON UNDERGROUND

This case history is partly based on the article 'HR Projects on the Right Track', which appeared in *People Management*, August 1995, and a discussion with Paul Farmer, the manager who managed the implementation of the project management initiative.

In exploring linkages between project management and project-based learning, the involvement of an HR team in a project management initiative is clearly of interest. One such recent initiative was in a Management of Change Programme at London Underground.[2]

THE APPROACH

During 1993, after closely examining how it operated and the service it provided, the HR team planned to extend the use of project management across their activities. Seven HR departments were involved in the introduction of project management, which was front end supported by training. It was agreed that the main focus should be on the hard skills of planning and monitoring, since there was already a growing familiarity with the softer skills of leading and organizing teams. As part of the hard skills, a computerized system 'Microsoft Project' was introduced.

The training comprised a two-day programme introducing concepts and techniques, with a further two days on the use of the software package. The system was introduced through a short guide on how projects should be set up, tackled and controlled.

Some difficulties were experienced with the software package. However, bringing in an expert coach from outside on a temporary basis helped in overcoming difficulties and with increasing motivation.

Ground rules for the HR team provided some structure. They were proposed by Paul Farmer, who was leading the initiative, and were based on his previous project management experience.

THE HR TEAM GROUND RULES

All HR team projects have:

- an owner – the HR lead person
- a leader – someone who leads the project or chairs meetings
- mixed diagonal teams across the HR team and the business

- a project proposal
- a charter with interim deliverables
- a Gantt chart scheduling the projects
- a resource plan with costs
- regular reporting
- a closing report that asks whether the benefits were achieved.

The value of the ground rules is that they give teams scope to deliver, including monitoring at the stages. In addition, terms of reference for project teams were created by the leaders and their teams.

EVALUATION OF THE PROJECT MANAGEMENT SYSTEM

Following the implementation of the project management system, an evaluation study was carried out by Frances Bee, an external consultant.

The most widely quoted benefit was the improvement in the quality of planning. This has helped in moving from a predominant mode of 'being good at dealing with incidents – crisis management' to 'being good at minimizing these incidents'. Another benefit was the improvement in communications with customers, which included senior managers in passenger services and professional engineers, and within the project teams – particularly in teamwork. Communications improvement has helped reduce friction within the HR centre functions and the seven business centres.

The approach also provided a rational basis on which to negotiate scope, context and timescales and helped in presenting a professional image, which is especially important for internal consultants.

Another finding was the extent to which project management skills learnt had been transferred or reinforced. While applications were encouraging, the results emphasized the importance of the timeliness of training, particularly for computer skills. The use of the expert coach proved to be a way of achieving value for money through IT training in that the projects supplied the context for skill practice and development. This, of course, requires the availability of suitable projects, which were not always forthcoming.

The briefing sessions were considered useful in dispelling any confusions about reasons for the project initiative; in essence, the initial communication had not been sufficiently clear and there had not been a common understanding. There were concerns about how much flexibility would be permitted, with some reluctance to change deadlines and issues of handling problems or agreeing change. The briefing sessions thus helped people to see the scope and relevance of the project initiative.

Again, with hindsight, Paul Farmer saw the need to be thorough in introducing project management, initially getting people to think 'project management', then to be flexible and not to go too hard on cost but to focus more on quality – but not quality at any cost! In fact, the resource plan with costings was one of the ground rules which was not adhered to. In addition, the closing reports were rather patchy, with the motivation being to get on to the next project.

Another point identified by Paul was related to the initial development of project teams, where it was seen to have been preferable to have used Belbin's team roles framework,[3,4] as part of developing teamwork earlier in the process.

Moreover, it was identified that concentrated coaching of project leaders would have contributed significantly to the effectiveness of outputs, particularly in their role as project sponsors. Project leaders had a strong drive to get into the 'task' aspects, while ignoring the softer HR aspects.

As with many change management initiatives, the experience of introducing project management emphasized the need to 'sell' such change in a focused way, relating to individuals' work and clarifying objectives and expected outcomes. The important issues of tailoring training to individual needs and for training to be timely were also emphasized.

Projects often provide opportunities for recognition and increased visibility. This was especially the case on longer projects with steering groups.

A CENTURY OF NEW PROJECTS

By the first full quarterly monitoring report in January 1995, there were over 100 projects registered on the system. The range of exercises reflected the diversity of work within the HR team.

For example, there was a series of projects investigating the different reward systems that could be used for London Underground staff. These were small research projects that were run internally by the strategy and employee relations departments within the HR team.

At the other end of the spectrum were major projects, such as the latest phase of the drugs and alcohol project, which organized the implementation of the new regulations in this area. Personnel Services used the project approach to manage large exercises such as recruiting staff for the Jubilee line extension.

204

Training Services ran a project that reviewed safety training. Although it was managed by a small team, the exercise involved consultation with managers from all parts of the business. They used the system to plan and monitor a major downsizing of the department, which involved a complex set of activities ranging from negotiations with staff and unions to the organization of assessment centres.

The Employee Development Department's portfolio included projects on a wide range of development issues, including succession planning and career counselling.

Finally, there were more traditional projects, for example a computer project (the introduction of a local area network for the HR team) led by the Management Information Systems team and an accommodation project being run within the facilities department.

The introduction of project management has demonstrated how such a system can be deployed for achieving individual and group objectives and how it can help in developing the necessary skills of managing change.

STATES OF GUERNSEY CIVIL SERVICE

The following case study was provided by Graham Robinson of Kennedy Robinson Business Development, it is part of a more comprehensive initiative.[5]

Between November 1994 and May 1995 the States of Guernsey Civil Service Board conducted a pilot programme for 12 of its Executive Officers which was built around four major projects conducted on behalf of four Chief Officers. The origins of the programme are to be found in a highly successful Senior Officer Management Development Programme which had included a Performance Improvement Project (PIP) which teams of participants had undertaken within their home organizations. These earlier projects had varied in quality and in the level of contribution that they had made, both to improved performance and to the learning of the managers involved. The most successful projects were those which focused on 'business' problems of significance, where there was a real sense of need, where the projects were seen as stretching, and where the project teams had a realistic sense of their capabilities and were prepared to acknowledge mistakes.

The least successful projects were those which were either over- or underambitious where the members of the group found difficulty in confronting and managing conflict or where the project's subject matter, though important, was seen as being peripheral to critical business issues.

When, in 1994, the designers of the programme were requested to develop a programme for Executive Officers, it was agreed that it should:

- be developed on action learning principles
- be built around a core of sponsored projects
- be supported by a framework of taught modules conducted in parallel with the projects.

If the projects were to be successful, both in terms of their learning objectives and in making a useful contribution to the 'business' of their sponsors, it was felt that they would require top management commitment, to contain an element of risk (both to the participants and to the sponsor him or herself) and that the participants should deliver them to an organization other than their own.

The reason that it was felt that the project should contain an element of risk was that it had been noted that the least successful projects in the original programme had been those where little damage to credibility, performance or prestige would be done in the event of failure.

Some nine Chief Officers of Civil Service departments or Trading Boards were approached with a request that they might volunteer to sponsor a project within their own organization on which a team of three or four participants would spend several hours each week for a period of six months.

Eventually, four Chief Officers each agreed to sponsor a project on an issue of business significance to them and with a commitment to present the project and its findings to their respective boards to determine the implementation action that would be taken as a consequence of the findings or outcomes of each project.

THE PROJECTS

The four projects on which the participants eventually elected to work were as follows:

Project 1: Measuring Morale (sponsored by the Chief Executive, Board of Health)

A project team was invited to investigate and to make recommendations to the Board as to ways in which it might *define* and develop means of measuring levels of morale among its staff. The team was encouraged to consider a variety of possible approaches and the experience of other organizations in using instruments such as attitude and climate surveys, briefing groups and so on, and to identify the benefits and pitfalls associated with such approaches.

Project 2: Pay Arrangements for UK Parity Groups (sponsored by the Chief Industrial Relations Officer, Civil Service Board)

For three specialist groups of Guernsey public servants (police, nurses and prison officers) pay rates have traditionally been tied to those for such groups in the UK. The mainland government announced its intention to introduce both performance-related pay and an element of local pay determination for these groups. A project team was asked to investigate and:

- develop a clear understanding of how such schemes would work in practice on the mainland
- identify what changes would be necessary to the States performance management systems in order to introduce the schemes to Guernsey
- obtain the views of the relevant managers on the prospect of moving their staff to performance-related pay.

Project 3: Business Plan 2000 (sponsored by the Chief Executive, Guernsey Post Office)

Postal authorities worldwide are facing increased competition in many areas of their business, not only from the private sector but also from alternative media and other postal authorities.

A project team was asked to investigate various approaches to the development of business planning frameworks and to recommend an approach to cover:

- corporate goals and strategy
- an analysis and modelling approach to cover the business environment, internal systems, resource requirements etc. of the Post Office
- key elements of the planning framework
- risks and sensitivities
- milestones.

It was recognized that, in order to develop their approach, the team would need to meet and discuss the key issues involved with the Chief Executive and members of the Post Office senior management team.

207

Project 4: Corporate Identity (sponsored by the Chief Executive, Boards of Industry, Agriculture and Milk Marketing, Horticulture and Sea Fisheries)

The four bodies identified above share a single Chief Executive and 'happen' to be co-located on a single site. Various initiatives had been taken to rationalize the organizational support functions in the interests of efficiency, effectiveness and value for money.

A project team was invited to investigate a range of options and to make recommendations to the Chief Executive as to the steps that would need to be taken to develop and promote a new corporate image, based on the concept of a Guernsey Centre for Industry.

The outputs of the project were expected to include:

- options for addressing the issue of common identity and corporate image
- a specific action plan for the consideration of the Chief Executive
- a process ensuring the commitment of key staff to the proposed course of action.

THE APPROACH

Each of these projects was significant enough to have merited a dedicated project team or consultancy assignment commissioned by the sponsoring organization on its own behalf. To offer these as projects to be undertaken by teams of middle managers drawn from organizations other than the sponsoring one, with little or no prior project experience and who did not know one another at the beginning of the programme, ensured that the criteria of risk were met.

The programme itself had been loosely designed around a series of six modules which, it was anticipated, should keep pace with the stages of the projects themselves. The loose design was consciously chosen in order to establish a balance between programmed learning and opportunities for learning from questioning insights (the Ps and Qs of action learning).

Thus the launch module covered:

- understanding the Action Learning approach
- developing project teams:
  - learning styles
  - work preferences
  - team roles

- negotiating contracts with the tutorial team
- negotiating contracts between project teams
- negotiating contracts between team members.

The emphasis placed on contract negotiating was critical. The projects were challenging, demanding of time over and above the participants' normal jobs and (as has been noted) carried a significant risk of failure. Therefore, it was important that there was a realistic sense of the commitments and expectations that the different 'players' could have of one another. After the launch module, each team was required to negotiate a contract with their project sponsor. This was vitally important and led to some significant modifications to the project specifications, without fundamentally changing them. These negotiations, included the amount of access the teams would have to their project sponsor, milestones and review points and the form that the project output would take (that is, formal report only or presentation and report; to the Chief Executive alone or to the full management team and so on).

The subsequent modules covered issues such as:

- project planning and control
- contextual issues (including policy developments) likely to be of relevance to the projects
- problem analytical techniques
- resource management
- negotiating, influencing and interpersonal skills
- planning and managing change
- report writing and presentation skills and so on.

However, most of the time spent on modules was devoted to dealing with questions raised by the teams themselves as they tackled their projects. Each module was characterized by short inputs from the tutorial team, project reviews, generation of questions and identification of inputs that would be required at subsequent modules.

A key integrating role was provided by the Set Advisor who acted as facilitator to each project group and to the programme as a whole. It fell to her to debrief the tutorial team after each module to ensure that inputs were developed, or modified, to meet needs identified by the participants. These debriefings led to some significant shifts in emphasis as the programme progressed. For example, one member of the tutorial team is a specialist in business planning. His initial involvement, however, was on the basis of his project management and project planning capabilities. Not unreasonably, the members of Project Team 3 (investigating business planning frameworks) were anxious to use this particular tutor as much as possible, while the other teams were anxious lest they were short-changed on his project knowledge and skills. Similarly, another member of the tutor group had considerable knowledge of survey methodology but was also utilized for his team development and project negotiation knowledge.

For the participants, the programme was extremely challenging. Action learning was unfamiliar to them, while the projects themselves were high profile, ambitious and largely outside the realms of their prior experience. They found the apparent lack of a structured learning process unsettling and, at first, found the need to structure and manage their own time puzzling and confusing. During the earliest modules, much of the time that was not programmed tended to be 'wasted' in general discussion and social banter. This helped to develop team identity and some healthy 'hostility' towards the tutors ('Why aren't you teaching us more?' 'Action learning is a soft option for trainers' and so forth). But it also led to increasing anxiety as milestones approached and slippage appeared to be increasingly likely.

As this slippage built up, it was inevitable that more demands were met by giving up increasing amounts of private time. This too generated tensions between participants, some being more willing or able to meet timescales than others. Gradually each group came to terms with these pressures and conflicts, each one developing processes – some formal others less so – for coping.

As the due date for project presentation to the sponsors approached, attention turned more and more to report writing and presentation skills. The team had generated masses of data, some of which they were extremely proud of since it reflected boldness and ingenuity on their part. For example, the group involved in 'measuring morale' had made contact with the former Personnel Director of a major multinational company who had given them a great deal of advice and guidance. They were anxious to show off their newly acquired knowledge in their report.

However, while it had been invaluable in leading them to their final conclusion, it was not directly relevant to the conclusion itself and, therefore, of less interest to the sponsor.

OUTCOMES

The Programme's conclusion had two elements. The first of these involved reporting back to the sponsors. In some cases this involved a formal presentation to the whole of the sponsoring organization's management team. In others, the approach was less formal and involved a meeting between the sponsor and the project team members to discuss the report which was a requirement of each of the teams. In reporting back to their sponsors the project teams were unaccompanied by any members of the tutorial group. The aim was for them to accept full responsibility for the outcomes of their project, their recommendations and the sponsor's reactions to them.

The second element involved the teams in presenting 'the story' of their project, including what they had learned as a consequence of undertaking it, to a panel comprising the States Supervisor (Head of the Civil Service), the Head of Personnel and Establishments and two senior politicians. The sponsors also attended this session, giving their reactions and their implementation proposals.

The overall conclusions were very positive and included some significant learning points for the programme designers.

1. Action and project-based learning requires a degree of tolerance for ambiguity and uncertainty that is not to everyone's taste. While this reflects management reality, it is a significant contributor to the risk element in the projects and needs to be recognized from the outset.
2. The tutorial element of the programme needs to contain sufficient project planning and control training to enable the participants to manage their projects realistically, but without causing them to feel that the techniques are controlling them.
3. Participants have considerably greater sources of energy and ingenuity than they are willing to give themselves credit for. Often, this only becomes manifest when tutors resist the temptation to be 'helpful'. Participants do not thank them for being so resistant.

LEARNING POINTS

Among the key learning points noted by participants were the following:

- Improved teamworking skills; time management; working to deadlines.

- Learning from dealing with 'real world' issues and problems in 'real time'.
- Improved presentation skills and confidence.
- Working with colleagues with diverse backgrounds and experiences; using these characteristics as a major asset.
- Learning not to have unrealistic expectations when collecting information from external providers.
- Developing negotiation and assertiveness skills.
- Data collection and analytical skills.

Against these positive elements, some participants felt that the experience was interesting but overdemanding, spread over too long a period and that its learning benefits would possibly be limited to situations in which project working was the most significant requirement.

KEY POINT SUMMARY

- Learning takes place throughout a project. Learning must be captured on a continuous basis, rather than just depending on an end-of-project learning review.
- Learning is possible from both successful and failed projects.
- Projects provide vehicles for increased understanding of the way roles and functions 'fit'.
- Benchmarking can be a useful means of understanding the complexities involved in managing change.
- There can be great value in capturing the outputs from major change projects in checklist form, which may provide templates for other departments or functions about to experience similar change processes, e.g. merging of departments.
- Strong involvement and commitment by project sponsors can greatly help to secure wider implementation of project recommendations, often resulting in major beneficial change.
- Once initiated, projects raise the expectations of the various stakeholders; it is essential that project owners' self-interest is 'delivered' in line with expectations.
- Increasingly, tasks in organizations are being achieved by teams, so the value of teamworking in carrying out projects is an investment for the future.

- Projects provide opportunities for individuals to take more responsibility for their own learning and development.
- Group projects can allow for innovation and opportunities to try something new.
- Successful experience of carrying out a group project can engender commitment to wider adoption of teamworking.
- Benchmarking activities in projects can be useful to help identify the complexities involved in managing change.
- Project groups set up to bring about learning and change can be ambassadors for cultural change.
- A key element at the end of the project is a closeout report. These are valuable for capturing and transferring learning, even though motivation is often to move on to the next project. Priority must be given to their completion.
- The introduction of project management can help to develop skills in managing change.
- Building in 'risk' as one of the criteria in project selection can contribute to successful outcomes, i.e. risk to credibility, performance or prestige.
- Group projects can raise the risk level where team members come from organizations different to the sponsoring one, do not know each other and have little or no prior project experience.
- It is important for team members to negotiate contracts with the sponsor, with the tutorial team and with each other.
- The lack of a structured learning process within an action learning approach can be unsettling to participants who have come to expect 'being taught'.
- Action and project-based learning require tolerance of uncertainty. This in itself is a risk element which needs to be recognized from the outset.
- Training in hard skills and techniques should be offered to participants but not be seen as methods of controlling them.
- Projects are opportunities for learning because they deal with 'real world' issues and problems in 'real time'.

REFERENCES

1. Grieve, I. (1994), 'Inland Revenue – Managing the Change Challenge', *Industrial and Commercial Training*, **26**, (4).

2. Bee, F. and Farmer, P. (1995), 'HR Projects on the Right Track', *People Management*, August.
3. Belbin, R.M. (1984), *Management Teams: Why They Succeed or Fail*, Oxford: Butterworth-Heinemann.
4. Belbin, R.M. (1993), *Team Roles at Work*, Oxford: Butterworth-Heinemann.
5. Robinson, G. and Hurley, C. (1996), 'Mangement Development and Inspiration in the Guernsey public sector', *Industrial and Commercial Training*, **28**, (3), pp 19–25.

10 The International Dimension

There is immense scope for developing project-based learning internationally. In this chapter we draw together some early experiences of this emerging area from the following perspectives:

- Differences in national culture can have a significant impact on the acceptability of project-based learning as a methodology.
- In the increasingly global setting in which managers operate, projects can provide a means of benchmarking performance.
- At first degree level, it is increasingly becoming common practice internationally to include a project element as part of the curriculum. For first management appointments, the project-based learning methodology has a useful fit.

The following theoretical considerations of cross-cultural working and practical case material underpin the above perspectives.

CULTURAL DIMENSIONS

A valuable starting point for examining the impact of national culture upon the effectiveness of management development is to draw upon the work done by Geert Hofstede, in the 1960s and 1970s, concerning international differences in work-related values.[1] He developed a theory of culture applicable to management, based upon a comparison of the values of some 116,000 employees and managers in 64 national subsidiaries of the IBM Corporation. Hofstede defined culture as 'the collective programming of the mind which distinguishes one group or category of people from another'.

He determined that cultures differed between nations along four work-related dimensions; that the position of a country on these dimensions allowed some predictions to be made concerning the processes and theories of management applicable within the national societies.

He developed an index of relative scores for each dimension, with about one hundred points between the lowest and highest scoring country. Figure 10.1 below shows the names given to the four dimensions and provides a summary of scores.

Two of Hofstede's cultural dimensions are relevant for management development. The other two dimensions, individualism–collectivism and masculinity–femininity, can also affect development preferences, though we do not believe they are as important as those discussed below.

POWER DISTANCE

'Power distance' measures the extent to which the less powerful members of a society accept an unequal distribution of power. Inequality exists in all cultures, but the degree to which it occurs and is tolerated varies between one culture and another. In organizations, the level of power distance is

PD	=	Power distance
UA	=	Uncertainty avoidance
ID	=	Individualism
MA	=	Masculinity

	PD	UA	ID	MA
USA	40	46	91	62
Germany	35	65	67	66
Japan	54	92	46	95
France	68	86	71	43
Netherlands	38	53	80	14
Britain	35	35	89	66
Turkey	66	85	37	45
Israel	13	81	54	47

Figure 10.1 Culture dimension scores for selected countries

related to the degree of centralization of authority and the degree of autocratic leadership. A centralized, autocratic organization has a high level of power distance; a decentralized, participative organization has a low level.

In a development situation, the power distance dimension would describe the degree to which participants are self-directed or trainer-directed. Cultures with small power distance scores value learner-centred learning, placing a premium on the participant initiative. The effectiveness of training in these cultures is related to the amount of communication between trainer and participants as well as among participants. Knowledge can be acquired from any competent person. On the other hand, cultures with large power distance scores value trainer-centred learning, placing a premium on order. Training effectiveness is considered a product of the knowledge and expertise of the trainer; knowledge is to be obtained from the trainer.

UNCERTAINTY AVOIDANCE

'Uncertainty avoidance' measures the extent to which members of a society feel threatened by unstructured, unpredictable situations and the extent to which they try to avoid these situations. Societies and organizations with strong uncertainty avoidance scores seek to avoid ambiguity and provide greater structure by establishing more formal rules; rejecting deviant ideas and behaviour; accepting the possibility of absolute truths.

In a development environment, the uncertainty avoidance dimension would describe the degree to which participants seek to structure information and avoid ambiguity through generalized principles and a search for absolute truth. In cultures with weak uncertainty avoidance, participants are comfortable with unanswered questions and may be encouraged to seek innovative approaches to problem solving. Intellectual disagreements are viewed as stimulating. On the other hand, in cultures with strong uncertainty avoidance scores, trainers are considered experts; intellectual disagreements are disrespectful; participants are rewarded for accuracy in problem solving and conformity with trainer-established principles.

What can be learnt by applying the concepts of power distance and uncertainty avoidance to the use of projects in a multi-cultural setting? In experiential training, such as project-based development, learning is expected to take place independent of the trainer. Participants learn from one another. Power, responsibility, and knowledge are shared by the participants and the trainer. There is little difference between the power of the trainer and the power of the participants, suggesting an orientation towards a low power distance value.

Experiential training is centred on problem solving and learning how to learn, rather than on absolute truths. The outcomes are not predictable but grow out of the interaction of the participants, requiring periods of considerable ambiguity. Experiential training techniques assume tolerance for ambiguity and, in Hofstede's framework, orientation towards a low Uncertainty Avoidance value orientation.

Thus, examination of the culture dimension data in Figure 10.1 would suggest that countries with low power distance scores, such as the USA, Germany, the Netherlands and Britain, will be more naturally disposed towards project-based management development initiatives. These countries vary, however, in their uncertainty avoidance scores, Germany having a relatively high score. We believe that additional time and effort should be given to establishing the scope and purpose of project initiatives in high uncertainty avoidance countries such as Germany.

The initial aim should be to bring to the surface and deal with any worries or ambiguities which may be present initially and to ensure ownership of the process by participants and others involved. For countries with high power distance scores, such as France, we recommend that careful thought is given to the political considerations within the organization which the project may encounter, in particular any impacts on the power and standing of senior managers involved in the project.

The aim should be to ensure that the learning environment for the participant is not unduly disrupted by, for instance, clashes of political interests.

The above issues and other related considerations concerning the cultural relativity of training techniques have been further developed by Joyce Francis.[2]

USE OF PROJECTS AS A PRECURSOR TO A DEVELOPMENTAL MODULE

In addressing issues arising from differences in national culture, differences cannot always be recognized directly. Many differences relate to

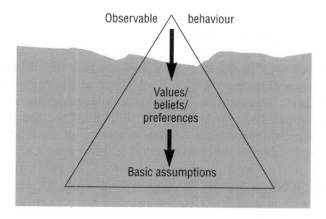

Figure 10.2 The cultural 'iceberg'

what is assumed or unstated. The 'iceberg' model shown in Figure 10.2 illustrates a useful way of visualizing this.

Cultural differences arise largely from the part of the 'iceberg' that is under the water and are thus not directly visible. For an individual or group to become familiar with cultural differences requires time to be spent in the location where the culture is different; to feel and articulate the differences through direct experience (i.e. experiential learning).

One approach is to use a project as a means of giving the participants the opportunity of experiencing the cultural differences *in advance* of a developmental module. Whereas projects are used as a means of applying and reinforcing learning *following* a module within a developmental pro-gramme, in this case the project work is used before the module has taken place. This provides the opportunity to identify early the impact of cultural differences in business situations and to consider approaches for handling them. Subsequently, during the module, the differences can be discussed and further examined.

Allowing sufficient time is a key requirement for developing cross-cultural awareness and skills. It can take perhaps two years for an individual to acclimatize to a new culture. During the period of weeks for the pre-module project and the module itself, we would not expect the participant group to become fully familiar with the cultural differences. However, the extra learning provided by experiencing the difference in advance of a module can provide a significant stimulus to the learning process, as the BTR example illustrates.

219

BTR – THE PAN EUROPEAN MANAGER

A pre-module approach to the timing of projects was taken in this case. The 'Pan European Manager' module took place at the mid-point of the BTR–DEP (Europe) programme – a multi-modular programme for managers of high potential within BTR.* The objectives for the module included improving understanding of the influence of national cultures when working in a mixed culture group and gaining practical experience of developing a pan-European business initiative. The participants in the programme included managers from Germany, Holland, Belgium and Switzerland, as well as from the UK, whence the majority originated. The objective of the project work was to provide practical experience of cross-cultural working, relating to specific issues, shortly before participating in the 'Pan European Manager' module which took place in Brussels. Project groups were formed from a mix of nationalities, each group addressing an agreed topic.

AN EXAMPLE

A project undertaken by one of the groups, centred on the working practices of Dunlop BTR Hydraulik in Germany, included the following three stages:

- Initial formation and briefing of the group, followed by agreement of the project topics with the programme specifier, Alex Dickinson, Senior Human Resources manager at BTR.
- Detailed planning and work on the project work in Germany by the group members.
- Presentation of project outcomes and recommendations at the start of the module in Brussels.

The host within the project group was Bernard Feldhaus, from Dunlop BTR Hydraulik, who summarized the aims for the project as follows:

Project Outline

Review the role of the Employers' Association and unions in Germany, including identifying any differences in opinion between

---

* Provided by Sundridge Park.

blue and white collar staff concerning:

- Working hours
- Employment conditions
- Team spirit
- The importance of sales and PBIT (Profit before Interest and Taxation)

It also included consideration of the general characteristics of the management style and behaviour in Germany.

The schedule of activities in Germany for the project group included:

- a tour through BTR Operations in Essen, Overath and Gummersbach
- a day spent at head office, in the workshop and at the sales office, including discussions with a sales representative
- a day of discussions with the Employers' Association in Essen and seeing a German court in operation
- a visit to the IG METALL Union Headquarters in Gummersbach.

A set of topics was identified by the project group for discussion with staff from different functions within the business. The topics selected were:

- Willingness to relocate and acceptability of commuting distances
- The importance of a formal education
- The dress code
- Working hours and the working environment
- Bonuses and gifts
- What constitutes a 'good day'
- Job descriptions
- Teamworking
- The role of women
- The use of technology
- Knowledge of BTR
- Awareness of company performance

Responses obtained from the various staff groups varied according to individual circumstances, as would be expected, but did serve to highlight some German cultural characteristics and preferences. Examples are given below:

The importance of a formal education

- Academic education is not as important as experience
- A formal education is not essential to success
- Academic qualifications are not important

The emphasis on pragmatic, result-orientated values comes through here. This also illustrates the low power distance culture of the Germans.

The dress code

- 'The boss' must wear a jacket and a tie – if not, he must have a very dominant character
- Dress does not matter unless you are very senior
- Casual dress on most days; only wears a tie when he feels like it

The responses show the more flexible attitude to dress code in German business compared with many British organizations.

The role of women

- Would be unusual to have a woman boss; if she was attractive it would make him very nervous
- No women on the shop floor but there should be
- Women could not do his sales job – too much travelling
- Working for a woman could be difficult but so could working for a different man
- The role of women is more stereotyped in Germany than in the UK, but the person is more important than the gender

As these responses suggest, the acceptability of women in Germany in managerial roles has some way to go. A linkage to the relatively high uncertainty avoidance culture could, perhaps, be inferred!

INTERNATIONAL BENCHMARKING OF PERFORMANCE – SCOTTISH NUCLEAR

The following paragraphs are largely based on extracts from a paper presented at the AMED 1993 Research Conference – Management Learning in an Electricity Generating Company by M. Hamilton, Heriot-Watt University Business School and P. James, Ashridge Research Group.[3]

For many organizations, benchmarking is carried out as a diagnostic activity preceding a managing change initiative. Benchmarking can, of course, provide project learning for managers. In the electricity generating industry, Scottish Nuclear Limited successfully integrated 20 soft benchmarking projects with two management programmes (senior and middle levels) with a common goal of responding to the question 'what does Scottish Nuclear have to learn from this utility?' The utilities are world class organizations in Europe, Japan and the USA, although not necessarily models of best practice.

Each team was asked to:

- decide on their approach
- prepare a costed project plan
- research information about the utility and the country
- contact and visit the utility
- prepare a report and make a presentation to the directors of Scottish Nuclear Limited.

The management development programme was designed to:

- enhance commercial awareness, enabling managers to respond more effectively to threats and opportunities in a privatized electricity industry
- develop a sense of purpose and share understanding among managers
- develop specific skills and competencies, e.g. people skills.

The utility projects were aided by an international orientation, including sessions on the European electricity industry and Japanese management styles, together with an emphasis on action learning within the programme.

An assumption of the programme was that the electricity industry and nuclear power in particular is becoming more international in nature. Indeed, Scottish Nuclear has already developed international linkages and the utility project was designed to develop understanding of international changes and foster linkages with overseas utilities.

The programme gave support to those carrying out projects through sessions on information sources and developments in the international electricity industry, scope for group discussions and rehearsals of project presentations.

There was a range of benefits for both individual managers and the organization as a whole. For individual managers, benefits included:

- a sharper understanding of the strategic issues facing Scottish Nuclear and the industry
- being in a different role by acting as ambassadors for their company
- the challenge of managing a project with an open brief
- the experience of researching and formulating appropriate questions
- the oft-quoted challenge of managing their own jobs while carrying out the project, requiring effective planning and time management
- increased self confidence through taking individual and team initiatives
- managers recognizing in themselves the need for change through a process of self-discovery.

Moreover, several managers have been promoted and feel that the programme was a valuable preparation for their increased responsibility.

Organizational benefits included:

- capturing and valuing of new ideas among the wealth of information available from the benchmarking visits
- much greater commercial awareness and sense of common purpose throughout the company
- having a cluster of people who know a considerable amount about strategies and policies in other countries and how Scottish Nuclear will need to embrace continuous change over the next few years to survive and prosper.

PROJECTS IN EARLY MANAGEMENT APPOINTMENTS – RENONG BERHAD

Renong Berhad is one of Malaysia's leading strategic investment companies which steers an integrated group of 12 other public-listed companies. Renong, via its subsidiaries and associate companies, is an integrated infrastructure group involved in engineering, construction and infrastructure development; expressways and tolls operations; hotel, property and township development; telecommunications, power engineering and information technology; building material supplies; oil and gas services; transportation; financial services.

Two years ago, the Renong Management Trainee Scheme was launched

224

with the purpose of developing a pool of qualified managers for the future. Malaysian graduates are recruited to the scheme from local and overseas universities, including several in the UK. The scheme comprises several secondments spread over a two-year period. An integral part of the scheme is the Young Manager Programme, designed and delivered by consultants from Sundridge Park Management Centre.

The design is based on Sundridge's Younger Manager Programme, with the main difference being group rather than individual projects. Over 20 management trainees have attended each of the two programmes so far completed.

The project-based learning element of the programme has been a resounding success and here we describe some of the projects undertaken and their outputs. An important reason for the success in developing managers through projects is that many have undertaken an educational process (particularly in the UK) which has included a project element. What follows are extracts from reports prepared by the trainees on which presentations to sponsors were based.

PROJECT EXAMPLES

MERLIN HOTELS GROUP

The Merlin Hotels Group was undergoing a strong competitive challenge from a sharpening of the market profile, in which the highest standards of service and facilities were increasingly demanded. Based on this, the Group planned for all hotels within the group to be upgraded under a strategic alliance with ITT Sheraton.

An integral part of this upgrading exercise was an improvement to the standard of service of the Group's hotels. It was recognized that the quality of service would be perceived by the extent to which the group has a 'service culture'. It was also clear that it is the front-line employees who exemplify the culture.

Purpose of the project

The project's purpose was to determine the *service culture* of the front-line employees of the Merlin Group, identify its strengths and weaknesses and suggest recommendations to improve it to a 'total service culture'.

In addition, in choosing the project, the criteria which were considered important were that it:

225

- was significant to the trainees' areas of operation
- offers a challenge
- contains a 'people' element
- requires involvement, co-operation and commitment of other colleagues
- is linked to a planned and ongoing change
- will yield worthwhile benefits to the trainees' organization.

The *methodology* involved research at four characteristically different hotels to obtain a fair representation of conditions at all hotels in the Group.

Research was conducted through:

- project sponsor briefings plus interviews with General Managers
- briefings of heads of departments
- interviews with heads of departments
- questionnaire sessions with front-line employees
- observation.

It was found that the inclusion of observation can result in an increased level of objectivity.

Meetings with the project sponsor, Chris Gorring, initiated by team members were particularly useful. There were four meetings in all. The first considered project possibilities related to the criteria for choice. The second meeting confirmed the project's scope, budget and action plan, with the sponsor offering the benefit of his vast experience in the hospitality industry, particularly in the context of the questionnaire. The third meeting confirmed avenues for research plus help/advice on research methodology. The fourth meeting provided the sponsor with a summary of research findings.

General Managers of the hotels were also important stakeholders, and again their opinions and advice were valued. Further stakeholders were the heads of departments within each of the hotels, all of whom were interviewed. A great deal of valuable data was gained, including their ideas for achieving the required upgrading.

For front-line employees, questionnaires were seen as the most cost-effective means of data collection. Competitive benchmarking was viewed as important, and observation tours of several competitor hotels were carried out. Areas that were surveyed included:

- cleanliness and hygiene
- courtesy
- speed of service
- ambience
- competency
- value for money.

Findings indicated the need for improvements across the board. Changes recommended in order to achieve excellent standards of service centred around the need for a Human Resource organization and infrastructure. It was recommended that an HR infrastructure was set up at corporate and operational levels.

RECOMMENDATIONS

The project group made specific recommendations for enhancing the service culture of the front-line employees through concentrating on four key areas:

- recruitment processes and procedures
- remuneration
- service performance audit programme
- morale and esprit de corps.

For *recruitment processes and procedures*, it was recommended that more of the 'right kind of people' should be recruited, particularly those with a positive attitude toward their own learning.

Development programmes producing well-trained, motivated, self-believing, professional employees were recommended to provide consistent and effective services. Such programmes would also include multi-skilling with cross-departmental exposure, thus providing for a well-rounded experience. Such programmes would also need to be complemented by the formulation of proper career paths.

On *remuneration*, the need for pay to be competitive was highlighted. Linked to this was the need for *performance audit* with performance indicators and appropriate recognition for achievement. It was believed that such a programme would also help in identifying and selecting suitable employees for promotion and advancement.

For *morale and esprit de corps*, there were recommendations for building a spirit of co-operation and unity among front-line employees. These included flexibility in management styles to be responsive to employees' needs and sensitivities, investment in employee welfare programmes and mechanisms to improve communication and rapport, including 'meeting the employees' meetings.

LEARNING POINTS

During the group presentation, the participants emphasized the following points:

- Networking skills – building and expanding networks will have value in the future.
- Interviewing skills, with particular reference to listening and questioning skills.
- Planning and time/self-management in sequencing the project stages, monitoring progress and completing the project satisfactorily within the deadline.
- Making best use of the sponsor, drawing on his experience.

PARK MAY BERHAD

Park May Berhad is a management and investment holding company, with the majority of its subsidiaries and associate companies involved in bus commuter services, coach building and property investment. The company is upgrading and improving its nationwide fleet and transportation network to meet the higher expectations of today's commuter. In 1996, the company will have added 30 new executive coaches and 285 modern buses to its Cityliners existing fleet. This strategy is setting new standards in comfort and changing the face of the transport business. Linked to this strategy, is the company's decision to buy out the management of Foh Hup Omnibus Co Ltd (Foh Hup).

Foh Hup is facing stiff competition in a very difficult business environment, with management failing to adapt to the progressive change in their service sector. In addition, close government controls of the industry through tight regulations have added to pressures on Foh Hup. Having bought out the management of Foh Hup, a restructuring programme with a turnaround strategy is to be implemented such that Foh Hup can become an efficient and reliable provider of a public transport system in the city.

228

PURPOSE OF THE PROJECT

The project purpose was to analyse critically the situation and present a proposal for implementation to management, while applying knowledge and skills acquired from the first module of the Young Manager Programme.

The project team divided the project into three main stages: planning; data collection and analysis; report and presentation, including recommendations and conclusions.

Analysis drew out several issues.

COMPETITION AND FLEET REPLACEMENT

Foh Hup's low capital investment had allowed competitors to enter the market with new fleets. Consequently competitors, while initially using alternative routes, now compete directly on main routes.

FINANCE

Foh Hup's cash position is not strong with large debts to creditors and lawsuits in process. In addition, government controls on fares and increased operating costs had led to cost cutting in order to secure some profits. This failed.

OPERATOR'S SUPPORT SERVICE

The operator's support service was inadequate to meet needs, with limited facilities able to cater only for small repairs and with no proper plan for preventive maintenance. The outcome was too few vehicles to meet passenger demand, coupled with an attendant fall in revenue, while having to pay fixed costs on idle vehicles.

HUMAN RESOURCES

Turnover is high, with conductors and drivers being attracted by more lucrative employment. There is also high absenteeism and misconduct, possible indicators of poor motivation.

Following the data collection of Foh Hup, a SWOT analysis was carried out within the context of the takeover. Moreover, a detailed competitor analysis was undertaken looking at fleets, routes and operations, from which the project team put together two strategies, short and long term.

SHORT-TERM STRATEGY

The short-term strategy centred on immediate critical issues currently faced by Foh Hup, with action plans for up to a year following the acquisition. It covered the following points:

- Restructuring of the fleet including replacement, refurbishment and purchase of new buses.
- Expanding operations which would include extending current routes to a new catchment area and amalgamating routes operated by Park May subsidiaries.
- Human resource restructuring, to include reviews of organization structure, recruitment, salary and staff benefits. It was recommended also that training and staff development should be introduced.
- Restructuring of workshops and depots in order to provide for proper planned schedules on maintenance and repairs. This would also include programmes for preventive maintenance.

LONG-TERM STRATEGY

The long-term strategy raised the need for a number of new initiatives:

- Introduction of new routes, in particular covering areas where the company has no presence.
- Development of modern bus interchanges, which would become more important with the introduction of new routes and the extension of current routes. Interchanges could be self-financing through developing commercial centres.
- An automated ticket system to enable tighter cash control and reduce operating costs by eliminating conductors.
- Manpower planning, requiring proper projection of needs to avoid staff shortages. Further reinforcement of training and staff development, was also proposed
- Organization restructuring, towards a leaner management structure, which would lead to decentralization while promoting the scope for synergy between Park May and Foh Hup. Such structural change is seen to be more responsive to problem solving, with 'fast' and 'flexible' being used to describe the new structure.

LEARNING POINTS

The project team identified the following learning points:

- the experience and value of working as a team
- the development of key relationships in working with Park May and Foh Hup managerial/supervisory staff
- application of analytical skills in carrying out a critical analysis of the company situation
- increased understanding of company strategy and its implementation.

UNITEERS COMMUNICATIONS

Uniteers Communications Sdn Bhd (UCSB) was incorporated in 1989. Its primary function is to market and sell telecommunications equipment. It has achieved this by entering into a non-exclusive distribution agreement with OKI Japan to distribute OKI phones. Other products include keyphones, videophones, videocameras and camcorders.

The OKI cellular phone has been the most prominent product since it was first launched in the market, contributing more than 90 per cent of UCSB's turnover.

OKI was one of the pioneers in cellular phones in Malaysia. But with the pressure of new competitors, OKI started to lose its grip on the market and no longer holds a significant market share. In addition, due to the dynamic and competitive nature of the telecommunications industry, competitors have resorted to price cutting in order to protect or build on market share. For UCSB, there was also the problem of low brand awareness of OKI compared with competitors such as Motorola. Following several revisions to pricing strategy over the past few years, sales declined further which created a problem of slow moving stock. In-house trading then took precedence in order to clear existing stock. Thus uncompetitive pricing, together with an over-dependence on in-house trade, defines company weaknesses and the losses experienced.

PURPOSE OF THE PROJECT

The purpose of the project was to investigate what is wrong and what can be done.

The project team described the main problem as corporate decline following the adoption of inappropriate and undynamic strategies. This had two components:

- *Business orientation adopted*: Analysis confirmed the perceived image of the company as being sales-orientated instead of marketing orientated, and thus not addressing the full marketing mix.
- *Inappropriate strategic planning.* The study revealed the short-sightedness of a strategy concentrating on the cellular tele communications industry, despite the declining long-term profit potential as a result of the ever-growing competition.

METHODOLOGY

The methodology adopted was to identify symptoms, then to determine and test possible causes of each symptom. In this way it was envisaged that analysis of possible causes would help to identify the root of the problem. Recommendations were made identifying alternative solutions and then choosing the best solution.

SYMPTOMS AND CAUSES

Symptoms were identified as follows.

- Drop in sales
- Non-committed dealers
- High staff turnover
- Excessive stocks and high cost of inventory

DROP IN SALES

The drop in sales occurred over the last few years and, following strong competitor activity, led to OKI's fall from joint leader in cellular phones with Motorola to an also-ran, especially with regard to the introduction of more advanced systems.

NON-COMMITTED DEALERS

Observations from visits showed little effort to display the OKI brand and there was a low level of commitment. Lack of discounts was emphasized, with some dealers seeing no future in OKI.

HIGH STAFF TURNOVER

The high rate of turnover was because of UCSB's unrealistic expectations that staff would sell more OKI phones which are simply not competitive in the market. Salaries and incentives were also uncompetitive.

EXCESSIVE STOCKS AND HIGH COST OF INVENTORY

The arrangement with OKI of Japan required UCSB to take stock in bulk which became a burden when sales dropped sharply. UCSB was left with a large holding of obsolete stocks and its attendant holding costs.

Causes of the problem were identified using the five Ps model of Product, Price, Place, Promotion and People, a model which had been introduced and applied in marketing sessions on the first module. The results from applying this model were the following:

- *Product.* The five-stage product lifecycle approach was used:
  - Introduction
  - Growth
  - Maturity
  - Saturation
  - Decline

  OKI phones are now felt to be between the saturation and decline phase, having relied solely on an outdated system like analogue. The opportunity of introducing a new product range just before he saturation stage has been missed by UCSB.

- *Price.* Competitive analysis showed that the OKI price was high and far from competitive, thus contributing to the drop in sales and leaving OKI trailing its competitors.
- *Place.* The intention of nationwide coverage is not sufficiently recognized by the sales force who are too stretched to achieve it.
- *Promotion.* Again the stages in the buying process (also covered in the first module) of Awareness–Interest–Decide–Action were applied to OKI in relation to promotion and advertising.

  'Awareness' was found to be very low (15 per cent), aided by only a brief initial advertising campaign but without any follow through.

  'Interest' has not been established for OKI, i.e. not a brand which people will be proud to use or which will enhance their image. Again, a lack of advertising has contributed to OKI not establishing itself as

233

the 'in thing'. 'Desire' to buy has not been stimulated through lack of any promotional activities, in comparison with competitors who have used promotional methods widely. In addition, observations showed that very little incentive was provided to dealers with minimal promotional material and low profit margins.

The 'action' that should result from good promotion tends to be 'inaction'.

- *People.* There is a serious deficit in training through lack of exposure to modern selling techniques. Because of this, considerable time spent with customers is wasted and many sales calls are unproductive.

  Another factor contributing to lower sales is the lack of support for the sales force which means that sales people spend too much time in non-customer facing activities.

Other possible causes were:

- an organization structure which did not promote speedy decisions, an essential requirement in an industry typified by rapid change
- too strong a focus on internal markets (Renong) with such internal dependency acting against growth
- the marketing concept is not internalized since there is no marketing department, so the organization depends on its sales department for marketing!
- lack of support from OKI Japan, characterized by unfavourable terms in the agreement including slow response to the need for price changes, inadequate training and poor advertising support.

POTENTIAL ALTERNATIVE SOLUTIONS

Three solutions seemed to be available:

- *Continue with an expanded product range.* In exploring this alternative, the project team again applied the five Ps model. Pricing was seen as the key, but with the stiff competition in the market becoming more intense, trying to recover by making up lost ground appeared unlikely to be successful.
- *Cease UCSB's operations.* In evaluating this alternative the project team applied the Five Forces model (Michael Porter)[4] to diagnose systematically the principal competitive pressures in the market. The five forces are:

234

- rivalry among existing competitors
- power of buyers
- power of suppliers
- threat of new entrants
- threat of substitutes.

Each of the forces were considered unfavourable to UCSB. Profit potential looked particularly gloomy and the company would be prone to cannibalization by other market players. Ceasing operations could avoid further losses. Another reason for ceasing operations would be that cellular telecommunications is not synergistically complementary to the infrastructure business in which the parent company, United Engineers Malaysia, specializes.

- *Introduce other communications products.* It is suggested that a future lies in satellite communication products and that it would be sound strategically for UCSB to venture into this lucrative satellite-related business.

In considering this alternative, the project team carried out a SWOT analysis of UCSB (another example of using a technique from Module 1). It also explored products which UCSB could offer and their market options, together with a proposed strategy. In this strategy, it is proposed the company should learn from its mistakes in respect of the OKI strategy.

RECOMMENDATIONS

A combination of the second and third alternatives was proposed, since it was believed that a new telecommunications business could offset business losses from OKI. It was further proposed that whatever option(s) are chosen, a thorough planning process should be undertaken and a strong marketing orientation adopted.

LEARNING POINTS

- Using the project as a means of applying and testing specific models introduced during the first module, namely the five Ps model of Product, Price, Place, Promotion, People; the Five Forces model (Porter); SWOT analysis.
- Distinguishing between symptoms and root causes of problems.

- Learning was also evident in the process of observation, interviews, collection, collation and analysis of data.

KEY POINT SUMMARY

- The influence of national cultures and, in particular, the implicit assumptions that are contained within cultures, should be taken into consideration when using projects in an international context. The 'power distance' and 'uncertainty avoidance' culture dimensions (Hofstede) provide useful insight into how best to plan and introduce projects which involve different nationalities.
- The impact of differences in national culture cannot easily be identified simply by direct observation of behaviour. Differences in values and beliefs need to be brought to the surface and discussed, in order to develop mutual understanding and effective working.
- It requires time and experience in the location of another culture to develop cross-cultural awareness and skills. Projects which are designed as a pre-cursor to a developmental stage of a programme can accelerate the learning process and provide a major stimulus overall.
- Benchmarking as an activity can provide project-based learning for managers, particularly in looking outside national boundaries, e.g. broadening one's perspectives of international strategies and policies. Such projects are increasingly important in the context of greater global competition, where national boundaries no longer provide commercial protection, even for national utility supply organizations.
- Projects are an integral part of the formal education process in which many younger managers from different parts of the world will have participated, often involving a period in Europe or the USA. Therefore, further development of these managers using projects works well as it corresponds to a learning process with which they are familiar.
- Projects can make a significant impact on an organization's development when focused on analysis of business issues, problems and strategies.
- Business-focused projects provide for learning transfer of 'hard' skills and techniques, such as the Five Ps model (Product, Price, Place, Promotion, People), Porter's Five Forces model and SWOT analysis.

Such projects provide scope for identifying and understanding the differences between symptoms and causes of problems and achieving appropriate solutions.

REFERENCES

1. Hofstede, G. (1990), *Culture's Consequences*, London: Sage.
2. Francis, J.L. (1995), 'Training Across Cultures', *Human Development Quarterly*, Spring.
3. Hamilton, M. and James P. (1993), 'Management Learning in an Electricity Generating Company, A Paper', AMED Research Conference.
4. Porter, M.E. (1985), *Competitive Advantage*, The Free Press: New York.

Epilogue: The Project-Orientated Organization

Sometimes the future seems to have arrived too soon, with too much change, too quickly and with too much complexity. This can be very disorientating. Managers undertaking projects, particularly where the project takes them outside their domain, are frequently at the forefront of change. Where such change can be integrated with learning, then individual learning and the potential stock of organizational learning is greatly enriched.

Much has been written in recent years concerning the organizations and business environment that will emerge as we approach the end of this century. Charles Handy, in his book *The Age of Unreason,*[1] describes the impact of the shamrock form of organization, based on a core of essential executives and workers, supported by outside contractors and part-time help. This way of organizing, in big businesses and public sector institutions, will grow rapidly. He also describes the transition towards individuals having a 'portfolio' of work categories directed towards differing activities and sources of income. In this environment, individuals will be contributing differing activities to several organizations, depending on the nature of the organization's shamrock of requirements and the available portfolio of individual offerings.

The significance of this for project-based learning and development is:

- Achieving business objectives and operational requirements will increasingly be accomplished by employing a mixture of internal and external resources, managed as a set of parallel running projects. Resources will come and go, i.e. be allocated and relinquished, in accordance to the needs of the business. Organizations will need to take steps to capture and build on the learning that takes place during a project, as there will be fewer permanent core staff to act as the repository of organizational learning. Indeed, older staff may be moving from a core role to a part-time role and developing the portfolio aspect of their work.

- Our understanding of the term 'organization' will become less clear, as the boundaries within and between organizational activities become fuzzier. The concept of the 'virtual' organization, consisting of internal and external components, will make it more difficult to locate the centre of expertise for a given business activity.

- Existing businesses in the developed world will be under increasing pressure from competitors emerging in the developing world. One route to competing effectively will be a shift towards higher added value, low volume offerings, which cannot be provided readily by the developing world. For success, the importance of capturing knowledge and developing the knowhow base ever more rapidly will be paramount. Information technology, including the electronic superhighways envisaged in the USA and the European Union, can make an important contribution to this. However, encouragement of creativity and innovation within organizations will have greater impact. Project-based learning and development provides a vehicle for releasing and focusing creative energy and for breaking the mould of organizational inertia.

- The continuing advances in the availability and sophistication of IT systems will provide additional means for supporting project-based learning and development activities. Part of any learning activity is the opportunity of interacting with the sponsor, coach and others involved in the learning process. IT systems can provide the means of extending the interactive learning environment across distance, enabling dialogue to take place at times which suit the needs of the manager and the project.

Much of this 'futures scenario' for organizations lends strength to the development of learning through individual and group projects. The harnessing of information technology and the acceleration of technological change will require an effective integration best achieved through project working. In addition, the higher priority which will increasingly need to be given to new product development, quality, customer service and changing customer needs, can provide scope for projects containing essential learning for individuals, groups and organizations.

240

MANAGEMENT BY PROJECTS

The growth of project management is an established fact. Evidence abounds among the main external providers of management training and development. Without exception, programmes and courses in project management are an expanding part of their portfolios.

The flattening of organization structures, through delayering and right-sizing, accompanied by a move from hierarchical to flexible network structures is bringing with it the phenomena of project orientation. Projects are being increasingly deployed as a means of achieving business objectives, to such an extent that management by projects is being articulated as a central management strategy; a strategy which reflects the relentless increase in complexity with which companies are having to cope. Companies are having to adapt continuously their strategies, structures and cultures. Moreover, their relationships with customers and suppliers are constantly in a state of flux.

The size and duration of projects can vary widely. Successfully managing a network of projects in progress simultaneously will require a project-orientated management strategy.

Project-orientated companies need to allocate people resources effectively, so that projects 'deliver' successfully through a balance and blend of the hard skills of planning, organizing, directing and controlling and the softer skills of influencing, persuading and teamworking – in Harrison's terms, a combination of 'task' and 'role'. However, it is likely that these emerging project-orientated companies may rewrite some of the cultural definitions. In these companies, there will be reciprocal influence between projects and business strategies, with speed and flexibility being key descriptors.

Indeed, different sub-cultures can be defined, usually, by functions, e.g. Sales, Finance, Operations. In project-orientated companies, it is likely that there will again be subcultures reflecting different values and beliefs. Thus, managing cultural diversity may still be a significant requirement. Of course, there may be synergies and competitions, both in culture and actual projects. Managing synergies/competitions between projects can be aided by grouping projects into clusters. Such clusters can be differentiated by separating them into different categories, for example:

- client – same or different
- timescale – short or long

- focus – internal or external
- use of technology – high or low
- risk level – high or low
- size – large or small
- independent of – interdependent with (the outcomes of one project may influence or have input to another).

Project-based learning differs from project management, but there are important similarities and links. Burke[2] defines a project as 'a group of activities that have to be performed in a logical sequence to meet pre-set objectives outlined by the client' and project management is defined as 'making the project happen'.

Project management employs systems such as Gantt charts, Critical Path Method (CPM) and Programme Evaluation and Review Technique (PERT). All of these can be employed in carrying out projects as part of a project-based learning initiative. The size and complexity of the particular project will tend to determine which systems are appropriate to use.

Another similarity is the closeout report in project management. One element of this is an evaluation of the project against the project objectives, together with recommendations for future projects. Again, where project-based learning is becoming an established learning methodology, then such closeout reports can be of value in identifying suitable individual/group projects.

The model produced by Stewart[3] in offering a framework for the management job – Demands, Constraints, Choices – can profitably be applied to a project, as described in Chapter 6. Indeed, the analysis of constraints is part of the well-established methodology of project management. But the other two elements of the model can also be applicable in project-based learning. Identifying the demands – the 'musts' – is essential at the scoping stage. It is, however, the exploration of choices where potential for learning lies. Analysing demands in detail, to explore how they may be met, can help the project owner to develop the methodology. Similarly, and possibly more powerfully, challenging identified constraints with a view to exploring scope for change can often open up or flex the boundary of the project. In the context of management jobs, it is the choice element which can release potential for growth and development. Applying the model to projects can help project owners to open up new possibilities for learning.

IMPACT OF TECHNOLOGY

In considering how technology may influence the way we learn in the future, we should reflect on the degree to which the ubiquitous television has already caused a shift in methods of obtaining our entertainment. The movement from participation by large groups in cinemas to small groups at home has had dramatic impact on the entertainment industry. TV entertainment is still predominantly a 'broadcast' phenomenon – the programme is transmitted to all viewers at the same time – although the video recorder has provided the means for varying the time at which we choose to view.

INDIVIDUAL PERSPECTIVES ON TECHNOLOGY-BASED LEARNING

Present developments in the telecommunications industry make possible and commercially viable the provision of 'teleshopping' and 'video on demand' services. The significance of this in the context of learning is the interactive nature of the services, i.e. it has become possible for users to have a dialogue with an 'intelligent television', at the time of day which suits them.

Such interactive, on-demand, type of facilities are well suited to the support of project-based learning and development. We are already aware of the benefits obtained by small groups of managers meeting at a time and place of their choice with their coach, to review progress and exchange ideas concerning their projects. We do envisage that such face-to-face gatherings will continue to be important. However, we also believe that the availability of on-demand, interactive, multi-media facilities will result in significant changes in the learning environment and approach adopted in organizations. Project-based learning, with its inherent flexibility in terms of scheduling and the direct link to the work context, will be at the forefront of such change.

ORGANIZATIONAL PERSPECTIVES ON TECHNOLOGY-BASED LEARNING

The organizational, rather than individual, context is fundamental in introducing computer-mediated communication (CMC) and computer-mediated learning (CML) based approaches. The imperative is for the organization to become conversant with the medium. Some barriers to its introduction are technophobia – fear that it will cost more money, fear of the unknown, fear about possible job losses and the so-called 'extra' work involved in personal learning and course development.

With an increasing emphasis on 'the learning organization', there is room for CMC to play a part in extending the concept of continuous organizational learning. The ready availability of CMC facilities to an organization, together with study programmes appropriate to its needs, can enable employees to take greater responsibility for their own individual development.

These issues are associated closely with those of organizational development, changes in organizational culture and the empowerment of employees, together with promotion of self-managed learning programmes on a group and individual basis. The notion of organizational networking is important in this area.

As the nature of 'the way we do business around here' changes, so management attitudes towards the underlying training and development strategies also needs to change to embrace more innovative approaches. The central issue is one of 'letting go' and devolving power to the people who provide and 'consume' training/learning/development activities.

LEARNING AND DEVELOPMENT APPROACHES

One of the potential strengths of CMC is the emphasis which it can place upon action learning. Learners are more likely to adapt to, or adopt, new approaches if the relevance of CMC studies to their place of work and to day-to-day problems can be emphasized.

Arguably, this places a greater premium on real-life, case-based materials, short activities and audits in curriculum and course development. It also provides potential scope for collaborative ventures between academic and other organizations.

Another area where CMC can potentially play a role is in the coaching and mentoring aspects of management development. At the individual level, CMC can add further dimensions to the essential personal face-to-face or phone/fax contacts between mentors and individual mentees, by providing contact with a wider mentee network and taking part in small syndicate discussion and problem-solving groups, whether as part of a formal course or not.

Adverse trends in labour markets, both in academia and elsewhere in the public and private sectors, will encourage growing moves towards

244

part-time or short-term contracts. The use of flexible workforces and the rise of portfolio working is on the increase, as is the need to keep up to date and abreast of current developments in professional terms.

CAPTURING LEARNING OUTCOMES

A step-jump difference that these technologies may provide is the ability to capture learning which arises as part of the outcome of project activities and, going further, to allow interactive access to the knowledge base at the stage where new projects are being initiated.

Thus, the learning benefits from projects can be captured, retained and used widely within the organization. This, in turn, will help organizations improve their responsiveness to changing business needs.

To quote Reg Revans and his Action Learning gospel, 'the rate of learning should be equal to or greater than the rate of change in an organization'. If technology is influencing and increasing the rate of change in organizations, then technology may become an essential component in ensuring that the rate of learning keeps pace so that organizations can flourish and compete effectively.

Project-based learning takes hold when project owners are involved in action. Carrying out the diagnostic stage of a project can be relatively risk-free. It is only when there is involvement in implementation that the high ground of learning can be claimed, as Revans has often pointed out.

Frustration is a stimulus to learning: 'Without frustration there is no need, no reason to mobilize your resources, to discover that you might be able to do something on your own.'[4]

Projects are inevitably linked to change and when properly chosen can provide opportunities for project owners to increase their understanding of organizational change processes and, to a degree, bring about desirable change. For many, the project experience is a microcosm of the growing part of their role as managers of change.

But change processes, to be effective, require the practice and development of interpersonal skills. It is here that the project group can be of great benefit. Project owners can practise interpersonal skills within the group, and receive feedback, as a reinforcement for using such skills in moving the project forward within the organization.

After all, important business problems are not solved by an injection of technical/functional skills, but are capable of solution by giving priority to the complexity of interpersonal processes.

245

Project-based initiatives, particularly group projects, can be part of a company's strategy for loosening up the structure of an organization, generating structural flex and moving towards a situation of greater involvement and participation at all levels.[5] Once project-based learning has proved its value, then the project group approach can underpin thrusts in certain business activities such as product development, productivity improvement and strategic planning. The opportunities are immense at individual, group and organizational levels.

ORGANIZATIONAL LEARNING

A seminal work in the area of organizational learning is Peter Senge's *The Fifth Discipline*,[6] in which learning organizations are described as:

> Organizations in which people continually expand their capacity to create the results they truly desire, where new and expansive patterns of thinking are nurtured, where collective aspirations are set free, and where people are continually learning how to learn together.

In this book, Senge describes five disciplines which are required for building a learning organization. These are entitled:

- systems thinking
- personal mastery
- mental models
- shared vision
- team learning.

Systems thinking is designated as the fifth discipline, the discipline that integrates the other four disciplines into a coherent body of theory and practice.

The following sections review each of the five disciplines and make the connections with our approach to project-based management development.

SYSTEMS THINKING

Senge calls systems thinking the fifth discipline, the cornerstone of how learning organizations think about their world. He says: 'The essence lies in a shift of mind, from seeing parts to seeing wholes . . . from reacting to the present to creating the future . . . seeing interrelationships

246

rather than linear cause–effect chains and seeing processes of change rather than snapshots.'

In his book, Senge describes how cause and effect in complex human systems are not closely related in time and space. By 'effects' he refers to the obvious symptoms that indicate there are problems, by cause he refers to the underlying system that is most responsible for generating the symptoms and which, if recognized, could lead to changes producing lasting improvement. The problem he identifies is that most of us assume, most of the time, that cause and effect *are* close in time and space.

Projects allows us to see beyond the 'parts'; to look at the 'whole' of a business situation and, in so doing, taking the opportunity to explore complex interrelationships, recognize processes of change and take on a pro-active role in creating the future.

Senge also refers to the complexity of today's business environments and the difficulties managers face in managing a business. He distinguishes between *detail* complexity and *dynamic* complexity, highlighting how with *dynamic* complexity, situations where cause and effect are subtle, effects of interventions over time are not obvious. Conventional forecasting, analysis and planning tools which focus on *detail* complexity usually fail to produce dramatic breakthroughs in managing a business. Senge argues that 'the real leverage in most management situations lies in understanding dynamic complexity, not detail complexity'.

In investigating, it becomes apparent that one of the changes in the business environment is the *speed* at which change is taking place. Earlier this century, the 'dynamic complexity' of a business situation was such that change tended to occur over a longer period than now, perhaps tens of years. Today, it occurs in perhaps two or three years. This underlines the massive increase in the rate at which change takes place and hence the importance of understanding dynamic complexity.

Projects provide a framework for exploring and learning from both the detailed complexity and the dynamic complexity of a situation. During the period of months that a project entails, it is possible for the manager to recognize and develop an understanding of the circle of events that constitute a 'system' in a business situation, thus moving away from the limitation of straight-line thinking. By recognizing the balancing processes which are at work, which ultimately determine the 'steady state' in which an organization functions and which identify the explicit and implicit goals and values within the balancing processes, it is possible for the manager to arrive at the best leverage for achieving change. 'To change the behaviour of a system, you must identify and change the limiting factor', says Senge.

Projects provide the opportunity for the manager to recognize the systems at play in an organization and to start to change the thinking that produced a problem in the first place, as part of a pro-active initiative towards developing the learning organization.

PERSONAL MASTERY

Senge comments that: 'Personal mastery is the discipline of continually clarifying and deepening our personal vision, of focusing our energies, of developing patience and of seeing reality objectively. As such, it is an essential cornerstone of the learning organisation.'

In explaining the importance of personal vision, Senge develops the principle of 'creative tension' arising from the gap between current reality and our vision. The gap is the source of creative energy which can help us move towards our vision, but can also pull our vision back towards reality. He says: 'Mastery of creative tension leads to a fundamental shift in our posture toward reality. Current reality becomes the ally not the enemy. An accurate, insightful view of current reality is as important as a clear vision.'

By developing managers through projects, we create the opportunity for clarifying and deepening personal vision and also for gaining an accurate understanding of current reality. Gaining practice and developing skills for dealing with the emotional tension which may arise in the context of the project, without lowering the goals of their personal vision, is a key aspect of learning and personal development for managers.

Using projects to nurture a climate where personal mastery can be practised helps to build organizations in which it is safe for people to create visions, challenge the status quo and face up to aspects of current reality that some people may seek to avoid.

MENTAL MODELS

Senge describes mental models as deeply ingrained assumptions, generalizations, pictures or images that influence how we understand the world and how we take action.

New insights may fail to be put into practice because they conflict with our mental models. The discipline of managing mental models – bringing

248

to the surface individual mental models and making them explicit – helps accelerate individual and organizational learning.

Managers throughout an organization form the target audience. Projects can create the means of encouraging managers to adopt different mental models that reflect better the competitive and work place realities. Developing managers through projects provides the opportunity to develop the skills which are required, including:

- skills of reflection, slowing down our own thinking processes so that we are more aware of how we form our mental models
- face-to-face interactive skills for conversing with others.

Such skills are especially important where there are complex situations and conflicting views.

Projects allow for the opportunity to bring new mental models to the surface and to move forward through shared learning.

SHARED VISION

Senge comments: 'The practice of shared vision involves the skills of unearthing shared "pictures of the future" that foster genuine commitment and enrolment rather than compliance.' By working together in the context of a project, a shared vision can be developed, creating a shared sense of purpose. Senge uses the analogy of a hologram to describe how individuals may share personal visions within the context of the whole vision represented by the hologram image. Each person involved in a common project can relate to the whole vision, via differing personal perspectives arising from individual visions.

TEAM LEARNING

Senge sees team learning as vital to organizational learning because teams, not individuals, are the basic learning unit in modern organizations: unless teams can learn, the organization can not. Team learning builds on the disciplines of developing shared vision and of personal mastery.

Projects can be the vehicle for individuals in a work group to engage in dialogue and gain new insights. The whole group explores the differing perspectives of a project. The resulting dialogue can enable individuals to become aware of the incoherence in the thoughts of others and to move towards a shared, more coherent way forward.

249

OTHER LEARNING ORGANIZATION PERSPECTIVES

The learning company, as defined by Burgoyne, Pedler and Boydell, 'is an organization that facilitates the learning of all its members and continuously transforms itself'. This definition is also a model for the experimentation of learning and discovery. This innovative vision accords well with breaking new ground and discovery, which is so elemental in project-based learning.[7]

In their exposition of the learning company, the authors propose several practices for achieving a balanced corporate learning process. Among these, some have clear links with, and can be realized through, project-based learning, as the following examples show:

- Giving feedback from which receivers can learn. Our approach to project-based learning includes presentations, focused partly on learning outcomes, at the end of which sponsors give feedback as part of an assessment process.
- Setting up enabling structures (those that are simple enough to allow learning and accommodate its consequences). The infrastructure established for project-based learning, where different stakeholders with different interests are involved, ensures that learning is captured and applied.
- Providing a learning climate (a culture that supports shared learning from experience). Group projects, focusing on significant business issues and change, can make a contribution to developing such a learning climate.
- Investigating processes that support self-development for individuals. The whole ethos of project-based learning encourages both individuals and groups to take responsibility for their own learning, while contributing to organizational and bottom-line outputs.
- Stimulating internal exchange (mutual adaptation between people, departments and sections). Projects frequently span interfaces and encourage mutual learning.
- Establishing reward flexibility (reward systems as incentives to learning). The increasing visibility of participants involved in change projects puts learning and development into the spotlight, frequently resulting in rewards through increased credibility, recognition and sometimes role expansion.

MAKING IT HAPPEN

CRITICAL MASS

While there are different definitions of a learning organization, the real challenge is in 'making it happen' which entails thinking about what the organization needs to be in order to succeed in the future.

Organizations learn only through their individual members. Learning for the organization occurs through the sharing of insights, knowledge and experience. Policies and procedures need to facilitate learning transfer. In addition, there needs to be a sufficient 'critical mass' of members with new knowledge and skills to ensure that true organizational learning happens. A project-based learning initiative in an organization can help to build such a critical mass, where both learning and learning transfer are valued.

ORGANIZATION CULTURE

The culture of an organization can impact on the capture and transfer of learning. Trends such as delayering and rightsizing create a climate of insecurity, an environment in which individual learning of new knowledge and skills is 'held close' by people as an aid towards maintaining job security.

An identification and understanding of barriers to learning is an important prerequisite to any effort to inculcate a continuous learning culture – a culture which values experimentation, risk taking, empowerment, teamwork, sharing of knowledge, learning and customer feedback.

ASSUMPTIONS CHECKLIST

Whether or not organizations adopt a particular model of a learning organization as a guiding vision, there are clearly some fundamental assumptions to which they should be committed, for instance:

- learning is of value
- learning flows in all directions in an organization
- learning is continuous with no beginning and no end
- people need access to as much information as possible
- mistakes and difficulties are key learning opportunities
- new ideas, from whatever source, are valuable and need to be accessed

- the quantity and quality of learning can be increased if deliberately encouraged
- openness in relationships can promote exchange and development of ideas
- shared learning with others is easiest to sustain
- people's capacities to learn can be enhanced.

All of these assumptions can be accommodated easily in project-based learning.

SEIZING THE INITIATIVE

Managers need to seize opportunities for their own development. In today's rightsized organizations, being reactive to learning and development opportunities is no longer an option. Moreover, the impact of delayering has led to an increase in project-based approaches in tackling key business issues. The people development specialist can occupy a key position in recognizing opportunities for projects which, while solving business problems or exploiting opportunities, can provide learning benefits to individual managers. When a project is identified as the most suitable method for tackling a business issue, it is likely that some senior person will have a strong interest in the outcome. Indeed, projects may be set up by sponsors for whom the output will be critical to achieving one of their objectives. The challenge for managers is to be covertly observant for project opportunities which, if taken, are likely to yield learning and career benefits. The message is clear: 'get yourself a project'.[8]

CLOSING REFLECTIONS

Rapid change and how we can best learn and grow to achieve success in the future, from both an individual and organizational perspective, has been this chapter's theme.

In Chapter 1 of this book we introduced the concept of projects as 'twin track' vehicles, which provide a means for achieving both learning and tangible operational benefits. Expanding further on this theme, within the context of achieving successful change, we believe that developing managers through projects provides a staged, multi-level means for making progress, in the following way:

STAGE 1: EXPLORING NEW TERRITORY

The early stage of a project is concerned with exploring and understanding, gaining new experiences. Project owners begin to see more clearly the assumptions that are being made by themselves and others, and the consequences of those assumptions. Outcomes at this stage may emerge in the form of new shared language, expressions and structures to describe the situation. Individuals may begin to behave differently, but the basic rules and assumptions remain as before.

STAGE 2: TESTING NEW OPTIONS

Using the new expressions and ideas arising in Stage 1, the project owner and others involved start to question the existing assumptions and to experiment with new ways of working. As the project progresses, new 'rules of action' begin to emerge, reflecting the development of new assumptions. In this way the project acts as a shared vehicle for communicating and applying new ideas at a higher, more tangible level. The parties involved are at a steep point in the learning curve and, under stress, may find it difficult to articulate precisely what they are accomplishing.

STAGE 3: OPERATING ANEW

The operating anew stage is where the project is largely completed. The project owner, sponsor and other parties involved have started to benefit from the tangible and intangible outcomes from the project. The vehicle of the project has delivered tangible results, perhaps in the form of a new production method, with time or cost savings. However, other intangible and less obvious deliverables, in the form of changes in values, rules of action and operating assumptions, have also arisen.

It is the latter set of deliverables which are essential for success in times of continuing change, for it is only through people and how they work together that there can be movement forward.

The dictionary provides definitions of a project as 'a scheme' or 'a means of focusing ideas'. Thus the word project involves both a practical and conceptual aspects. These definitions reflect our own belief in the duality of value in developing managers through projects.

KEY POINT SUMMARY

- During these times of rapid change, projects are becoming central to our whole way of working, enabling individuals and organizations to manage a portfolio of parallel, rapidly developing and time-constrained business activities. In this context, we advocate that projects provide the natural vehicle for achieving not only work place results, but also individual and organizational learning.
- Projects are an inherently flexible means of confronting a changing variety of business needs. They can be organized to deliver the appropriate balance of 'hard' skills and techniques as well as addressing 'softer' cultural and interpersonal issues.
- Rapid developments in the use of information technology will continue to transform our working and learning environment. The ability to interconnect and communicate between individuals and among groups electronically provides a supportive environment for work place performance and learning through projects.
- Technology provides a new capability for capturing the learning which arises from project work and for supporting the process by which an organization adapts and competes in the global marketplace.
- Conceptual frameworks of how organizations learn have become better understood and articulated by leading authors such as Peter Senge. We believe that project-based learning fits well with these conceptual frameworks and provides the means for achieving learning and organizational development.
- Projects are vehicles for delivering both learning and tangible operational benefits. Intangible, less obvious deliverables in the form of changes in values, rules of action and operating assumptions also arise. It is these intangible deliverables that are necessary for success in times of continuing change.

REFERENCES

1. Handy, C. (1991), *The Age of Unreason*, London: Business Books Ltd.
2. Burke, R. (1992), *Project Management – Planning and Control*, 2nd edn, Chichester: J. Wiley.
3. Stewart, R. (1982), *Choices for the Manager*, Maidenhead: McGraw-Hill.
4. Revans, R.W. (1982), *The Origins of Action Learning*, Bromley: Chartwell-Bratt.

5. Smith, B. (1979), 'Projects at Nabisco', *Journal of European and Industrial Training*, **3**, (3).
6. Senge, P.M. (1992), *The Fifth Discipline*, London: Century Business.
7. Burgoyne, J., Pedler, M. and Boydell, T. (1995), 'Feeding Minds to Grow the Business', *People Management*, September.
8. Smith, B. (1995), 'Project Yourself Into The Future', *BJC Today*, Spring.

Index

ABB Zamek, case history 91–4
Accidental learning 22
Achieving Management Potential, Inland
  Revenue 189–90
Action learning 28, 213, 244
  Inland Revenue 190
  Sundridge Park Management Centre 64
Activist learning style 18, 24
Advantages *see* Benefits
The Age of Unreason (Charles Handy) 239
Allied Domecq, Sundridge Park
  Management Centre training course
  113–31
Argyris, Chris, quotation from 24
Assessment of projects 127, 130, 183–5
  Allied Domecq 127, 129
  Gestetner 172–3
  Guernsey Civil Service 205–6
  Inland Revenue 195
  Lloyd's Bank Insurance Services   177
  London Underground 203–4
  Park May Berhad 230–31
  Renong Berhad 228
  Sundridge Park management
    Centre 73–82, 110, 149–55
  Uniteers Communications Sdn Bhd 235
  Volvo Concessionaires 165

Barrett, Gavin, *Forensic marketing* 179
Bee, Francis, consultant 203
Benchmarking
  Renong Berhad 226
  Scottish Nuclear Ltd 223–4
Benefits of projects 8, 15–17, 37–8, 186–7,
  253, 254
  CMCS Dairy Division 94–5

European Air Catering Services Ltd 96–7
financial services group 99–100
Gestetner 171
Guernsey Civil Service 211–12
ICI 134, 146–7
Inland Revenue 200–201
Lloyd's Bank Insurance Services 181
London Electricity 98
London Underground 203
Longman Training 101–3
methodology 108
Pacific Rim, Sundridge Park 104–11
planning 106, 107
Polish power group 91–4
Scottish National Ltd 224
sponsors 80
Sundridge Park Management Centre,
  76, 77–81
Volvo Concessionaires 164–5
Boydell, T 250
BTR-DEP (Europe), cross-cultural training
  220–22
Burgoyne, J 250
Burke, J 242
Business Process Re-engineering (BPR)
  32–3
  Dairy Division CMCS 94–5
  Polish power group 91–4
Businesses *see* Organizations

Capabilities *see* Skills
Case histories
  business restructuring, Polish power
    group 91–4
  customer requirements, London
    Electricity 97–9

market potential, Longman Training
101–3
overhead value analysis, financial services group 99–101
rationalization, Dairy Division CMCS
94–5
training scheme, European Air Catering
Services Ltd 96–7
Change
in organizations 4–5, 33, 213, 239–40,
241, 244, 246–9, 252, 254
Allied Domecq 115–17
empowerment 32, 244
Inland Revenue 189, 197–8, 201
Lloyd's Bank Insurance Services 175
mergers 195–6
and people 33
and projects 9, 33, 51, 57, 117, 213,
240–41, 247–8
Classification of projects 52–3
CMCS Dairy Division, rationalization, case
history 94–5
Coaching 23–4, 43, 244
Companies see Organizations
Comparisons see Benchmarking
Competencies see Skills
Competition in companies 240
Complexity in organizations see
Organizations, change
Computer-mediated learning (CML) 243–4
Conditions for projects 10fig, 61–2, 241–2
Consortium Alliance for Learning 168
Consultants, training see Sundridge Park
Management Centre
Continuous development 4, 12
Cost effectiveness 4–5, 32–3, 147
Volvo Concessionaires 167
Coulson-Thomas, C 7
Culture
national culture 215–19
in organizations 5, 29, 31–3, 51, 241, 250,
251
public sector 189
Inland Revenue 197–8, 201
Volvo Concessionaires 165
and projects 219
'service culture', Merlin Hotels Group
225, 227
Customer requirements, London
Electricity, case history 97–9

Dairy Division CMCS, rationalization, case
history 94–5
Database of projects, Sundridge park 137,
149
Decision-making, Allied Domecq 116
Developing Tomorrow's Top Managers
programme, Sundridge Park 63–4,
86–8
financial services group, case history
99–101
sample projects 64–5, 91–4, 99–101
Development, continuous 4, 12
Difficulties see Pitfalls
Directors see Managers
Distance learning 23
Dress at work, German attitudes 222
Dunlop BTR Hydraulik, cross-cultural
training 220–22

Education, German attitudes 222
Electricity industry, international 223
Elements of projects 7
Empowerment 31–2, 244
European Air Catering Services Ltd, train-
ing scheme, case history 96–7
Evaluation see Assessment
Executives see Managers
Experiential training 218
External training
(see also Off-the-job training; Sundridge
Park Management Centre)
programmes 57–87
projects 33–7, 38

Farmer, Paul, London Underground 202–4
Fayol, project management 63
The Fifth Discipline (Peter Senge) 246–9
Financial services group, overhead value
analysis, case history 99–101
Foh Hup Omnibus Co Ltd 228–31
Forensic Marketing (Gavin Barrett) 179
Formal management type 22
Foundations of Business programme
133–57, 134fig
sample projects 138–46
France, attitudes to work 218
Francis, Joyce 218

Germany, attitudes to work 218, 220–22
Gestetner, training course 168–75

Girolami, Sir Paul, on innovation 52
Glaxo 52
Government departments 189
    Guernsey Civil Service, case study
        205–12
    Inland Revenue, case study 189–201
Group projects 31, 182–3, 213, 245–6, 250
Group support 7, 27–8, 50, 56
    (*see also* Teamworking)
    Inland Revenue 190
    voluntary 27–8
Guernsey Civil Service, management pro-
        gramme 205–12
    sample projects 206–8

Handy, Charles, 239
Harrison, R 27, 241
Heraclitus, quotation from 4
Hofstede, Geert, national culture 215–18
Hogg, Sir Christopher, on failure 128–9
Honey and Mumford learning styles *12fig*,
    18–20, 63
Human resources development *see* People
    development specialists

IBM Corporation 215
ICI, Foundations of Business programme
    133–57, *134fig*
    sample projects 138–46
ICL, self-managed learning 27
Informal managerial type 22
Information technology, use of 8, 240,
    243–5, 254
    ICI training course 137, 149
    London Underground 202
Infrastructure for projects 41, *42fig*, 45–6,
    48fig, 54, 125, 250
    change 51
Inland Revenue, training programme
    189–201
    mergers 195–7
    sample projects 193–200
Innovation 52, 240
    at Volvo Concessionaires 165
Integrated managerial type 22
International comparisons *see*
    Benchmarking
International management training 215–41
    France 218
    Germany 218, 220–22

Malaysia 224–35
International Training Services 190
Interpersonal skills 47

Johari Window 29

Kennedy Robinson Business Development
    205
Kingsway Group, Sundridge Park training
    courses 65–72
Knowledge 5
Kolb, D A 12
Kotter, J 6, 63

Leadership skills 30–31
Learning
    (*see also* Projects, assessments)
    accidental 22
    action 28, 213, 244
        Inland Revenue 190
        Sundridge Park Management Centre
        64
    context of 3, 22
    distance 23
    methods 23–31
    off-the-job 7, 13, 15–16, 23, 38
    organizations 3, 13, 27, 246, 250, 251–2,
    254
    from people 14
    planned 22, 24
    potential 15–16
    processes 3, 11–15, 22, 28
        Honey and Mumford *12fig*, 18–20, 63
    programmes 57–8
        Allied Domecq 117, *118fig*, 119–20
        ICI Foundations of Business 133–57
        Volvo Concessionaires 159–68
    from projects 212–13, 245, 249, 250, 254
    self-managed 6, 12, 27, 51–2, 217
        ICL 27
        Inland Revenue 190
        self-development 26–7, 51, 217, 250, 252
            Inland Revenue 192
    teams 249
    transfer 11–12, 14, 245, 251
        London Underground 203
        Volvo Concessionaires 166
    workplace applications 4, 6–7, 13, 24, 45,
    49
Learning cycles, Honey and Mumford

12fig
Learning logs 14
Learning styles *12fig* 13, 18–20, 63, 103
    activist 18, 24
    pragmatist 19–20, 24
    reflector 18–19, 24
    theorist 19, 24
Lex Services plc *see* Volvo Concessionaires
Line managers 41
    (*see also* Managers; Sponsors)
    ICI 134, 136
    relationship with sponsor 45–6
    relationship with trainees, Volvo
        Concessionaires 166
Lloyd's Bank Insurance Services, group
    training 175–182
London Electricity, customer require-
    ments, case history 97–9
London Underground, management pro-
    gramme 202–5
    sample projects 204–5
Longman Training, market potential, case
    history 101–3

Malaysia
    Park May Berhad 228–31
    Renong Berhad 224–7
    Uniteers Communication Sdn Bhd 231–5
Management development 5–6, 57
    (*see also* Teamworking)
    action learning 27–9, 213, 244
        Inland Revenue 190
        Sundridge Park Management Centre 64
    coaching 23–4, 43, 244
    leadership skills 30–31
    mentoring 25–6, 244
        European Air Catering Services Ltd
            96–7
        Lloyd's Bank Insurance Services 176
        Strathclyde Business School 35
    national cultures 215–19
    needs 21, 58, 63, 103
        Allied Domecq 116
        Gestetner 169
        Inland Revenue 189, 192
        Volvo Concessionaires 159–61
    self-development 26–7, 51, 250, 252
        Inland Revenue 192
    types *22fig*
Management styles *22fig*

Management training 5
    (*see also* Learning; Projects)
    Allied Domecq, case history 113–31
    application to work 4, 6–7, 13, 24, 45, 49
    European Air Catering Services Ltd,
        case history 96–7
    Kingsway Group, case history 65–72
    international context 215–41
    learner-centred 12
    programmes 57–87
        (*see also* Sundridge Park Management
        Centre for other companies)
        Guernsey Civil Service 205–12
        Inland Revenue 189–201
        Volvo Concessionaires 159–67
    in UK 3–4
Managers
    (*see also* Line managers; Sponsors;
        Trainees)
    as coach 24
    mental models 249
    personal mastery 248
    power-sharing 24, 251
    relationship with mentors 25
    senior managers, Allied Domecq 113–31
    support of learning
        Lloyd's Bank Insurance Services
            176–8
        Volvo Concessionaires 163–4, 166
    training needs 58, 63
Mental models 248–9
Mentoring 25–6, 244
    European Air Catering Services Ltd
        96–7
    Lloyd's Bank Insurance Services 176
    Strathclyde Business School 35
Merger, Inland Revenue 195–7
Merlin Hotels Group, 'service culture'
    225–7
Methodology of projects 43, 47, 49–50,
    107–8, 242
    (*see also* Planning)
    Allied Domecq 119
    ICI 137, 144
    Lloyd's Bank Insurance Services 180–81
    London Underground 202–3
    pitfalls 107
    Renong Berhad 226
    Strathclyde Business School 36
    Uniteers Communications 231

Mintzberg, H 6
Mission statements 5
Motivation *see* Empowerment
Motorola 231
Mumford, A *12fig*, 18–20, 22, 27, 63

National culture 215–19
    and projects 236
Networks 50, 56, 72, 125, 186–7, 201
    Allied Domecq 119
    difficulties 123
    Gestetner 171
    Lloyd's Bank Insurance Services 179
Next Steps initiative 189
North West Senior Managers Programme,
    Inland Revenue *190–91fig*

Obstacles *see* Pitfalls
Off-the-job learning 7, 13, 15–16, 23, 38
    (*see also* Management development;
    Projects; Sundridge Park
    Management Centre)
    programmes 57–8
        Allied Domecq 117, *118fig*, 119–20
        ICI Foundations of Business 133–57
        Volvo Concessionaires 159–68
OKI Japan 231–5
Opportunistic managerial type 22
Organizations
    change 4–5, 33, 213, 239–40, 241, 244,
        246–9, 252, 254
        Allied Domecq 115–17
        empowerment 32, 244
        Inland Revenue 189, 197–8, 201
        Lloyd's Bank Insurance Services 175
        mergers 195–6
    competition 240
    culture 5, 29, 31–3, 51, 241, 250, 251
        (*see also* National culture)
        public sector 189
            Inland Revenue 197–8, 201
        Volvo Concessionaires 165
    innovation 52, 165, 240
    learning 3, 13, 27, 246, 250, 251–2, 254
    mental models 248–9
    mission statements 5
    personal mastery 248
    'power distance' 216–17
    projects 78, 240, 247, 248, 254
        CMCS Dairy Division 94–5

European Air Catering Services Ltd
    96–7
    Polish power group 92–3
    Scottish Nuclear Ltd 223–4
public sector, case studies 189–214
    Guernsey Civil Service 205–12
    Inland Revenue 189–201
    London Underground 202–5
    'shamrock' structure 239
shared visions 249
staff 239–40, 244–5, 254
systems thinking 246–8
'uncertainty avoidance' 217–18
Owners of projects *see* Trainees

Pacific Rim project, Sundridge Park
    104–11
Park May Berhad, management pro-
    gramme 228–31
Pedler, M 27, 250
People
    and change 33
    learning from 14
People development specialists 4, 14, 38–9,
    252
    (*see also* Management development)
    Business Process Re-engineering 33
    changing role 5, 52
    development needs 21, 51–2
    empowerment 32
    London Underground 202–5
    relationship with participants 41
    support groups 50
    teamworking 29–30
Personal mastery 248
Personnel staff *see* People development
    specialists
Pitfalls in project work 53–4
    CMCS Dairy Division 94–5
    European Air Catering Services Ltd
        96–7
    financial services group 99–100
    Gestetner 170
    ICI 141
    London Electricity 98
    methodology 107
    planning 105, 106
    Polish power group 91–4
    presentations 108–9
    for sponsors 54–5, 81

Sundridge Park 76–7, 79
Planned learning 22, 24
Planning 63, 105–7
  (*see also* Methodology)
  Gestetner 169
  Lloyd's Bank Insurance Services 180–81
Poland, power group restructuring, case
  history 91–4
'Portfolio', work categories 239–40, 244–5,
  254
'Power distance', national culture 216–17
Power-sharing 24, 251
Pragmatist learning style 19–20, 24
Presentations 38, 61–3, 108–10, 127–9, 250
  Allied Domecq 119–20
  Guernsey Civil Service   211
  ICI 137, 139–40
  Inland Revenue 200–201
  Lloyd's Bank Insurance Services 178
  Volvo Concessionaires 162
Programmes *see* Management training,
  programmes
Project-based learning, definition 6
Project management 241–242
  (*see also* Projects, planning; Projects,
  methodology)
  London Underground 202–5
Project owners *see* Trainees
Projects
  (*see also* Presentations; Sponsors;
  Trainees)
  assessment 127, 130, 183–5
    Allied Domecq 127, 129
    Gestetner 172–3
    Guernsey Civil Service 205–6
    Inland Revenue 195
    Lloyd's Bank Insurance Services
      177
    London Underground 203–4
    Park May Berhad 230–31
    Renong Berhad 228
    Sundridge Park 73–82, 110, 149–55
    Uniteers Communications Sdn Bhd
      235
    Volvo Concessionaires 165
  benefits 8, 15–17, 37–8, 186–7, 253, 254
    CMCS Dairy Division, 94–5
    European Air Catering Services Ltd
      96–7
    financial services group, 99–100

Gestetner 171
Guernsey Civil Service 211–12
ICI 134, 146–7
Inland Revenue 200–201
Lloyd's Bank Insurance Services 181
London Electricity, 98
London Underground 203
Longman Training, 101–3
methodology 108
Pacific Rim, Sundridge Park 104–11
planning 106, 107
Polish power group, 91–4
Scottish National Ltd 224
sponsors 80–82
  Gestetner 171
  Sundridge Park 150–55
    questionnaire 157
  Sundridge Park 76, 77–81
trainees 77–8, 245, 250
  Gestetner 173–4
  Scottish Nuclear Ltd 224
  Sundridge Park 150–55
    questionnaire 156
  Volvo Concessionaires 164–5
and change 9, 33, 51, 57, 117, 213,
  240–41, 247–8
choice of 9*fig*, 10–11, 42, 57–8, 104,
  125–6, 130
  Allied Domecq 120, 122–3
  CMCS Dairy Division, case history
    94–5
  ICI 134
  Lloyd's Bank Insurance Services 177,
    180
  Strathclyde Business School 35
  Sundridge Park Management Centre
    43–4, 58–9, 64–5, 70–72, 74–5
  Volvo Concesionaires 162, 168
classification 52–3
conditions 10*fig*, 61–2, 241–2
and cultural differences 219
database, Sundridge Park 137, 149
external courses 33–7, 38, 57–87
  (*see also* Off-the-job-training;
  Sundridge Park Management Centre)
group projects 31, 182–3, 213, 245–6, 250
infrastructure 41, 42*fig*, 45–6, 48*fig*, 51,
  54, 125, 250
methodology 43, 47, 49–50, 107–8, 242
  Allied Domecq 119

ICI 137, 144
Lloyd's Bank Insurance Services
180–81
London Underground 202–3
pitfalls 107
Renong Berhad 226
Strathclyde Business School 36
Uniteers Communications 232
national culture 236
outline of 7–9, 59–60
pitfalls 53–4
CMCS Dairy Division, 94–5
European Air Catering Services Ltd
96–7
financial services group, 99–100
Gestetner 170
ICI 141
London Electricity, 98
methodology 107
planning 105, 106
Polish power group, 91–4
presentations 108–9
Sundridge Park 76–7, 79
planning 63, 105–7
Gestetner 169
Lloyd's Bank Insurance Services
180–81
relevance to workplace 11, 13, 24, 45, 49,
56, 103, 121–2, 123–5, 130, 241
Allied Domecq *121fig*
Kingsway Group examples 70–72
Volvo Concessionaires 167
reports 108–9, 149–55
results 62, 242
(*see also* assessments)
Inland Revenue   198–9
Renong Berhad 227
Sundridge Park 149–55
Uniteers Communications Sdn Bhd
234–5
scope 8–9, 42, 48, 55, 60
topicality 31
ICI 134
as vehicles 8, 123, 200, 252
workshops, Sundridge Park
Management Centre 60–61
Prospect Centre, project assessment 183–4
Public sector organizations, case studies 189
Guernsey Civil Service 205–12
Inland Revenue 189–201

London Underground 202–5

Questionnaires *see* surveys

Reflector learning style 18–19, 24
Renong Berhad, management programme
224–8
Repertory grid interview, Volvo
Concessionaires 159
Reports 108–9, 149–55
Resources for trainees 53
Results of projects 62, 242
(*see also* assessments)
Inland Revenue   198–9
Renong Berhad 227
Sundridge Park 149–55
Uniteers Communications Sdn Bhd
234–5
Revans, R W 27, 245
Review of projects *see* Assessment of pro-
jects
Robinson, Graham 205
Role play 23
Ruskin, John, quotation from 117

Scope of projects 8–9, 42, 48, 55, 60
Scottish Nuclear Ltd, cross-cultural train-
ing 223–4
Self-development *see* Self-managed learn-
ing
Self-managed learning 6, 12, 24, 51–2
ICL 27
Inland Revenue 190
self-development 26–7, 51, 217, 250, 252
Inland Revenue 192
Senge, Peter, 246–9
Senior Management Programme, Inland
Revenue 190
Senior Officer Management Development
Programme, Guernsey Civil Service
205
'Service culture', Merlin Hotels Group 225,
227
Sets 28
'Shamrock' structure in organizations 239
Shared visions in organizations 249
Skills 5, 28, 47
decision-making, Allied Domecq 116
interpersonal 47
leadership 30–31

Longman Training, 101–2
programmes 57
teamworking 29–30, 31, 50, 249
    BTR-DEP (Europe) 220–22
    cultural differences 220
    empowerment 32
    European Air Catering Services Ltd
    96–7
    Gestetner 168–75
    Guernsey Civil Service 205–12
    group projects 182–3, 213, 245–6, 250
    Inland Revenue 197–201
    Lloyd's Bank Insurance Services
    175–82
    Volvo Concessionaires 159–68
    Volvo Concessionaires 165
Smiles, Samuel 26
Sponsors for projects 7–9, 25, 41, 130,
186–7
    benefits of projects 80–82
    Gestetner 171
    Sundridge Park 150–55
        questionnaire 157
    empowerment 32
    European Air Services Ltd, case history
    97
    Gestetner 170–71
    Guernsey Civil Service 206
    Lloyd's Bank Insurance Services 176,
    180
    London Electricity, 99
    Longman Training, 103
    pitfalls 54–5, 81
    project choice 44
        ICI 134, 136
    relationship with line manager 45–6
    relationship with trainee 44, 46, 47, 53–4,
    60, 79–80, 81, 103, 123, 126, 130
        ICI 136
        Lloyd's Bank Insurance Services 178
    roles 42–5, 81, 201
        Gestetner 170
        ICI 136
    Renong Berhad 226
    Strathclyde Business School 35
    Volvo Concessionaires 161
Staff, 'portfolio' work categories 239–40,
244–5, 254
States of Guernsey Civil Service see
    Guernsey Civil Service

Stewart, R 6, 242
    project integration *121fig*, 122
Strategic investment company, Malaysia
224–7
Strategy, projects for 52
    Allied Domecq 113, 117
Strathclyde Business School
    accreditation, Volvo Concessionaires 167
    use of projects 33–7
Sundridge Park Management Centre
    ABB Zamek 91–4
    action learning 64
    Allied Domecq 113–31
    CMCS Dairy Division 94–5
    database of projects 137, 149
    Developing Tomorrow's Top Managers
        programme 63–4, 86–8
        financial services group, case history
        99–101
        sample projects 64–5, 91–4, 99–101
    European Air Catering Services Ltd
    96–7
    financial services group 99–101
    Gestetner 168–75
    ICI Foundations of Business programme
    133–57, *135fig*
        sample projects 138–46
    The Kingsway Group 65–72
    Lloyd's Bank Insurance Services 175–82
    London Electricity 97–9
    Longman Training 101–3
    Pacific Rim project 104–11
    Park May Berhad 228–31
    programmes 58–87
    project assessments 73–82, 149–55
    project choice 43–4, 58–9, 64–5, 70–2,
    74–5
    project workshops 60–61
    Renong Berhad 224–7
    sample projects 10–11, 64–5, 70–72,
    104–11
    surveys 73–82, 149–55
        questionnaires 156–57
    Volvo Concessionaires 159–68
    Younger Manager Programme 58, *59fig*,
    63, 84–5
        The Kingsway Group 67
        Pacific Rim project 104–11
        Renong Berhad 224
        sample projects 64–5

Volvo Concessionaires 159, 163
Support groups 7, 50, 56
  Inland Revenue 190
  voluntary 27–8
Surrey European Management School,
  surveys 7
Surveys
  London Electricity, case history 98
  Sundridge Park Management Centre
    73–82, 149–55
    questionnaires 156–57
  Surrey European Management School 7
  Volvo Concessionaires, questionnaire
    159
Systems, projects for 52–3
Systems thinking 246–8

Teamworking 29–30, 31, 50, 249
  BTR-DEP (Europe) 220–22
  cultural differences 220
  empowerment 32
  European Air Catering Services Ltd
    96–7
  Gestetner 168–75
  Guernsey Civil Service 205–12
  group projects 182–3, 213, 245–6, 250
  Inland Revenue 197–201
  Lloyd's Bank Insurance Services 175–82
  Volvo Concessionaires 159–68
Technology and learning 243–4, 245, 254
  (see also Information technology)
Theorist learning style 19, 24
Topicality 31
  ICI 134
Transfer of learning 11–12, 14, 245, 251
  London Underground 203
  Volvo Concessionaires 166
Trainees 9, 41, 186–7
  (see also Learning; Projects)
  authority 53, 63
  benefits of project work 77–8, 245, 250
    Gestetner 173–4
    Scottish Nuclear Ltd 224
    Sundridge Park 150–55
      questionnaire 156
  choice of 124–5
    Allied Domecq 119
  empowerment 32
  high fliers, Kingsway Group 66
  Lloyd's Bank Insurance Services 177–8

projects 47–8
relationship with line managers, Volvo
  Concessionaires 166
relationship with participants 47, 50–51,
  54, 130
relationship with sponsor 44, 46, 47,
  53–4, 60, 79–80, 81, 103, 123, 126, 130
  ICI 136
  Lloyd's Bank Insurance Services 178
resources 53
skills 47
Training see Management development;
  Management training
Twin-track approach 8, 26, 252

'Uncertainty avoidance', national culture
  217–18
Uniteers Communications Sdn Bhd, management programme 231–5

Value for money see cost effectiveness
Volvo Cars UK see Volvo Concessionaires
Volvo Concessionaires, internal training
  course 159–68

Women in the workplace, German attitudes 222
Workplace
  dress, German attitudes 222
  relevance of training 4, 6–7, 13, 24, 45,
    49
  relevance of projects 11, 13, 24, 45, 49,
    56, 103, 121–2, 123–5, 130, 241
    Allied Domecq 121fig
    Kingsway Group examples 70–72
    Volvo Concessionaires 167
Workshops, Sundridge Park Management
  Centre 60–61

Younger Manager Programme, Sundridge
  Park 58, 59fig, 63, 84–5
  The Kingsway Group 67
  Pacific Rim project 104–11
  Renong Berhad 224
  sample projects 64–5
  and Volvo Concessionaires 159, 163